James Joyce
Interviews and Recollections

JAMES JOYCE

Interviews and Recollections

Edited by

E. H. MIKHAIL

Professor of English
University of Lethbridge

Foreword by

FRANK DELANEY

St. Martin's Press   New York

1805246
DLC

5-23-91

Selection and editorial matter © E. H. Mikhail 1990

First published in the United States of America in 1990

Printed in Hong Kong

ISBN 0–312–02416–9

Library of Congress Cataloging-in-Publication Data
James Joyce: interviews and recollections.
  Bibliography: p.
  Includes index.
  1. Joyce, James, 1882–1941—Biography.
2. Joyce, James, 1882–1941—Friends and associates.
3. Novelists, Irish—20th century—Biography.
I. Mikhail, E. H.
PR6019.09Z6345   1990   823'.912[B]   88–18177
ISBN 0–312–02416–9

Contents

Foreword

FRANK DELANEY

'A man of small virtue, inclined to alcoholism', said James Joyce to his doctor, a self-portrait which offered no more than a thumbnail's glimpse. He put half a truth in it, or, rather, half of the truth: alcohol did play a part in his life, a merry and pain-provoking part, but to say he possessed only 'small virtue' either makes him disingenuous, or begs definition.

Virtue, in Joyce's Ireland (and ever since) took the form of domestic good behaviour while obeying the Ten Commandments and the Six Precepts of the Church, which ranged from 'To hear Mass on Sundays and all Holydays of Obligation' through to 'To contribute to the Support of our Pastors'. According to these lights, then yes, James Aloysius Joyce, 'Jaysus James', possessed less than small virtue.

See him, though, against standards. Any writer who spends a thousand hours on one chapter, as Joyce did with the *Oxen of the Sun* segment of *Ulysses*, any writer who considers two completed sentences a pleasing reward for a whole day's work, as he told a friend in Zurich, cannot be allowed to accuse himself of lacking virtue. In his description of himself, alcoholism excepted, he has to be considered an unreliable witness.

Of course, he would never allow his *persona* to be perceived easily or clearly. To begin with, he did not wish to be observed in his writings; part of his intention – not entirely mischievous – would keep the professors busy, he declared, 'for centuries'. As a further branching of these gardens paths, he chose to write, as he insisted, about 'the hundred-headed rabble of the cathedral close', and said 'nobody in any of my books is worth more than a hundred pounds'. The disingenuousness clicks on – he himself stood apart, aloof, withdrawn, a stork of an observer, and did not, in going about his daily life, associate himself with his proletarian raw material.

The descriptions of Joyce's physical appearance seem to confirm this statuesque distance from his subject-matter. In the impressions gathered throughout this book he stands as 'a tall blind beautiful gentleman' (James Stephens), 'a tall cathedral-spire of a man' (Nancy Cunard), 'And the blond face, the neat moustache and the air of personal aloofness were a little chilling' (Kenneth Reddin).

Joyce seems deliberately to have beggared description when it came to himself; after all, his writing famously eschewed direct portrayal. Nowhere in multitudinous *Ulysses*, and never under any circumstances in *Finnegans Wake*, did he write a conventional descriptive passage; reality, he saw, did not need to be reported, it entered the mind, especially the unconscious, effortlessly.

In any case, since the small, ordinary, recurrent and bubbling realities of life provided the fodder of his art, any sort of traditional faithful description – especially of himself, the artist – would have defeated his purpose, made it superfluous. His biographer, Richard Ellmann, put it well: 'The life of an artist, but particularly that of Joyce, differs from the lives of other persons in that its events are becoming artistic sources even as they command his present attention. Instead of allowing each day, pushed back by the next, to lapse into imprecise memory, he shapes again the experiences which have shaped him.'

Joyce, accordingly, wrote no autobiography. Facts can only be inaccurate. Art, for the artist, can be the only record. Life can only be seen in all truth if taken in, swilled about, filtered and released through the imagination of the artist. Invention, or re-invention, constitute valid reportage, since all observation is subjective.

So, an anthology of interviews and recollections collected from friends, acquaintances, chance encounters, would, presumably, have had an anti-value to Joyce. To those who draw inspiration from him, however, this material has considerable value. Even if he questioned the validity of it, or the necessity of it, Joyce would have understood the appeal of it. An early part of the reputation which *Ulysses* garnered in Dublin sprang from the fact that people rushed to discover whether they could see their own reflections there, so close did Joyce get to the bone of the city's humanity. One citizen, when asked many years later how he felt about being a character in *Ulysses*, replied with indignation, 'I am not a character in fiction, I am a real person.'

Consequently, any effort to get close to Joyce, to uncover him, to Portray the Artist as a young, middle-aged or elderly man, as a calm or inspired or curmudgeonly man, as a boulevard, family or solitary man would surely, somewhere have appealed, if only to his more perverse humours, in a 'set-a-thief-to-catch-a-thief' sort of way. How interesting, too, that so many people felt so compelled to record their impressions of him; time after time in the following pages, a kind of urgency starts up, as if those who saw, met or knew him felt they had something to tell, and immediately and in detail. Few writers seem to have inspired such compulsive observation.

Perhaps we now feel the need to have the same sort of ordinary information about Shakespeare, or Milton, say, or even Chekhov (a small school of such recollection has grown around Hemingway, but for entirely different reasons). Search across literary recollection and the same obsession with an author's life – how many theses has he spawned? – will be difficult to find. Joyce seems to have made people want to notice him, through a combination of the curiousness of his works, his undoubted accepted genius which transcended all critical pettiness and envy, through the folklore which grew up around him – 'an espionage agent, a film magnate, a cocaine-sniffer, a mystic and a madman', as he put it to his patron – and through his remarkable presence.

The biographical facts of his life, while not exactly mundane, could never, in themselves, have excited such attention or curiosity. A Dubliner, born in 1882 in Brighton Square (in reality the square is a triangle), oldest surviving child of a feckless, romantic and ultimately ne'er-do-well father and a sweet, ultimately sickly mother, the boy had a brilliant scholastic career with the Jesuits and at University. He developed a student interest in Ibsen and mastered the playwright's dialect of Dano-Norwegian sufficiently to write him an admiring letter. After early excursions abroad, and some mild literary skirmishings in Dublin and London he left Ireland forever (apart from two short vacations) in October 1904. He took with him Nora Barnacle, the scullery-maid with whom he first walked out on 16 June of that year, who would become his lifelong companion and bear him two children. They fetched up in Trieste, where they knew extreme poverty, and would continue to, in spasms, for the rest of their lives. They lived in Zurich and Paris, then Zurich again, where Joyce died in 1941. Nora buried him in Fluntern cemetery, on a hill above the city, near the zoo; she said she liked to think of him lying there listening to the lions roaring.

Artistically, James Joyce's life remains one of the most remarkable. He wrote no book that was not, on publication day, hailed as a masterpiece. His four major creations – he also published poems, drama, works in progress – all set intellectual standards which have defied changing fashions and educational trends. *Dubliners* (1914) cast glances at fellow-citizens; *A Portrait of the Artist as a Young Man* (1916) traced the emergence of adult sensibility; in *Ulysses* (1922) he wrote the book of life's day; and in *Finnegans Wake* (1939) the book of life's night.

Professor Mikhail makes the point in his Introduction that 'the number of people who knew or dreamed they knew Joyce strains credulity'. In itself, this fact responds to Joyce's capacity as an artist. The books he wrote, and the statements he made about life, connect so intensely with the spirit that he made the reader part of the world. He understood and described the plight of the human being more roundly than any writer since – or perhaps other than – Shakespeare.

He understood our essential solitariness and the need for each man to make himself important, to come to terms with his own uniqueness, and that in this lies our genuine little immortality. He understood that we are what we do, that we are the daily round of borrowing and begging and stealing and whingeing and praising, profane and obscene and a little sacred and weak and ambitious, 'Karma', or 'The True Faith', or 'Life Force', ungilded, plain, undramatic, lurching, feeling the way between tragedy and comedy, getting by, 'human being'. No wonder, then, that he inspired such compulsive recollecting, conveying as he did, in artistic re-creation, the very system of life. More than one modern writer has admitted trying – and failing – to find a corner of human experience Joyce has not uncovered.

So – a man of small virtue, inclined to alcoholism'? On reflection, Joyce may have been stating an ambition in that remark – to be, like the ingredients of his art, an ordinary member of mankind. Plainly, and as this assembly of Interviews and Recollections demonstrates, he was not.

Acknowledgements

My gratitude is due to the following for assistance, support, encourage-ment, information, editorial material or notification of certain items that appear in this book: Professor William A. Armstrong, Miss Lorraine Bailes, Mr Robert Chapman, Dr M. Gudrun Hesse, Miss Rosemary Howard, Mr David Jarvis, Dr William Latta, Mr James McMurray, Mr Robert Nicholson, Professor Robert O'Driscoll, Mr Ralph Payne, Mr Alec Reid, Mr Robert Reid, Dr Gaston R. Renaud, Mr Kenneth Robinson and Dr Richard Wall.

The book benefited greatly from the comments and suggestions made by Dr Christopher Murray; and from the translations of German texts into English by Dr Peter Preuss.

I am greatly indebted to Miss Nancy Baker for research assistance, and to Mrs Charlene Sawatsky for her kindness and patience in the final preparation of the manuscript.

Several publications have been of immense help to me, particularly: Richard Ellmann, *James Joyce*, 2nd edn (London and New York: Oxford University Press, 1982); Thomas Jackson Rice, *James Joyce: A Guide to Research* (New York: Garland, 1982); Robert H. Deming, *A Bibliography of James Joyce Studies* (Boston, Mass.: G. K. Hall, 1977); and Thomas F. Staley, 'James Joyce', in *Anglo-Irish Literature: A Review of Research*, ed. Richard J. Finneran (New York: Modern Language Association, 1976), supplemented in *Recent Research on Anglo-Irish Writers*, ed. Richard J. Finneran (New York: Modern Language Association, 1983).

Thanks are due to the University of Lethbridge for granting me a sabbatical leave, without which this book could not have come into existence.

It is also a pleasant duty to record my appreciation to the staff of the University of Lethbridge Library; the National Library of Ireland; Trinity College Library, Dublin; the British Library, London, the Newspaper Library, Colindale; and the New York Public Library.

The editor and publishers wish to thank the following, who have kindly given permission for the use of copyright material:

Atheneum Publishers, an imprint of Macmillan Publishing Co. and

Collins Publishers, for the extracts from *Harold Nicolson: Diaries and Letters, 1930–1939*, ed. by Nigel Nicolson; © 1966 William Collins Sons & Co. Ltd;

Blackie and Son Ltd, for the extracts from *Claybook for James Joyce* by Louis Gillet (London and New York: Abelard-Schuman, 1958);

Lady Bliss, for the extract from *As I Remember* (1970) by Arthur Bliss;

Edward Booth-Clibborn, Executor of the Nina Hamnett Estate for the extract from *Laughing Torso: Reminiscences* by Nina Hamnett (London: Constable, 1932);

Chatto & Windus, for the extract from Sybille Bedford's *Aldous Huxley*;

Chilton Book Co., for the extracts from Nancy Cunard, *Nancy Cunard: Brave Poet, Indomitable Rebel, 1896–1965*, ed. Hugh Ford (Philadelphia: Chilton, 1968);

Joan Daves and Dell Publishing Co., for the extracts from *The Collected Essays and Occasional Writings of Katherine Anne Porter* by Katherine Anne Porter; copyright © 1955, copyright renewed © 1983 by Katherine Anne Porter; reprinted by arrangement with Delacorte Press and Seymour Lawrence; all rights reserved;

Fred Dennis, for the extracts from 'Shakespeare and Co., Paris' and 'How I Published *Ulysses*', by Sylvia Beach;

Ann Elmo Agency, Inc., for the extract from Richard Aldington's *Life for Life Sake*;

Envoy Publications, for the extract from Joseph Hone's 'A Recollection of James Joyce', *Envoy*, 5 May 1951;

Evening Herald (Dublin), for the extracts from the interview with Eileen Joyce Schaurek, 'Pappy Never Spoke of Jim's Books', published 15–16 July 1963;

Farrar, Straus & Giroux, Inc., for the extracts from *Silent Years* (1953) by J. F. Byrne;

Oliver Gogarty, for the extract from *Mourning Becomes Mrs Spendlove* (1948) by Oliver St John Gogarty;

Harper & Row, for the extracts from *Many Lives – One Love* (1972) by Fanny Butcher, copyright © 1972 by Fanny Butcher;

Horizon Press, for the extract from *My Thirty Years' War* by Margaret Anderson;

Hutchinson Publishing Group Ltd, for the extracts from *The Wild Geese: Pen Portraits of Famous Irish Exiles* by Gerald Griffin (London: Jarrolds, 1938);

Irish Digest (Dublin), for Kees van Hoek's 'I Met James Joyce's Wife' (1950);

Irish Independent (Dublin), for the extract from 'I Introduced Joyce to a Dublin Newspaper Office' (1962) by Piaras Béaslaí;

Irish Press (Dublin), for the extract from 'Sisters of James Joyce Mourn for Two Brothers' (1941);

Peter Lennon, for the extracts from 'James Joyce's Nurse Remembers' which appeared in the *Irish Digest* (Dublin, 1962);

J. B. Lippincott Co., for the extract from Sisley Huddleston's *Back to Montparnasse: Glimpses of Broadway in Bohemia* (1931);

Macdonald & Co. Ltd, for the extract from Frank Budgen's *James Joyce and the Making of 'Ulysses'* (London: Grayson & Grayson, 1934);

Macmillan Publishers, for the extract from William K. Magee (pseud.: John Eglinton), *Irish Literary Portraits* (1935);

Macmillan Publishing Co., Inc., for the extract from *The Road Round Ireland* (1926) by Padric Colum;

The New Yorker, for the extracts from 'The Joyces' by Giorgio Joyce, © 1935, 1963 *The New Yorker Magazine*, Inc.; 'Ecce Puer' by Stephen Joyce, © 1947, 1975 *The New Yorker Magazine*, Inc.; and 'Sister' by May Joyce Monaghan, © 1964 *The New Yorker Magazine*, Inc.;

The New York Times, for the extract from 'A Sister Recalls Joyce in Dublin' by May Joyce Monaghan, *New York Times* (1964);

North Point Press, for the extracts from *Being Geniuses Together* by Robert McAlmon and Kay Boyle (1968);

Random House, for the extract from Virgil Thomson, *Virgil Thomson* (New York: Alfred A. Knopf, 1966);

Alec Reid and the James Joyce Museum, Sandycove, Co. Dublin, Ireland, for an unpublished interview with James Joyce by Robert Reid (1928);

Charles Scribner's Sons, for the extracts from *A Moveable Feast* by Ernest Hemingway, copyright © 1964 Mary Hemingway;

the Society of Authors, on behalf of the copyright-owner Mrs Iris Wise, for the extracts from 'The Joyce I Knew' by James Stephens (*The Listener*, 24 October 1946);

Southern Illinois University Press, for the extracts from James Stern, 'James Joyce: A First Impression' in *A James Joyce Miscellany*, Second Series, ed. by Marvin Magalaner, copyright © 1959 by Southern Illinois University Press;

Time and Tide (London), for the extract from Sylvia Lynd's 'Some Recollections of James Joyce' (1941);

University of Tulsa, for the extracts from 'James Joyce: Two Reminiscences' by Antonio Fonda Savio and Letizia Fonda Savio, which appeared in *James Joyce Quarterly*, 9 (Spring 1972); 'Recollections of Joyce' by Alessandro Francini Bruni, which appeared in *James Joyce Quarterly*, 14 (Winter 1977); 'My First English Teacher' by Mario Norido, which appeared in *James Joyce Quarterly*, 9 (Spring 1972); 'James Joyce: An Occasion of Remembrance' by Nora Franca Poliaghi, which appeared in *James Joyce Quarterly*, 9 (Spring 1972); and 'Visits with James Joyce' by P. Beaumont Wadsworth, which appeared in *James Joyce Quarterly*, 1 (Summer 1964);

Michael Yeats, for the extract from 'The Younger Generation is Knocking at my Door' by W. B. Yeats.

Every effort has been made to trace all the copyright-holders but if any have been inadvertently overlooked the publishers will be pleased to make the necessary arrangements at the first opportunity.

Introduction

The title of this book, *James Joyce: Interviews and Recollections*, seems ironical, for Joyce always shunned interviewers and avoided journalists, principally on account of their habit of inaccuracy. His friends were always careful not to quote him for publication, although he was never averse to publicity, so long as he could manage it himself.

Nor was Joyce a conversationalist in the ordinary sense. In fact, he was a remarkably silent man, 'silence, exile and cunning' being, according to *A Portrait of the Artist as a Young Man*, his three vaunted weapons. No one can say that Joyce, any more than J. M. Synge, had what is called conversation. According to Richard Best, 'If you made a remark about some literary man to Joyce, let us say you said, "Oh, I think that Meredith is a wonderful writer," he might say, "Ho, ho, ho, ho," like that; he had a way of guffawing.'[1] Eugene Jolas writes that Joyce was never an easy conversationalist, 'and had a tendency to monosyllabic utterances. He did not relish being questioned on any subject. . . . When he was in the mood, his talk, given in his mellifluous Dublin speech, was a ripple of illuminating ideas and words.'[2] Sylvia Beach remembers that 'he was not liked at dinners and things like that because he had no small talk; but with people he knew, he was a delightful man'.[3] George Antheil, for instance, recalls that 'Conversation with Joyce was always deeply interesting';[4] and Morley Callaghan records an evening in Paris in which Joyce 'immediately became too chatty, too full of little bits of conversation, altogether unlike the impression we had been given of him'.[5]

Joyce was a self-centred man. Progressively, since he was in school, he had been getting further out of touch with life and more and more intrigued with words. Unlike Oscar Wilde and Brendan Behan, who were too busy living to write, Joyce, like Sean O'Casey and W. B. Yeats, gave the totality of his life to his art. He did not find his diversion in his friends because of the exigencies of his work. However, he was not unsociable; he was capable of strong, but few, friendships. C. P. Curran found that Joyce 'lived rather much to himself in the College. He had three or four particular cronies';[6] and Elliot Paul concluded that no one was intimate with him.

Men . . . cannot get near him or his thoughts except through long acquaintance, carefully nourished and developed. He does the best

xv

he can to be approachable, but like a rare violin ... longs for company as much as he dreads it.[7]

According to Morril Cody, Joyce was always *Mister* Joyce even to some of his best friends, like Sylvia Beach, for instance: 'This was partly because he kept a certain distance from those around him, aloof always from familiarities of name or spirit.'[8] No one could see him or talk with him without an awareness of his unusual qualities. Workmen, when he walked unwittingly into an area where construction was in progress, warned him gently and called him 'professor' or 'doctor'. To his neighbours he seemed to be a studious and quiet man

> whose habits are steady and who is eccentric only in the matter of going away from home each day at dinner-time. His family, the members of which never enter his study when he is working there, sometimes wonder if he is aware of their existence at all. . . .
>
> So Joyce will continue his daily routine, loving music and wine and all the life not denied him, remote from his admirers and contemporaries, a solitary, in many ways a pathetic figure, but one whose inner life is rich beyond the understanding of unimaginative men.[9]

Until the publication of Richard Ellmann's definitive *James Joyce* in 1959 there had been no satisfactory biography of Joyce. In *Silent Years*, J. F. Byrne deplored the mediocrity of the biographical work that had been done on Joyce: 'I knew Joyce so well that I wouldn't recognise him from the pen pictures of his biographers.'[10] Herbert Gorman's 'authorised' biography, for example, was written with Joyce's co-operation but with hardly anyone else's. Hence it was partial, inaccurate and distorted. When Gorman announced that his biography was ready in the summer of 1939, Joyce wished to see first the complete typescript 'and of course the subsequent proofs'. He objected strongly to the suggestion that his father had been financially irresponsible or flamboyant and insisted that passages suggesting that John Joyce had suffered from these vices be struck out. Gorman, similarly, suffered other interferences in writing about Joyce's marriage. Helen Joyce makes only the briefest appearance, and Lucia Joyce's mental illness could not be mentioned at all.

Nor is a biographer's job made easier by the existence of a large number of friends and acquaintances in the life of his subject. The number of people who knew or dreamed they knew Joyce strains credulity. Some recollectors of Joyce try to impress just by dropping his name.[11] Nevertheless, a volume of recollections of Joyce would show him from different points of view and would result in a composite portrait in which certain traits appear prominently. Some such collections have already appeared in print. Ulick O'Connor's *The Joyce We Knew* (1967) contains four contributions by contemporaries who were born within a year or two of Joyce's date of birth. W. R. Rodgers's *Irish Literary Portraits* (1972) includes edited transcriptions of BBC interviews with several of Joyce's contemporaries recorded in 1950. John Ryan's *A Bash in the Tunnel* (1970) stresses that it is a book by '*Irish writers*' about an '*Irish writer*'.

> Joyce was quintessentially an Irishman to the extent that Wilde, Shaw or Yeats could never be. This was the great source of his genius, the inexhaustible mine from which he could hew *Ulysses* and *Finnegans Wake*. To understand Joyce at all, this fact has to be faced. In seeing Joyce through the eyes of the Irish (not always smiling) we shall see the man more clearly and, I believe, understand the writer more fully.[12]

Willard Potts, on the other hand, argued in *Portraits of the Artist in Exile* (1979) that Joyce felt much more at ease with Europeans than with his fellow Dubliners.

> In many ways continental Europe, where he found his chief literary inspiration, wrote all his major work, and spent most of his adult life, had a greater significance to him than did Ireland.[13]

This book attempts to show Joyce as an international figure, since his outlook had always been cosmopolitan. The exigencies of space, however, allow only for the inclusion of a limited number of writers. I have aimed mostly at selecting those recollections that have not been reprinted as well as those that are not readily accessible. The pieces, arranged in chronological order, cover almost all the stages of Joyce's life, so that as many facets as possible could be presented.

NOTES

1. Quoted in *Irish Literary Portraits*, ed. W. R. Rodgers (London: British Broadcasting Corporation, 1972) p. 28.
2. Eugene Jolas, 'My Friend James Joyce', *Partisan Review*, 8 (March–April 1941) 82.
3. Peter Lennon, 'James Joyce's "Nurse" Remembers', *The Irish Digest* (Dublin), 74 (June 1962) 63.
4. George Antheil, *Bad Boy of Music* (Garden City, N.Y.: Doubleday Doran, 1945) p. 153.

5. Morley Callaghan, *That Summer in Paris: Memories of Tangled Friendships with Hemingway, Fitzgerald, and Some Others* (New York: Coward-McCann; Toronto: Macmillan, 1963) p. 138.

6. Quoted in *Irish Literary Portraits*, p. 27.

7. Elliot Paul, 'Farthest North: a Study of James Joyce', *Bookman* (New York), 75 (May 1932) 157.

8. Morrill Cody, 'James Joyce in the Twenties', *Connecticut Review*, 5 (April 1972) 12.

9. Paul, 'Farthest North', 163.

10. J. F. Byrne, *Silent Years: An Autobiography with Memoirs of James Joyce and Our Ireland* (New York: Farrar, Straus and Young, 1953) p. 144.

11. See, for example, Louis J. Walsh, 'With Joyce and Kettle at U.C.D.', *The Irish Digest* (Dublin), 12 (June 1942) 27–9, in which there is only a very slight reference to Joyce.

12. John Ryan (ed.), 'Introduction', *A Bash in the Tunnel: James Joyce by the Irish* (Brighton: Clifton Books, 1970) p. 14.

13. Willard Potts (ed.), 'Introduction', *Portraits of the Artist in Exile: Recollections of James Joyce by Europeans* (Seattle and London: University of Washington Press, 1979) p. xi.

A Note on the Text

In the extracts given, spelling errors in the originals have been silently corrected, American spelling and punctuation have been anglicised, and the spellings of names have been rendered consistent throughout.

Chronological Table

1882 2 Feb: James Joyce born at 41 Brighton Square West, Dublin.
5 Feb: Baptised at the Church of St Joseph, Terenure.

1884 Family moves to 23 Castlewood Avenue.

1887 May: Family moves to 1 Martello Tower, Bray.

1888 26 June: Joins his parents in singing at an amateur concert at the Bray Boat Club.
1 Sept: Enters Clongowes Wood College, Co. Kildare.

1891 before Feb: Takes piano lessons.
June: John Joyce (father) withdraws James from Clongowes because of increasing financial troubles.
after 6 Oct: Writes poem, after Parnell's death, entitled 'Et Tu Healy'.

1892 early: Family moves to 23 Carysfort Avenue, Blackrock.

1893 Family moves to 14 Fitzgibbon Street.
6 Apr: Enters Belvedere College.

1894 8–14 Feb: John Joyce sells his remaining Cork properties.
Spring: Wins one of the top prizes at school.
Summer: Goes with father on a trip to Glasgow.
late: Family moves to 17 North Richmond Street.

1895 7 Dec: Enters the Sodality of the Blessed Virgin Mary.

1896 25 Sept: Chosen prefect of the Sodality of the Blessed Virgin Mary.

1897 Easter: Experiences period of piety.

1898 Sept: Enters University College Matriculation course.
27 Sept: Writes an essay on 'Force'.

1898– Family moves several times for failure to pay rents.
1901

1899 18 Feb: Elected to the executive committee of the Literary and Historical Society.
Sept: Writes an essay on the painting 'Ecce Homo' by Munkácsy.
9 Oct: Offers to read a paper in January on 'Drama and Life' before the Literary and Historical Society.

1900 20 Jan: Reads his paper in the Physics Theatre.
1 Apr: 'Ibsen's New Drama', first published work, appears in *Fortnightly Review*.
16 Apr: Ibsen writes to William Archer praising Joyce's review.

23 Apr: Archer relays the message to Joyce.

May: Invites father to go to London with him.

Summer: John Joyce employed to straighten out the voting lists in Mullingar, and he takes James along. Writes a play and calls it *A Brilliant Career*.

30 Aug: Sends *A Brilliant Career* to William Archer with a letter saying, 'I am most anxious to hear your judgment upon it'.

15 Sept: Archer writes Joyce a long, helpful letter.

Writes a play in verse entitled *Dream Stuff*.

1901 Mar: Writes to Ibsen to greet him on his 73rd birthday.

14 Oct: Writes an article entitled 'The Day of the Rabblement', condemning the Irish Literary Theatre for its parochialism.

21 Oct: Article printed and distributed.

1902 1 Feb: Reads a paper on the Irish poet James Clarence Mangan to the Literary and Historical Society.

2 Mar: George Joyce (brother) dies of peritonitis, as James himself was to die.

Apr: Registers for the Royal University Medical School.

May: Paper on Managan published in *St Stephen's*.

June: Leaves University College.

Summer: Decides to make himself known in Dublin literary circles.

Oct: Begins the medical course for which he had registered in the previous spring.

31 Oct: Receives his Bachelor of Arts degree from the Royal University.

18 Nov: Writes to the Faculté de Médecine, Paris, to request admission.

1 Dec: Leaves for Paris on borrowed money.

4 Dec: Writes his first reviews for the Dublin *Daily Express*.

5 Dec: Goes to find out about the medical course.

7 Dec: Probably attends his first classes.

18 Dec: John Joyce takes a second mortgage on his house to enable James to come home.

22 Dec: Leaves Paris; calls on Yeats in London between trains.

23 Dec: Arrives in Dublin.

1903 17 Jan: Leaves Dublin for London.

23 Jan: Reaches Paris.

24 Jan: Acquires card of admission to the Bibliothèque Nationale.

6 Mar: Meets J. M. Synge.

13 Mar: Joyce and Synge part amicably, 'respecting and disdaining each other'.

10 Apr: Receives a telegram that his mother is dying.

11 Apr: Leaves Paris for Dublin.

24 Apr: John Joyce takes out a penultimate mortgage on his house to meet the heavy medical costs of his wife.

13 Aug: May Joyce dies.

3 Sep–19 Nov: Fourteen reviews appear unsigned in the *Daily Express*.

3 Nov: John Joyce takes out another mortgage on his house.

19 Nov: Suggests to Francis Skeffington that they might found a new daily newspaper of the continental type.

1904 7 Jan: Writes off in one day an autobiographical story, 'A Portrait of the Artist', and sends it to the editors of *Dana*, who reject it.

10 Feb: Finishes the first chapter of *Stephen Hero*, based on his rejected short story.

16 May: Sings at the Feis Ceoil (Festival of Music) and receives the bronze medal.

10 June: Meets Nora Barnacle.

15 June: The McKernans, with whom he had his room, encourage him to leave until he can pay his rent.

16 June: Several aspects of his life converge upon this day (which he afterwards chooses for the action of *Ulysses*), the most memorable being his first walk with Nora Barnacle.

20 June: His most public exhibition of drunkenness occurs.

10 Sept: Moves, with Oliver St John Gogarty, to the Martello tower at Sandycove.

9 Oct: Arrives (with Nora) in Paris, after deciding to leave Ireland.

11 Oct: Arrives in Zurich.

20 Oct: Arrives in Trieste, Italy (now called Pulj, in Yugoslavia).

31 Oct: Arrives in Pola, and starts teaching English at the Berlitz school.

1905 Mar: Arrives in Trieste, after deciding he has not liked Pola.

May: Grant Richards turns down *Chamber Music*.

27 July: Giorgio Joyce (son), born.

20 Oct: Stanislaus Joyce (brother) leaves Dublin to join James in Trieste.

3 Dec: Sends *Dubliners* to Grant Richards for consideration.

1906 17 Feb: Grant Richards accepts *Dubliners*.

24 Feb: The Joyces and the Francinis move into a house at 1 via Giovanni Boccaccio.

31 July: Arrives in Rome to work in a bank.

1 Aug: Starts work as a clerk at the bank.

16 Aug: Has used up the money advanced him by the bank.

1 Sept: Grant Richards writes that he could not now publish *Dubliners*.

12 Nov: Receives notice from landlady to leave the room.

20 Nov: Offers *Dubliners* to John Long.

3 Dec: Finds himself without a place to live.

8 Dec: Moves to two small rooms at 51 via Monte Brianzo.

1907 17 Jan: Elkin Mathews accepts *Chamber Music* for publication.

Feb: Tells the bank that he will leave at the end of February.

21 Feb: John Long rejects *Dubliners*.

7 Mar: Returns to Trieste.

22 Mar: Writes his first article in Italian for *Il Piccolo della Sera* (followed by the second on 19 May and the third on 16 Sept).

27 Apr: Gives a lecture on 'Ireland, Island of Saints and Sages'.

May: *Chamber Music* published.

26 July: Lucia Joyce (daughter) born.

1908 12 Feb: Renounces drinking.

May: Has an attack of iritis.

28 June: Announces a new plan to become a commission agent for Irish tweeds.

5 July: Considers training his voice again.

14 July: Thinks of entering for a civil service appointment.

4 August: Nora suffers a miscarriage.

25 Aug: Announces that the following April he will try for a teaching job in Florence.

1909 Apr: Sends *Dubliners* to Maunsel for consideration.

July: Secures payment in advance for a year's lessons from one of his pupils, and plans a visit to Dublin.

29 July: Arrives in Dublin.

19 Aug: Signs a contract for *Dubliners*.

25 Aug: Attends premiere of Bernard Shaw's *The Shewing-Up of Blanco Posnet* and writes an article on it for the *Piccolo della Sera*.

26 Aug: Goes to Galway to visit Nora's family.

8 Sept: *The Evening Telegraph* runs an article about his *Piccolo* review.

9 Sept: Departs from Dublin.

18 Oct: Leaves Trieste again for Dublin after deciding to venture into business.

21 Oct: Arrives in Dublin to open the first cinema in the city.

20 Dec: The Volta Cinema in Mary Street opens.

1910 2 Jan: Leaves Dublin for Trieste.

July: The Volta Cinema, having failed to break even, sold.

1911 Nov: Makes a new effort to gain a livelihood and inquiries about the possibility of teaching in an Italian public school.

1912   Feb: Finds himself unable to pay the rent and his landlord gives him notice.

Mar: Makes a little money by delivering a series of lectures at the Università Popolare.

24–26 Apr: Takes a series of written examinations at the University of Padua to qualify for teaching in public schools.

30 Apr: Takes an oral and an additional written examination.

8 July: Nora and Lucia arrive in Dublin on a visit.

14 or 15 July: Jim and Giorgio leave for London and then for Dublin.

11 Sept: The Joyces leave Dublin for Trieste. (This was to be Joyce's last visit to Dublin.)

11 Nov: Delivers the first of a series of twelve Monday night lectures, in English, on *Hamlet* at the Università del Popolo.

Dec: Sends off *Dubliners* to Martin Secker.

1913   Spring: John Joyce ships the family portraits to Trieste to be entrusted to the care of his eldest son.

Given a position at the Scuola Superiore di Commercio Revoltella.

25 Nov: Grant Richards writes to Joyce wishing to see *Dubliners* again.

Nov: Notes for *Exiles* show the conception of the play to be already formed.

1914   Jan: Holds a part-time job as English correspondent for Gioacchino Veneziani's paint factory.

15 Jan: Ezra Pound publishes an article in the *New Freewoman* entitled 'A Curious History' which embodies the material about the rejection of *Dubliners*.

29 Jan: Grant Richards agrees to publish *Dubliners*.

2 Feb: *A Portrait of the Artist as a Young Man* begins to be published in serial form in *The Egoist*.

15 June: *Dubliners* published.

16 June: Joyce has fixed upon this date as the date of *Ulysses* because it was the anniversary of his first walk with Nora Barnacle.

28 July: Austria declares war on Serbia; Joyce hastens to the British Consulate, but is assured that there is no reason for concern on the part of British subjects.

1915   Apr: Has *Exiles* in nearly final form.

12 Apr: Eileen Joyce (sister) gets married to Frantisek Schaurek.

15 May: Grant Richards decides not to publish *A Portrait of the Artist*.

June: Starts with family for Switzerland.

June (end): Arrives in Zurich.

30 Nov: Harriet Shaw Weaver offers to have the *Egoist* publish *A Portrait* in book form if no regular publisher could be found.

1916 11 July: The Stage Society rejects *Exiles*.

Aug: British Prime Minister grants Joyce £100 from the Civil List.

29 Dec: *A Portrait of the Artist as a Young Man* published.

1917 Mar: John Quinn sends him some money in return for the manuscript of *Exiles*.

1 Apr: The Stage Society asks to have *Exiles* again.

July: Grant Richards agrees to publish *Exiles*.

Aug: Decides to follow his doctor's advice and to winter in Locarno.

12 Oct: Leaves for Locarno.

1918 Jan: Brings family back to Zurich.

27 Feb: Receives a letter from the managing director of a Bank of Zurich asking him to call in connection with some money ('A client of the bank who is much interested in your work . . . wishes to give you a kind of fellowship').

Mar: *Ulysses* starts appearing in the *Little Review*.

Claud Sykes suggests they form a troupe to produce plays in English.

Apr: Rehearsals for *Exiles* begin. Joyce books the Theater zu den Kaufleuten for the night of 29th.

25 May: *Exiles* published.

July: Receives a letter from the British Consulate in Zurich asking him to volunteer for military duty; sends letter back.

9 Dec: His association with Marthe Fleischmann begins to occupy his mind.

1919 2 Feb: Meets Marthe Fleischmann.

28 Mar: Gives Marthe the German translation of *Exiles*.

7 Aug: *Exiles* presented in Munich.

1 Oct: Calls at the bank for his monthly stipend from Mrs McCormick, but the banker informs him that his 'credit is cut off'.

Oct: Takes his family to Trieste, where he reclaims his position at the Scuola Superiore di Commercio Revoltella.

1920 8 July: Goes to Paris to stay a week but remains for twenty years.

Sept: The New York Society for the Prevention of Vice lodges an official complaint against the July–August issue of the *Little Review* which contained part of the *Nausicaa* episode of *Ulysses*.

Dec: Sylvia Beach arranges for a meeting between him and Valery Larbaud, among the principal French writers of the 1920s.

1921   Apr: B. W. Huebsch formally declines the manuscript of *Ulysses*.
Sylvia Beach offers to publish the book by her Shakespeare and
Company bookshop.
7 Dec: Larbaud lectures on Joyce at Shakespeare and Company.

1922   2 Feb: *Ulysses* published on Joyce's fortieth birthday.
1 Apr: Nora, following a quarrel with Joyce, leaves with the
children for Ireland.

1923   Mar: Begins writing *Finnegans Wake*, the work which was to
occupy the next sixteen years of his life.
June: The Joyces arrive in London to spend the summer in
Bognor, Sussex.
Aug: The Joyces return to Paris.
Oct: Meets John Quinn for the first time.

1924   16 June: Scrawls in his notebook, 'Today 16 of June twenty
years after. Will anybody remember this date.'

1925   19 Feb: *Exiles* produced at the Neighborhood Playhouse, New
York.

1926   Feb: *Exiles* produced by the Stage Society at the Regent Theatre,
London.
Apr: Stanislaus Joyce visits James. (The relations of the two
brothers had been strained since 1919.)

1927   7 July: *Pomes Penyeach* published.

1928   Jan: Miss Weaver pays the Joyces a visit.
Sept: Collapses again with eye trouble, and can no longer see
print.

1929   25 Apr: Giorgio Joyce (son) makes his public debut as a singer.
May: First apologia for *Finnegans Wake*, entitled *Our Exagmination
round His Factification for Incamination of Work in Progress*, published.
Nov: His exertions for the Irish tenor John Sullivan begin.

1930   30 June: Attends a performance by Sullivan in the Paris Opéra.
10 Dec: Giorgio Joyce marries Helen Fleischman.

1931   19 May: Adrienne Monnier writes Joyce a letter (on which she
had meditated for a long time) in which she speaks openly of
the way that she and Sylvia Beach have, as they felt, been put
upon.
4 July: James and Nora get married at the Registry Office,
London.
29 Dec: John Joyce (father) dies.

1932   15 Feb: Stephen Joyce (grandson), born.
29 May: Giorgio Joyce and Mary Colum escort Lucia Joyce to
a doctor, who diagnoses her condition as a form of schizophrenia.
2 Sep: W. B. Yeats writes to him nominating him as a founding
member of an Academy of Irish Letters.
5 Oct: Turns down nomination

1934 Jan: Paul Léon persuades John Lane to publish an English edition of *Ulysses*.

Lucia runs away from home.

2 Feb: Lucia upsets James's birthday party by striking Nora, and her internment in a sanatorium could no longer be deferred.

July: Printers protest against certain passages in *Ulysses*.

1935 Dec: Lucia transferred to St Andrew's Hospital, Northampton, for blood tests.

1936 Mar: Lucia has to be carried out of the house in a strait-jacket.

1937 June: Attends a meeting of the PEN Club in Paris.

1938 July: Reveals the secret of the title of his new book, *Finnegans Wake*.

1939 May: *Finnegans Wake* published.

1940 Dec: Takes family back to Zurich.

1941 13 Jan: Dies and is buried in Zurich.

18 Jan: Charles Joyce (brother) dies.

1951 10 Apr: Nora Joyce dies.

1955 15 Apr: Stephen Joyce marries Solange Raytchine and lives in Paris.

16 June: Stanislaus Joyce dies.

1976 12 June: Giorgio Joyce dies.

1982 12 Dec: Lucia Joyce dies.

A Sister Recalls Joyce in Dublin*

MAY JOYCE MONAGHAN

'Jim, as we used to call him,' said Mrs Monaghan, 'was very gentle and quiet. I don't ever remember him going out with my father drinking. He didn't drink much.' Mrs Monaghan's father, John Stanislaus Joyce, is a leading character in his son's writings, and he is still remembered in Dublin as a drinker in the epic Irish tradition.

'My mother was very religious,' said Mrs Monaghan. 'My father was the opposite, anything but. He was a man about town. "I get more out of life than any white man" – so he used to say. He had a beautiful voice. So had Jim. My mother was a very good pianist. There always seemed to be music and playing and singing in spite of difficulties financially.

'My father amused Jim – with his wit and his vitality. My father was full of everything, whistling around, always wanting to live it up. You'd think he hadn't a care in the world. And ten of us there to be provided for. My mother was always trying to keep the men's souls right, trying to get them to go to mass and confession.

'Did Jim and his father ever fight? Jim wasn't a fighter, you know. His father would upbraid him for being out late: "Where were you last night? What hour did you get in?" "I was out with the poet" – Jim made that answer once. I think it could have been Padraic Colum.'

NOTE

Joyce's sister, Mrs May (Mary Kathleen) Joyce Monaghan (1890–1966), was in New York at the invitation of Mrs Frances Steloff, owner of the Gotham Book Mart and President of the James Joyce Society, to help celebrate the 82nd anniversary of Joyce's birth. She gave this interview at the Gotham Book Mart.

* Extracted from an interview in the *New York Times*, 3 February 1964, p. 25. Interviewed by Brian O'Doherty.

James Joyce at Belvedere College*

JOHN FRANCIS BYRNE

I sat in the same class with Joyce in room No. 3 in Belvedere College, from 1894 to 1895.[1] The large windows of this classroom gave south; and in the southwest corner there was the teacher's dais. At the west and east walls there were folding doors, opening respectively to the preparatory and middle grade classrooms. At the northeast corner in the north wall was the door to the corridor outside. In the room there were two rows of desks; four desks to the row, with a passageway between the rows. Each desk could accommodate four pupils. Joyce always sat near the window in the front desk of the left row, facing the teacher, and immediately under the dais. I sat always in the back desk of the right row, just one seat space from the door; that space next the door was occupied during that year by Joe Culhane; Joe's brother, Frank, sat in the back desk of the left row. I don't know about Joe, but Frank has been dead since 1927. He was Taxing Master in Dublin City and had been married to Maggie Sheehy, one of the four daughters of David Sheehy, the MP. One of these daughters is referred to by Joyce in the *Portrait of the Artist*. The eldest daughter, Hannah, married Skeffington; Mary became the wife of Tom Kettle, and Kathleen wedded Cruise O'Brien.

In this class there were about thirty boys, all of them good lads, and some of them really intelligent. There were two brothers, Keogh, who were obviously great chums. They lived over Rathmines way. The younger of these two brothers was one of the best and best-looking boys I ever knew – I think he was the youngest and he was certainly one of the brightest, in the class. He was small, but well-built and strong; with large blue eyes and curly golden hair. Towards the end of that school year this little fellow took sick and died. We were all very sad about it; at least I know I was. Joyce was a little boy, bright, well-looking, and apparently delicate. But he really wasn't delicate; he was virile enough physically. He was a bright boy, always the good scholar, and he was favoured by all the teachers, especially Dempsey,[2] the

* *Silent Years: An Autobiography with Memoirs of James Joyce and our Ireland* (New York: Farrar, Straus and Young, 1953) pp. 146–7. Editor's title.

English teacher, who, as I recall now over the intervening years, resembled Justice Holmes.

In some respects Joyce was precocious; in others he was, and remained, rather strangely simple. Dempsey liked him a great deal, but I think he liked the little fellow for his own sake, just as much as for his proficiency in English. Each Monday we were supposed to bring in an English composition, and of course all of us – well, very nearly all – complied. A few of the 'composers' would be asked by Dempsey to read their lucubrations, and among these James Joyce was one of the most frequently called upon. Joyce was a good reader, and the while he read, Dempsey would literally wriggle and chuckle with delight. Generally, the class, too, liked Joyce's efforts, but there were occasions when the floridity of his stuff made you feel as if you were in the hot-house out in the Botanic Gardens.

Joyce had a fine sense of humour, but his definitely favourite mirth rouser was when anyone pulled a boner. Always he sat in an elfin crouch waiting and hoping for a blunder. For instance, that day when the word 'pedestrian' came up and Dempsey asked the class, 'What is a pedestrian?' One kid's arm shot up like a semaphore.

'Well, Reuben, what is a pedestrian?'

'A pedestrian is a Roman soldier, Sir.'

Joyce's spontaneous shout – well, you couldn't describe it as a laugh – was more like a howl of agony, as if his little frame were being torn apart.[3]

NOTES

James Joyce readers know Stephen Dedalus, the protagonist of *Stephen Hero*, *A Portrait of the Artist* and *Ulysses*. Against Stephen's brooding spirit, Joyce counterposed Stephen's young friend Cranly, detached, critical and catalytic. Cranly is in reality John Francis Byrne, Joyce's lifelong friend. In 1910, Byrne went to New York, where he was a reporter, editorial writer and daily columnist.

1. Joyce entered Belvedere College in 1893 and stayed until 1898.

2. George Stanislaus Dempsey, the original of Mr Tate in *A Portrait of the Artist as a Young Man*.

3. For more information on Joyce at Belvedere College see Bruce Bradley, SJ, *James Joyce's Schooldays*, Foreword by Richard Ellmann (Dublin: Gill and Macmillan, 1982).

Reuben Didn't Admire James Joyce!*

FRANCIS AYLMER

– *And Reuben J., Martin Cunningham said, gave the boatman a florin for saving his son's life. A stifled sigh came from under Mr Power's hand.*
– *Oh, he did, Martin Cunningham affirmed. Like a hero. A silver florin.*
– *Isn't it awfully good? Mr Bloom said eagerly.*
– *One and eightpence too much, Mr Dedalus said wryly. Mr Power's choked laugh burst quietly in the carriage.*

Thus did James Joyce, in his *Ulysses*, lampoon the Dodds, father and son. Almost eighty years old, the 'young' Reuben, a retired Dublin solicitor, died last October in St Kevin's Hospital in his native city. He was up to then one of the few surviving characters from the pages of *Ulysses*. Another character, Dr Oliver St John Gogarty ('Buck Mulligan'), predeceased him a short while before.

Why was Joyce so splenetic against the Dodds?

My impression of Reuben Dodd was of a kindly, retiring man, living largely in those spacious days when Dublin was the third city of the British Empire. He bore no resemblance to the young man at whom Joyce scoffed. He seemed to be a fine Dublin gentleman of the old type.

Over a year ago he told me how 'Jim' (as he called him) Joyce came to hold that spleen against him. They were classmates in Belvedere College and Joyce brought a family vendetta against the Dodds to school with him.

About 1892 or 1893, as well as Reuben could remember, Joyce's father, John Stanislaus (originally a clerk in the old Collector-General's office in Fleet Street), borrowed £400 or £500 from the elder Reuben on a deposit of title deeds of a fairly valuable family property in Cork.[1]

Some times afterwards, Joyce, senior, requested the elder Dodd to give him back the deeds without repayment of the loan.

'But,' Reuben Dodd explained to me, 'my father was a very wide-awake man. He knew Joyce's father too well. And Joyce's father never forgave my father for insisting on payment of that debt.'

* Extracted from *Irish Digest* (Dublin), 61 (December 1957) 50–1.

And then he told me that he regarded 'Jim' Joyce, during his schooldays, as 'a disagreeable type'.

'He left Belvedere and went to some other school, and I have no recollection of him when he was knocking around Dublin. I need not tell you I never numbered him among my friends.'

Here is Reuben Dodd's impression of *Ulysses*: 'It was a scurrilous book all round, but the present generation could not appreciate it as I could, because I knew the characters in it. Of course, Joyce had a nasty mind.'

What did he think of Joyce's sense of humour? '*Ulysses*,' he said, 'has passages of unconscious humour, but nothing more'.

'Joyce,' he added, 'has no real intellectual stature. He was intellectual up to a point, and that was the point where blackguardism intervened.'

NOTES

While Joyce was at Belvedere College, his father's financial position was deteriorating and the sale of his properties in Cork was made necessary mainly by heavy debts to Reuben J. Dodd, a Dublin solicitor who lent money.

1. The sale of the properties took place in February 1894. See Richard Ellmann, *James Joyce*, 2nd edn (London and New York: Oxford University Press, 1982) pp. 37–8.

'The White Bishop'*

JOHN FRANCIS BYRNE

It was late in October 1898, that Joyce first dubbed me Cranly. This was one of the months during which he sat waiting for me, session after session while I played chess with Parnell.

After one of these sessions Joyce came over and stood beside me, waiting impatiently for us to go. For perhaps a minute or two I held a post mortem with John Howard on the game we had just played; when Joyce, taking me by the arm, intoned softly into my ear "Ite missa est," your Grace. Come on, Cranly; as you say yourself "Let us eke go" '

---

* *Silent Years: An Autobiography with Memoirs of James Joyce and our Ireland* (New York: Farrar, Straus and Young, 1953) pp. 43–4.

On the footpath outside, Joyce, still linking me, asked, 'Did you hear what I called you?'

'Yes, of course I did. You called me Cranly.'

'I like that name,' he said, 'do you mind me calling you by it?'

'No, I don't mind – only I'd just as lief be called Byrne or J. F.'

'Very well, then, I'll go on calling you J. F., but I'll think of you as Cranly. Do you know where I got that name?'

'Yes, I do. Since you came to University College last month you have heard me occasionally referred to as the "White bishop". And in the past few weeks there have been a couple of notices about a White Bishop who came here as Archbishop of Dublin five hundred years ago this very month of October. The other night I saw you reading about him in John D'Alton's book, the *Memoirs of the Archbishops of Dublin*.'

'Diseases of the Ox'*

JOHN FRANCIS BYRNE

In the *Portrait of the Artist* Joyce writes of 'Stephen pointing to the title page of Cranly's book on which was written "Diseases of the Ox".' This apparently trivial incident affords much material for rumination. Here is the story.

In July, 1899, something occurred to a cow owned by my farming friends in the County Wicklow; in the National Library I sought for, and with the help fo the librarian, Mr Lyster,[1] finally located a book in which I hoped to find some information that might be useful should a similar emergency occur. When the librarian handed me the book at the counter, he indicated a section or chapter in it with the title 'Diseases of the Ox', and although I was in serious mood, I immediately smiled. 'Diseases of the Ox' I read aloud, and remarked to Lyster, who also had a broad smile on his visage, 'Sounds funny, somehow, that title'. 'Yes, it does,' he agreed, 'but maybe it covers what you are looking for.'

I took the book with me and sat down at a table near the balcony door, and I had just begun to peruse it when Joyce came in and sat down beside me. At that period Joyce was cramming himself with the Norwegian language, and he had brought with him to our table a pile

* Extracted from *Silent Years: An Autobiography with Memoirs of James Joyce and our Ireland* (New York: Farrar, Straus and Young, 1953) pp. 58–9, 61, 63–4.

of books on Ibsen including some of his plays, a Norwegian dictionary and a Norwegian grammar. For a moment he was silent, but then he leaned over to look at the large book I had open before me. 'Good Lord, Byrne,' he ejaculated, 'what *are* you reading?' I didn't say anything but I turned the pages to the title of the chapter where printed in large type was 'Diseases of the Ox'. The instantaneous effect on James Joyce was the detonating expulsion of a howl that reverberated through the reading room; and no Assyrian ever came down more swiftly on a fold than did Lyster on Joyce, who was in a convulsion of laughter.

'Mr Joyce,' the librarian ordered, 'please leave the reading room.' By way of calling attention to an ameliorating circumstance, I pointed to the title, but Lyster snapped, 'Yes, Mr Byrne, I know, but Mr Joyce should learn to control himself, and I must ask him to leave the reading room, and to stay out of it, until he does.' Compliantly Joyce struggled to his feet, and I got up to go with him. 'I don't mean you, Mr Byrne. Of course, you can stay.' 'That's all right, thank you, Mr Lyster, but I'm afraid I'll have to help my friend out of the room. He would never be able to navigate as far as the turnstile.'

Outside of the library Joyce slowly regained his composure, but neither of us felt inclined to make an immediate return to the vicinity of that book. Instead, we went for a walk through the Green and, needless to say, we talked; and the one big question that interested us was why that title was so funny. Why, for instance, was it that if that title had been 'Diseases of Cattle', or 'Bovine Diseases', we would not have thought it a bit funny? But 'Diseases of the Ox' yes; for some obscure reason, it was funny. . . .

To retrace my steps once more after this digression, that incident in the National Library of Joyce's outburst of mirth at the title, 'Diseases of the Ox', occurred during the period when he was studying Ibsen and preparing his essay on that playwright – an essay which found prompt acceptance, on its very first offering, in the *Fortnightly Review*.[2] While Joyce was writing it, a period of about two months, he sat as usual beside me in the Library, and at his insistence I read it and re-read it as it progressed, and when it was finished I could have recited it verbatim. Whether it was a good thing for Joyce that his essay was accepted by the *Fortnightly*, and that it was accepted so promptly, is a point I won't discuss here. . . .

After his article on Ibsen had been published, Joyce's relationship with his few associates became impaired by either their jealousy or sycophancy; and so it happened that Joyce was forced during the next couple of years to rely more than ever on me for companionship.

Immediately after the publication of the Ibsen article, Joyce began occasionally, and when in the mood, to seek expression in writing short poems. In the production of these he was not prolific; and even as he sat beside me in the library he would write and rewrite and retouch, it might almost seem interminably, a bit of verse containing perhaps a dozen or a score of lines. When he had at last polished his gem to a satisfying degree of curvature and smoothness, he would write out the finished poem with slow and stylish penmanship and hand the copy to me. Many a time he said to me as he did this: 'Keep all these, J. F. – some day they'll be worth a pound a piece to you.' Joyce always said this jokingly; but I never took his remark as a joke for I was even then quite sure that, no matter what my own personal opinion of his bits of verse might be, these bits of polished verse in Joyce's equally polished handwriting would some day be collector's pieces.

The finished poems were invariably done on slips of good quality white paper provided free and in abundance to the readers of the National Library. The slips were approximately $7\frac{5}{8}$ inches in length by $3\frac{3}{8}$ inches in width. Joyce gave me copies of all the poems he wrote prior to October, 1902; and I kept all of them, as well as I could, for more than twenty years. Then, finding that many had been either lost, or, more likely, pilfered, and realising that they would probably be safer in a collection, I yielded to the importunities of John Quinn[3] and sold him the few originals I had left. With these I also sold to Mr Quinn a signed copy of Joyce's 'The Holy Office', which he gave to me on one of his visits to my place at 100 Phibsboro Road. The price I got for these several items averaged about six dollars. That certainly wasn't much; but still it was more than even Joyce had jokingly told me they would some day be worth.

NOTES

1. T. W. Lyster (1855–1922) worked at the National Library of Ireland from 1878 to 1920, being librarian from 1895.

2. 'Ibsen's New Drama', Joyce's first published work, appeared in the *Fortnightly Review* on 1 April 1900.

3. John Quinn (1870–1924), American lawyer and supporter of the Irish Renaissance.

My School Friend, James Joyce*

JUDGE EUGENE SHEEHY

From September 1892, to June 1899, I was a pupil of Belvedere College, Dublin. James Joyce came to Belvedere from Clongowes Wood College and was in a class, one year ahead of me, for the Intermediate examinations. He was aloof, icy and imperturbable. He took pleasure, too, in baiting his masters and the Rector.

One day when Father Henry, SJ, the Rector, was taking my class for Latin, Joyce was sent in by the English master, Mr Dempsey (the Mr Tate of *A Portrait of the Artist as a Young Man*), to report that he had been late for school. The Rector delivered quite a long lecture to Joyce, to which the latter listened in unrepentent silence.

When the lecture had finished, Joyce added, as if by way of afterthought and in a very bored manner:

'Mr Dempsey told me to tell you, Sir, that I was half an hour late also yesterday.' This led to a second telling-off, almost as long as the first, and when it had run its course Joyce took up the running again – this time almost with a yawn:

'Mr Dempsey told me to tell you, Sir, that I have not been in time for school any day this month.'

This method of confessing one's transgressions was calculated to break the heart of any headmaster, and I fear that at Belvedere Joyce added many grey hairs to Father Henry's head.

It was Father Henry whom Joyce burlesqued in the school play at Belvedere, so vividly described in his book, *Stephen Hero*. I was seated in the gallery of the school theatre when the play was produced and witnessed the performance. The Reverend Rector had many mannerisms and clichés.

Joyce, who was cast for the part of a schoolmaster in the school play, ignored the rôle allotted to him and impersonated Father Henry. He carried on, often for five minutes at a time, with the pet sayings of the Rector, imitating his gestures and mannerisms. The other members of

* *May It Please the Court* (Dublin: C. J. Fallon, 1951) pp. 8–29.

the cast collapsed with laughter on the stage – completely missing their cues and forgetting their parts – and the schoolboy audience received the performance with hysterical glee.

Father Henry, who was sitting in one of the front rows, again showed what a sportsman he was by laughing loudly at this joke against himself and Joyce received no word of reprimand for his impudence.

In the year 1889, when I was sixteen years old, I passed from school to the Royal University of Ireland.[1]

The lectures were few and afforded me ample time to browse elsewhere. The real Alma Mater at this time was the National Library in Kildare Street. We read for our examinations in the Library upstairs, but there were rather prolonged adjournments to the steps outside, where we heard the views on art and life and literature of Joyce, Kettle, Skeffington, Arthur Clery, John Marcus O'Sullivan, William Dawson, Constantine Curran and many other well-read and cultured men.

I remember a great occasion on which James Joyce read a paper on 'Drama and Life' for the Literary and Historical Society. He had previously submitted the script of his address to the Rev. President of the College for his approval. The latter, finding much to disagree with in Joyce's whole-hearted praise of Ibsen's plays, passed a blue pencil through some of the passages in the address.

Joyce, however, refused to read his paper if these passages were deleted. He discussed the matter with the President and to enforce his argument even lent him copies of the plays for his perusal. The result was that Joyce carried the day and read his paper without a word omitted.

Joyce took his Degree in the Royal University and I saw a good deal of him during his time in College. He treated both his lectures and examinations as a joke, and it is to the credit of the University and its Professors that, in spite of all this, he passed through successfully.

He told me, from time to time, how he enjoyed himself in the examination hall. He considered that the poet Cowper was only fit to write the rhymes which are found in Christmas crackers. When requested, therefore, to write an appreciation of *The Task*, he finished off two pages of scathing disparagement of its author with an adaptation of Hamlet's farewell to the dead Polonius: 'Peace, tedious old fool!'

Addison was another *bête noire*:[2] referring to his summons to Steele to 'see how a Christian can die', Joyce berated him as the world's greatest hypocrite, and lapsed into Chaucerian English to state that the great 'Atticus' himself was 'holpen nightly to his litter'.

It was, however, at his Oral Examination in English for his BA Degree that he excelled himself. One of the learned Professors put to him the question: 'How is poetic justice exemplified in the play of *King Lear*?'

Joyce replied: 'I don't know.'

The examiner, who had full knowledge of Joyce's literary ability, was not satisfied with this reply. 'Oh, come, Mr Joyce, you are not doing yourself justice. I feel sure that you have read the play.'

'Oh, yes!' replied Joyce, 'but I don't understand your question. The phrase "poetic justice" is unmeaning jargon so far as I am concerned.'

Joyce and I both attended the same class for Italian. Our lecturer was an Italian Jesuit named Father Ghezzi,[3] who had been in India for many years and spoke English perfectly. Joyce had a wonderful aptitude for foreign languages and spoke Italian like a native, though, at that time, he had never left Dublin.

My function in the class was to listen to Father Ghezzi and Joyce discuss philosophy and literature in Italian, and, for all I could understand of the dialogue, I would have been more profitably engaged in taking high dives from the spring-board at the Forty Foot hole in Sandycove.

A close companion of Joyce at the College was George Clancy, who was afterwards Mayor of Limerick and was shot by the 'Black and Tans'.[4] Clancy was a well-built and dark-haired son of Munster who was keen on Gaelic games and the restoration of our ancient language. He had a keen sense of humour and no guile. The simplicity and sincerity of his character appealed to Joyce and I suspect that the character described as Davin in *A Portrait* covers his identity.

He and Joyce, at French class, made merry at the expense of Professor Cadic.[5] Joyce would snigger whilst Clancy was translating into English a passage from a French textbook. Clancy pretended to take offence, demanded an instant apology, which was refused, and thereupon challenged Joyce to a duel in the Phœnix Park. The Professor intervened to prevent bloodshed; the performance ended with handshakes all round; and the guileless Frenchman never appreciated what a farce it all was.

One day Joyce entered the class-room about twenty minutes late and, ignoring the Professor's presence, went over to one of the large front windows of No. 86, threw it up, and stuck his head out. Monsieur Cadic, by a counter-stroke, in order to upset Joyce's equilibrium, went to the other window, threw it up and, putting his head well out, looked across at the offending pupil.

'*Bonjour, M'sieu!*' said the imperturbable Joyce. 'I was counting the carriages in Alderman Kernan's funeral.'

Joyce was an intimate friend, both at school and college, of my brother

Richard and myself, and he came very often to my father's house in Belvidere Place.

He was a tall, slight stripling, with flashing teeth – white as a hound's – pale blue eyes that sometimes had an icy look, and a mobile sensitive mouth. He was fond of throwing back his head as he walked, and his mood alternated between cold, slightly haughty, aloofness and sudden boisterous merriment. Sometimes his abrupt manner was a cloak for shyness.

Joyce could have been a great actor. Even in his late 'teens he was keen on dramatics and took part in family theatricals. I remember him playing in Belvidere Place the part of the English Colonel in Robertson's *Caste* and he played it to the life.

He acted also with my sister, Margaret, in the old XL Café in Grafton Street in a play written by her, called *Cupid's Confidante*, in which he played the part of the villain – Geoffrey Fortescue.

In charades in our house on Sunday nights he was the star turn. His wit and gift for improvisation came into ready play. He was also a clever mimic and his impassive poker face helped his impersonations.

I remember on one occasion a burlesque of *Hamlet* performed by him and William Fallon, Joyce played the Queen Mother to Fallon's Ophelia, and the performance would rival that of Jimmy O'Dea at his best.

As Ophelia, with appropriate comments, laid on the carpet some pieces of carrot and onion – the best substitutes for yew and rosemary – Hamlet's mother (who bore a striking resemblance to 'Mrs Mulligan of the Coombe') performed all the motions of a woman 'keening' at an Irish wake in the very ecstasy of grief.

Joyce had a beautiful tenor voice and one of his earliest ambitions was to be a singer. His mother sometimes came to our house and played on the piano the accompaniments to his songs. I remember her as a frail, sad-faced and gentle lady whose skill at music suggested, a sensitive, artistic temperament.

She was very proud and fond of James, and he worshipped her. I can still see him linking her towards the piano with a grave old-world courtesy. When she was not present he played by ear his own accompaniments.

He had a wide range of ballads, English and Irish. His favourite songs were: 'Take a Pair of Sparkling Eyes' from *The Gondoliers* and the Serenade by Shelley beginning 'I arise from dreams of thee'. He revelled, however, with a zest worthy of Falstaff in such rousing ballads as 'Blarney Castle', 'Bold Turpin Hero' and 'When McCarthy Took the Flure at Enniscorthy'.

Joyce had legends for some of the Dublin statues. Of that of Bishop Plunket[6] in Kildare Place, who has a finger thoughtfully on his brow, he said that the pose suggested: 'Now, where on earth did I put that stud?' And the statue of the poet Moore in College Green supplied with right forefinger raised the satisfied answer: 'Oh! I know'.

On one occasion my brother and I were walking together in Phisborough Road. We saw Joyce approaching us, waving aloft what seemed to be a small Venetian blind. He was followed, at some paces' interval, by his brother Stanislaus, who appeared to be hugely amused at James's antics. Joyce was very excited.

'Look what I have here,' he said. 'This is an Indian poem written in Sanskrit on ribbed grass, and I am going to sell it to the Professor of Oriental Languages in Trinity College.'

He opened up the book to show us the ribbed grass and the writing thereon. When he had the lattice work open in full length, a nursery maid in charge of a perambulator drove into him from behind, with the result that he fell back into the carriage of the pram. Joyce was not the least bit perturbed. Still holding the book wide open on his lap, he half turned to the nurse and said very calmly: 'Are you going far, Miss?'

He also loved to challenge others to do whimsical acts. One night I heard him wager Skeffington half-a-crown, that the latter would not purchase one halfpenny worth of gooseberries in the most expensive fruit shop in O'Connell Street and tender a golden sovereign in payment.

Skeffington took the bet and gave his miserly order to the lady shop assistant. When he offered the sovereign in payment the lady said in rather frigid tone: 'Could you not make it something more, sir?'

'No,' replied Skeffington, 'I can't afford it,' and he collected his gooseberries and his change.

Joyce witnessed all this from the door of the shop and whooped with glee at the peformance.

After Joyce left Dublin, I lost touch with him for some years, though he wrote to my father on the death of my brother Richard, and at another time sent me an Italian newspaper in which he had written an article – 'Il Fenianismo' – on the death of John O'Leary, the great Fenian leader.

One night in the year 1909 during a production by the Abbey Theatre of Shaw's *Blanco Posnet* I met Joyce again. He tapped me on the shoulder from behind with his walking-stick, and then greeted me nonchalantly, as if we had met the previous day. He told me that he had come to Dublin to do the critique of the play – which had been censored in Great Britain – for an Italian newspaper, *Il Piccolo Sera*.[7]

He also said that I would hear interesting news of him within the next few weeks. This had reference, I understand, to the fact that he was to be the manager of the first cinema in Dublin, the 'Volta' in Henry Street'[8]

The next and last time I met Joyce was in his flat in Paris in the year 1928, when he had become world-famous.

Everything in Joyce's rooms spelt 'Dublin'. There were pictures and sketches of old Dublin on the walls and even the design of the large rug, with which the floor was carpeted, portrayed the corkscrew course of the River Liffey.

He was delighted to meet me again, and his queries were all concerning the Dublin that he knew and loved.

'Where were now Tom and Dick and Harry!' – naming former companions that I had well-nigh forgotten, and he became quite impatient that I could not call to mind at once one Jack O'Reilly, who had faded from the Dublin scene for many years.

'And how does Sallynoggin look now?' and 'the shops along the chief streets?' And then he questioned me about some of Dublin's well-known characters.

He was thrilled to know that the statue of Smith O'Brien[9] had been moved from O'Connell Bridge, and was now in O'Connell Street.

'Why has nobody told me that before?' he said rather petulantly.

My sister, Mrs Sheehy Skeffington, told me that at a later date she had another such interview with Joyce. Half-dazed with his cascade of queries, she at length said to him:

'Mr Joyce, you pretend to be a cosmopolitan, but how is it that all your thoughts are about Dublin, and almost everything that you have written deals with it and its inhabitants?'

'Mrs Skeffington,' he replied, with a rather whimsical smile, 'there was an English Queen who said that when she died the word "Calais" would be written on her heart. "Dublin" will be found on mine.'

NOTES

Judge Eugene Sheehy (1883–?).

1. The Royal University was later reconstituted as the National University.
2. One especially disliked.
3. Charles Ghezzi.

4. Auxiliaries supplied by the British in 1920 during the Anglo-Irish conflict.
5. Édouard Cadic.
6. William Conyngham (1828–97), Fourth Baron Plunket, Archbishop of Dublin.
7. The correct title of the Italian newspaper was *Il Piccolo della Sera*. Joyce's review can be found in *Shaw: The Critical Heritage*, ed. T. F. Evans (London: Routledge & Kegan Paul, 1976) pp. 197–9.
8. The Volta Cinema was in Mary Street, not in Henry Street.
9. Smith O'Brien (1803–64), nationalist.

'An Extremely Clever Boy'*

GEORGE RUSSELL

Dear W. B. Y.,

. . .

I want you very much to meet a young fellow named Joyce whom I wrote to Lady Gregory about half jestingly. He is an extremely clever boy who belongs to your clan more than to mine and more still to himself. But he has all the intellectual equipment, culture and education which all our other clever friends here lack. And I think writes amazingly well in prose though I believe he also writes verse and is engaged in writing a comedy which he expects will occupy him five years or thereabouts as he writes slowly. Moore[1] who saw an article of this boy's says it is preposterously clever. Anyhow I think you would find this youth of twenty-one with his assurance and self-confidence rather interesting. He is I think certainly more promising than Magee.[2] . . .

Yours ever,
Geo, W. Russell[3]

NOTES

During the summer of 1902, Joyce decided to make himself known in Dublin

---

* Extracted from *Letters from AE*, selected and edited by Alan Denson (London and New York: Abelard-Schuman, 1961) p. 43.

literary circles. He approached first George William Russell [pseud. AE] (1867–1935), the poet who was a pivotal figure in the Irish Revival. Russell wrote to Joyce asking him, 'Could you come on Monday evening next to see me?' Following this meeting, which took place on 18 August 1902, Russell wrote this letter to W. B. Yeats, the poet.

1. George Moore (1852–1933), Irish novelist and playwright.
2. William Kirkpatrick Magee [pseud. John Eglinton] (1868–1961), Irish essayist and poet.
3. See Joseph Holloway's account of Joyce's interview with George Russell in *A James Joyce Miscellany, Second Series*, ed. Marvin Magalaner (Carbondale, Ill.: Southern Illinois University Press, 1959) pp. 107–8.

'The Younger Generation is Knocking at My Door'*

W. B. YEATS

I had been looking over the proof sheets of this book one day in Dublin lately and thinking whether I should send it to the Dublin papers for review or not. I thought that I would not, for they would find nothing in it but a wicked theology, which I had probably never intended, and it may be found all the review on a single sentence. I was wondering how long I should be thought a preacher of reckless opinions and a disturber who carries in his hand the irresponsible torch of vain youth. I went out into the street and there a young man came up to me and introduced himself. He told me he had written a book of prose essays or poems, and spoke to me of a common friend.

Yes, I recollected his name, for he had been to my friend who leads an even more reckless rebellion than I do, and kept him up to the grey hours of the morning discussing philosophy. I asked him to come with me to the smoking room of a restaurant in O'Connell Street, and read me a beautiful though immature and eccentric harmony of little prose descriptions and meditations. He had thrown over metrical form, he said, that he might get a form so fluent that it would respond to the motions of the spirit. I praised his work but he said, 'I really don't care whether you like what I am doing or not. It won't make the least difference to me. Indeed I don't know why I am reading to you.'

Then, putting down his book, he began to explain all his objections

* Richard Ellmann, *The Identity of Yeats* (London: Faber & Faber, 1954) pp. 86–9. Editor's title.

to everything I had ever done. Why had I concerned myself with politics, with folklore, with the historical setting of events, and so on? Above all why had I written about ideas, why had I condescended to make generalisations? These things were all the sign of the cooling of the iron, of the fading out of inspiration. I had been puzzled, but now I was confident again. He is from the Royal University, I thought, and he thinks that everything has been settled by Thomas Aquinas,[1] so we need not trouble about it. I have met so many like him. He would probably review my book in the newspapers if I sent it there. But the next moment he spoke of a friend of mine [Oscar Wilde] who after a wild life had turned Catholic on his deathbed. He said that he hoped his conversion was not sincere. He did not like to think that he had been untrue to himself at the end. No, I had not understood him yet.

I had been doing some little plays for our Irish theatre, and had founded them all on emotions or stories that I had got out of folklore. He objected to these particularly and told me that I was deteriorating. I had told him that I had written these plays quite easily and he said that made it quite certain; his own little book owed nothing to anything but his own mind which was much nearer to God than folklore.

I took up the book and pointing to a thought said, 'You got that from somebody else who got it from the folk.' I felt exasperated and puzzled and walked up and down explaining the dependence of all good art on popular tradition. I said, 'The artist, when he has lived for a long time in his own mind with the example of other artists as deliberate as himself, gets into a world of ideas pure and simple. He becomes very highly individualised and at last by sheer pursuit of perfection becomes sterile. Folk imagination on the other hand creates endless images of which there are no ideas. Its stories ignore the moral law and every other law, they are successions of pictures like those seen by children in the fire. You find a type of these two kinds of invention, the invention of artists and the invention of the folk, in the civilisation that comes from town and in the forms of life that one finds in the country. In the towns, especially in big towns like London, you don't find what old writers used to call the people; you find instead a few highly cultivated, highly perfected individual lives, and great multitudes who imitate them and cheapen them. You find, too, great capacity for doing all kinds of things, but an impulse towards creation which grows gradually weaker and weaker. In the country, on the other hand, I mean in Ireland and in places where the towns have not been able to call the tune, you find people who are hardly individualised to any great extent. They live through the same round of duty and they think about life and death as their fathers have told them, but in speech, in the telling of tales, in all that has to do with the play of imagery, they have an endless abundance. I have collected hundreds of stories and have had hundreds of stories collected for me, and if one leaves out certain set forms of tale not one story is like another. Everything seems possible to them, and because they can never be surprised, they imagine the most surprising things. The folk life, the country life, is nature with her abundance, but the art life, the town life, is the spirit which is sterile when it is not married to nature. The whole ugliness of the modern world has come from the spread of the towns and their ways of thought, and to bring back beauty we must marry the spirit and nature again. When the idea which comes from individual life marries the image that is born from the people, one gets great art, the art of Homer,[2] and of Shakespeare, and of Chartres Cathedral.'

I looked at my young man. I thought, 'I have conquered him now,' but I was quite wrong. He merely said, 'Generalisations aren't made by poets; they are made by men of letters. They are no use.'

Presently he got up to go, and, as he was going out, he said, 'I am twenty. How old are you?' I told him, but I am afraid I said I was a year younger than I am. He said with a sigh, 'I thought as much. I have met you too late. You are too old.'

And now I am still undecided as to whether I shall send this book to the Irish papers for review. The younger generation is knocking at my door as well as theirs.[3]

NOTES

In October 1902, George Russell introduced Joyce to W. B. Yeats (1865–1939). Yeats wrote this account of the meeting which he originally inteded to use as a preface to his book, *Ideas of Good and Evil*. The reliability of Yeats's account, however, has been questioned.

1. See William T. Noon, SJ, *Joyce and Aquinas* (New Haven, Conn.: Yale University Press, 1957). Yeats may be recalling Joyce's description of his soul as 'Steeled in the school of old Aquinas', in 'The Holy Office', 1904–5.

2. At this time, as Richard Ellmann has pointed out, Joyce had no interest in Homer. [*James Joyce*, 2nd ed (London and New York: Oxford University Press, 1982) p. 103.]

3. A reference to Solness's fear in Ibsen's *The Master Builder*. Fearful that he will be replaced and destroyed by the younger generation, Halvard Solness, an architect who stands at the top of his profession, has always guarded his commissions.

'Joyce has Grit'*

LADY GREGORY

15 November 1902. 'I have seen Joyce who came up to see me last night. His mind is quite made up for Paris. I think from any ordinary standpoint his action is wild, but with boys like Joyce there is always the overshadowing powers to consider. I think he has genius of a kind and I like his pride and waywardness. I have written to a friend in Paris about him but cannot be sure if anything can be done by him. Joyce's father is too poor and I think Joyce can only gather up money together to pay his fare over and keep him for two or three weeks. I think it likely if he could hold on for six weeks that he could find work. He is well educated, knows French and German and Italian and has a degree here. The cost of a medical degree in Paris is much less than in Trinity and if he could get tuition he would be able probably to pay his way. He can live cheaply and I can, through art students, put him in the way of finding financially possible lodging. I hope he will be all right. The more I know him the better I like him, and though I wish he could remain in Ireland still I would like to see him prosper somewhere. I am sure he will make a name somewhere.'

I wrote to Yeats from Coole in 1902: 'Joyce has been writing to me of his plans and I have him much on my mind. I am afraid he will find it hard to make a living by lessons in Paris, where there are so many English teachers. But I daresay Paris may be a good place for him – there is not enough give and take in Dublin – everyone, as Magee says, gets into a clique or two (perhaps he includes us!).'

And again, 'I wonder if Joyce has written to you. Poor boy, I am afraid he will knock his ribs against the earth, but he has grit and will succeed in the end. You should write and ask him to breakfast with you on the morning he arrives, if you can get up early enough, and feed him and take care of him and give him dinner at Victoria before he goes and help him on his way. I am writing to various people who might possibly get him tuitions and to Synge who would at least tell him of cheap lodgings.

* *Seventy Years: Being the Autobiography of Lady Gregory*, ed. Colin Smythe (Gerrards Cross, Buckinghamshire: Colin Smythe, 1974) pp. 425–6. Editor's title.

NOTE

On his graduation from University College, Joyce emigrated in December 1902 to Paris, where he was to undertake the study of medicine while supporting himself with some reviewing that Yeats and Lady Gregory had arranged. However, his mother's failing health prompted his return to Ireland in 1903. Lady Gregory (1852–1932) was a playwright, folklorist and one of the founders of the Abbey Theatre.

'Jim's Character is Unsettled'*

STANISLAUS JOYCE

[*1903*]

Jim's character is unsettled, it is developing. New influences are coming over him daily, he is beginning new practices. He has come home drunk three or four times within the last month (on one occasion he came home sick and dirty-looking on Sunday morning, having been out all night) and he is engaged at present in sampling wines and liqueurs and at procuring for himself the means of living. He has or seems to have taken a liking for conviviality, even with those whose jealousy and ill-will towards himself he well knows, staying with them a whole night long dancing and singing and making speeches and laughing and reciting, and revelling in the same manner all the way home. To say what is really his character, one must go beneath much that his passing in these influences and habits and see what it is in them that his mind really affects; one must compare what he is with what he was, one must analyse, one must judge him by his moments of exaltation, not by his hours of abasement.

His intellect is precise and subtle, but not comprehensive. He is no student. His artistic sympathy and judgement are such as would be expected in one of his kind of intellect – if he were not more than a critic, I believe, he would be as good a critic of what interests him as any using English today. His literary talent seems to be very great indeed, both in prose and in verse. He has, as Yeats says, a power of very delicate spiritual writing and whether he writes in sorrow or is

* *The Complete Diary of Stanislaus Joyce*, ed. George H. Healey (Ithaca and London: Cornell University Press, 1971) pp. 1–3.

young and virginal, or whether (as in 'He travels after the wintry sun')[1]
he writes of what he has seen, the form is always either strong,
expressive, graceful or engaging, and his imagination open-eyed and
classic. His 'epiphanies' – his prose pieces (which I almost prefer to
his lyrics) and his dialogues – are again subtle. He has put himself
into these with singular courage, singular memory and scientific minu-
teness; he has proved himself capable of taking very great pains to
create a very little thing of prose or verse. The keen observation and
satanic irony of his character are precisely, but not fully, expressed.
Whether he will ever build up anything broad – a drama, an aesthetic
treatise – I cannot say. His genius is not literary and he will probably
run through many of the smaller forms of literary artistic expression.
He has made living his end in life, and in the light of this magnificent
importance of living, everything else is like a rushlight in the sun. And
so he is more interested in the sampling of liqueurs, the devising of
dinners, the care of dress and whoring, than to know if the one-act
play – 'the dwarf-drama' he calls it – is an artistic possibility.

NOTE

Stanislaus Joyce (1884–1955) was close to his brother James, and after Joyce's
departure from Ireland permanently, Stanislaus joined him in his exile in Italy,
often criticising, editing, providing funds and devotedly attempting to improve
his brother's intemperate drinking. Stanislaus's unfinished autobiography
appeared posthumously in 1958 [*My Brother's Keeper: James Joyce's Early Years*,
ed. Richard Ellmann (New York: Viking; London: Faber & Faber, 1958].
   1. From 'Tilly', published in *Pomes Penyeach*.

James Joyce: a Portrait of the Artist*

OLIVER ST JOHN GOGARTY

A young man sat beside me in the electric tram as it sped up the slight
incline of Rutland Square on its way towards Glasnevin. I had been

* Extracted from *Mourning Becomes Mrs Spendlove* (New York: Creative Age Press, 1948)
pp. 41–58, 61.

introduced to him by some student friend so casually that to speak to him again was like introducing myself. I could see his clear profile with its straight nose that came out at an angle from a towering forehead. The skin of his face was thick and ruddy seen through the down of a golden beard. His eyelashes were long and chestnut coloured, flat at the roots as they swept upward over smoke-gray, clouded eyes. He weighed about one hundred and twenty-five pounds, if as much as that, for he was very slender. When he stood up, he was about my own height, which is five feet nine. In his hand he carried a roll of manuscript tied with a piece of string.

'You are Mr Joyce?' I ventured.

There was no reply. I felt embarrassed until I realised that his silence was due to a shyness as great as the diffidence of a lay brother in a monastery.

I was a Trinity College man, and Trinity College, being its only college, is synonymous with Dublin University. Joyce was attending classes given by the Jesuits in the great house where had dwelt Buck Whaley, one of those characters in whom the eighteenth century flared up and went out. As a 'Varsity man I had to be regarded, in self-defence, as a scion of the Ascendancy. Joyce's defensive attitude later assumed fantastic proportions.

I tried again: 'Are you going in my direction?'

'Apparently.'

It was not very promising but the silence was broken.

'I live near the Botanic Gardens. Where do you live?'

'Cabra.'

'I hope that they are poems that you have there?' I said, pointing to the roll of vellum.

'They are,' he asserted with a trace of challenge.

Such was the kernel from which our friendship grew.

I remember that it was spring because, when we walked in my garden weeks later, the apple trees were in bloom, and there is bloom in the first of the lyrics he reluctantly showed me. His manuscript consisted of twenty large pages. In the middle of each page was a little lyric that looked all the more dainty from the beautiful handwriting in which it was written; Tennysonian, exquisite things:

> My love is in a light attire
> Among the apple trees
> Where the young winds do most desire
> To run in companies.

We walked in that garden for many eager days. We talked of the poets, Yeats, Mangan, Ferguson and George Russell. Only the dead were commendable to Joyce.

One morning in the middle of one of my dissertations, 'Will you lend me your rifle?' he interrupted

This was rather disconcerting because I thought that I was talking rather well and agreeing with him by admiring Mangan's 'Veil not thy mirror, sweet Amine', to which he had drawn my attention some days previously. Besides, he was anything but a sportsman; yet, full of curiosity, I lent him my .22.

Not long afterward, he came to me as enthusiastic as he ever permitted himself to be. He had a great idea. He would rent the Martello Tower out at Sandycove. I would furnish it, and we would live defiantly and far from the madding crowd.

Now the Martello Tower was one of the many stone fortresses that the British government in the days of Napoleon built, characteristically, *after* the alarm of invasion was over. The south coast of England and the southeast coast of Ireland were studded with them. Nine or ten of them guarded Dublin Bay, even where landing was impossible.

The one we took was built of cut granite and shaped like a sculptor's mallet, from which the name 'martello' is said to be derived. It stood over the Forty Foot, a bathing pool in the granite cliffs about six or seven miles south of Dublin. It was entered by a ladder to a door halfway up the wall on the side farthest from the sea.

We went together to see it. Joyce produced a very large copper key about ten inches long. The door had not been opened for years, so we had some difficulty in getting in. At last the great metal door was opened. We descended a few steps and entered a large circular room. There was a clamour of wings as some pigeons flew up through the embrasures of the little windows. The roof was a strong cylinder of stone. Around the room went a deep shelf at arms' reach. A fireplace was opposite to the door. On the left side we saw a little door and, opening it, discovered a flight of steps in the thickness of the wall. Full of adventure we ascended. What a pleasant discovery! There was a platform of granite and a circular raised wall from which you could see over the battlements head high. There was the Hill of Howth that formed the northern arm of Dublin Bay lying purple in the light. Dublin lay to the west, a dull ruby under a canopy of smoke. The sight fascinated Joyce. For a long time he gazed at his native town, 'The Seventh City of Christendom'.

I was looking at Killiney Hill, the south guardian of the Bay. I rejoiced at the green, the deep green of the Hill where its cliffs of granite were climbed by pines.

'This will do for a table,' Joyce said, pointing to the gun emplacement, 'and we can sit in the step and move around with the sun. We can do as much sun-bathing as we wish. Nobody can see us here. We can see everyone when we look over the parapet.'

It was true. I looked over the parapet. I could see men bathing in the Forty Foot. I could see old Carson's sunburned body rolling in the waves on his way back from his two-mile swim to the Muglins. I could see Lyons and Jem, the fishermen, sitting under the Battery wall. We overlooked everything from our seventy-foot eminence.

When we were returning to the big room, we missed the door in the darkness and reached a semicircular cellar which had a copper-lined powder store and a cistern for water from the roof.

'We could stand a siege here,' Joyce remarked.

'It's a good retreat for those who like retreating.'

'We must take possession at once until you get in the furniture. Could you do it today?'

'I thought we had possession. Haven't you got the key?'

Joyce had an uncle who was a clerk in an attorney's office, and from him Joyce got a respect for the formalities of law.

'We must leave something here until we move in.'

When we ascended to the living room, very formally Joyce 'took possession' by laying his roll of poems on the shelf.

I was so delighted by the discovery of a residence that could be locked and left secure for a half a year if necessary, that I lost no time in getting beds, tables, chairs, utensils, washing basins and fish kettles and everything else that I could think of from my home. They were carted down next day.

The fishermen were set to clean out all vestiges that the wild pigeons had left and to put the place shipshape. Joyce's bed was to the right of the door, mine to the left. We had a table directly under one of the two window shafts where the light fell. The cooking things were piled up on the wide shelf to the right.

Joyce, who had once or twice said that he was suffering from inanition, had no fear of inanition now. Lobsters could be bought from the obliging Lyons or the morose Jem for twelve cents each, and mackerel for a cent each or two for a cent if they were not large. Milk, butter and eggs were so cheap that we could save for those nutritious pints of Guinness without which half Dublin would be half-starved.

Mr Murray who kept 'Murray's', the local tavern, was a blear-eyed little man with a broad forehead and a thin neck. His house was next to the railway arch, so, when he helped his clients, he could truthfully say, 'This is the best pint between this and "The Arch",' which was a well-known tavern seven miles away. When his wife died, a paraphrase from *Lycidas*, 'She must not float upon his watery beer, Unwept,' drew a thin smile from the lips of Joyce.

The problem of how to live without having to go to town every day

Joyce solved by taking a job as a teacher in a neighbouring school.[1] He had, at first, thought of forming himself into a company, the shareholders in which were to receive all the proceeds from his future writings. The idea was novel. The shareholders would have to keep and humour him. Already, I said, I could see them issuing an unbalanced sheet. It was left to the British government to invest the royal bounty of $500 a year in him, and to a Mrs Weaver, later, to put $100,000 into that stock. There were worse investments than in James Joyce, Inc.

At last all was ready. The fishermen had gone, the milk had been delivered. We had eggs and bacon in store. Joyce sighed with relief.

'What will we do now?' he asked.

'The first thing to do is to let me get rid of your beard,' I said. 'There is lovely soft water in the storage tank and we should use it even if it's too old to drink. You can offer up your whiskers to the Muses.'

It took very little persuasion because to use water from our own storage tank appealed to him. So I shaved Joyce for the first time in his life when, as Homer says, 'the youth of man is most comely'. He never forgot it, for, when he paid me the only kind of compliment he ever paid, and that is to mention a person in his writings, he described me shaving on the top of the tower. In fact, I am the only character in all his works who washes, shaves and swims.

Many friends bearing gifts came to stay with us for weekends. We had much to offer, for we were possessed of the freshest air nearest to the city. We could and did feast on the roof, using, as Joyce had at first suggested, the gun emplacement for a table. The gun had gone with its company long long ago.

We had at hand the best cure for any little indisposition that remained from overnight, a dive down and down through the green water of the Forty Foot, then breakfast of ham and eggs.

The insoluble problem of cleaning up and getting rid of grease was at last solved by me. Instead of spreading grease all over the crockery in the wash basin while trying to get it off a plate or two, I used metal plates and put them in the fire until they were sterilised, a method of dry cleaning that has been too long forgotten.

In our talks, Joyce laid down many rules for good writing. I wish I had listened and had not talked so much. One was, 'Don't exaggerate. Tell the truth.' Another, 'Describe what they do.'

When he could, he spent his time in the National Library. Here he taught himself Danish. It was little trouble to him to acquire a language. His memory was marvellous, and he had a good ear. He was also skilled in music. He once wrote me a letter in which he told of a plan to tour the coastwise towns of England singing old English ballads to the accompaniment of a lute by Dolmnetsch. That was in 1904. A singer has made a fortune by doing that very thing in recent years. Joyce's voice was clarion clear. John McCormack may not have heard it, for he described it as baritone. It was tenor. He would have won first prize at the Feis, which is the annual musical festival and competition, that year but for his bad sight that prevented him scoring at sight singing. As it was, he got the bronze medal which indignantly he threw into the Liffey.

Joyce at that time was undergoing an inward change which may explain some of his curious behaviour. Revolt and scorn were increasing within him as he brooded and pondered over *Ulysses*. He was the storm-tossed wanderer whose ingenuity would bring him to his kingdom. He was Stephen Dedalus, the crowned and curious artist. With Prussian strategy he defended himself by attacking. On Yeats's fortieth birthday he called on the poet, who was staying at the Cavendish Hotel. I give the account of this incident as I heard it.

After some ceremony, Joyce was admitted. 'How old are you?' he asked Yeats, although he must have known well Yeats's age from the newspaper accounts.

'This is my birthday. I am forty years old,' Yeats replied.

'Sorry. You are too old for me to help,' Joyce said insolently and turned on his heel. The incident impressed Yeats more than it offended him. He was enchanted by Joyce's eccentricity and audacity, though he did not suspect how far from being audacity it was in reality. But personalities could never affect Yeats's admiration for genius. It was he and Ezra Pound who secured from Mr Asquith for Joyce, who was then in Zürich, the royal bounty already mentioned. Of *Ulysses* Yeats wrote, 'The Martello Tower pages are full of beauty, a cruel, playful mind like a great, soft tiger cat.'

When I looked for the hidden model whom Joyce was imitating I was puzzled for a time, though I knew well that there must be some literary figure, probably beyond my ken, whom Joyce admired. At last I had it! Rimbaud.[2] I remembered how he would quote Rimbaud. I remember Rimbaud's revolt not only against the accepted forms of literature, but against language itself. Rimbaud! No one who studies Joyce should neglect this clue to his character and conduct at the time. And the time was 1905. He left for Flushing at the end of the year and, sure enough, I got a postcard photograph of James Joyce dressed in a long overcoat with muffler and black soft hat. Arthur Rimbaud!

Had my knowledge of European literature been more catholic, I would have recognised Rimbaud in Joyce sooner than I did. I had had quite a dose of Ibsen when Joyce Ibsenised himself translating the gloomy Norwegian.

Lady Gregory, who early had kidnapped Yeats and who was a disarming old lady, used as a conduit by Yeats to draw off his comic writings, had no use for Joyce. To her he was not 'out of the top drawer'; and she had all the snobbery of the shoneens of Galway.

One day an SOS was issued from the Abbey Theatre. It had run out of geniuses. Joyce, as great a genius as any save Yeats himself, applied in person to Lady Gregory. I was waiting outside some place at which she was staying – I think that it was in Molesworth Street. Joyce was not in long. Presently he appeared, full of gravity, an assumption of seriousness he kept for occasions when shot full of the slings and arrows. Gravely he inclined his head. Gravely he beat time with his forefinger and recited this impromptu limerick:

> There was an old lady called 'Gregory'
> Said, 'Come to me, poets in beggary';
>   But found her imprudence
>   When thousands of students
> Cried 'All, we are in that category!'

Thus we lived in privacy and profanity. I could take it easy on the roof, for I shunned work; Joyce could remain downstairs forever reading and rereading his 'Contra Gentiles', an early essay against everybody. I never saw him put pen to paper. He would often excuse himself 'to write a letter', which was his way of recording any turn of phrase he heard, or any one of my 'epiphanies', by which he meant unconscious 'giveaways'. If, for instance, I said I had no money and, later, revealed through some allusion that I had had some all the time, that would be an epiphany or a 'showing forth', a parody on the meaning of the church festival of that name.

This is but one example of his play on words. Why should I give others, when there are so many in his later works? Now, word associations and rebuses are no new thing in Irish literature. They are indigenous to monasteries and schools. The schoolmen of the ninth and the following centuries indulged in them *in excelsis*. It was in the schools that such equivoces as '*Mea mater mala sus est*' originated, a sentence that may be construed as 'My mother is an evil sow', or as 'Hurry, Mother! The sow is eating the apples'.

As for the association of ideas in such phrases as 'tight-breeched British artilleryman', which occurs in 'Gas From a Burner', that angry and unpublished poem he shot back at us from Flushing, at that time he was putting legions of them together. The Martello Tower was the nursery of *Ulysses*.

Sometimes when I would be lolling on the roof, getting a tan and feeling the sun pulsating on my skin, I would think of Joyce in the dark room underneath and invite him to come out into the air. It was no use shouting. Nothing could be heard in that room, so it would be necessary to go down the stairs, and put my head against the top of the door and call. I called, 'Kinch! Come up. It's a lovely day.'

'Why should I go up?'

'Because you are committing the Eight Deadly Sins by being "sullen in the sweet air". You know what your pal Dante does with such as you?'

'Go back to your sweet air.'

'Your mind will break your heart, dear Kinch.'

I went back. *Why do I put up with him at all? I asked myself. It must be the attraction of opposites that holds us together. But he is a bit of a weight. It is hard to make him smile except at some blunder of mine or others. Here I am with two madmen in the Tower. Narrumtour? Am I their keeper or companion? Then there is the fact that Endymion, the madman, likes only me. 'Show me your company'. My uncle was said to have been very wild and to have died in America. The first part of his history may be hereditary. What am I do do?*

Kinch calls me 'Malachi Mulligan'. 'Malachi wore the collar of gold', and he is envious of my canary-coloured waistcoat with the gold buttons. Besides, 'Malachi' is his way of hinting 'Mercury'; and 'Mulligan' is stage Irish for me and the rest of us. It is meant to make me absurd. I don't resent it, for he takes 'Kinch' – 'Lynch' with the Joyces of Galway, which is far worse. I might have called him 'Haughton', after the grandfather of Baldy Haughton who invented the 'drop' in hanging. And 'Haughton' would convey to him 'Haughty' or 'Plaughton' and 'Plutone'. He would have taken that, for he intends to put us all in his underworld one of these days. Meanwhile, who ever heard of Hermes having a drink with Pluto?

One Sunday we decided to go to Dublin, for we were in funds. We would knock about for a while and, in the evening, drop in on AE's Hermetic Society, which was founded and presided over by AE (George Russell) himself. This society intrigued Joyce; he could not get into it. The majority of its members were girls who worked in Pim's, the large Quaker dry-goods store in which AE was an accountant. This was the society that George Moore and I visited years later to find AE astride a bench in a little room crowded with intense females, and in the process of digging up from the World Memory a Fifth Gospel.

When Moore heard AE, with 'his fading knowledge of Hebrew' (sic), intoning 'Oom' or 'Amen' five times, he exclaimed impatiently, 'Why he's got it upside down,' an irreverence that had us both removed.

Joyce and I spent most of Sunday having quick ones in Davy Byrne's, Mooney's, Fanning's and Kennedy's with John Elwood, Vincent Cosgrove, Sweeney, the greengrocer, and Cocky Meade. About nine o'clock we thought that the Hermetic would be in full blast. We reached the tall forbidding office building in Dawson Street by the side door in the lane that leads through an arch to South Frederick Street. It was by this door, Joyce said, that the members were wont to enter unobtrusively. We pushed it in and struggled up the dark stairway. We found the door and entered. I struck a match. The place was empty except for some deal chairs and the form or bench on which the Master rode. I saw the gas bracket and lit the burner. So this was the temple of the secret society. Joyce came upon a suitcase behind him near the door, and he opened it out of curiosity. Ribbon-tied packages were revealed. Through the tissue paper I could see gauze or muslin materials.

'Ladies' drawers,' said Joyce, imitating a salesman. 'Here are the latest fashions, ladies, in all tones shapes and sizes.'

'What goes on in here?' I asked, thinking of the reputation of the Thrice Great Hermes.[3]

'Not what you think,' Joyce said. 'They belong to Maunsell's manager's travelling bag. He probably arrived from Belfast only to find that the Society was not in session this Sunday. So he dumped his samples here, and will pick them up in the morning. Only he will have to sell them this week without the spiritual support of AE.'

The gas from the burner went out. We stumbled down the stairs, and into the street. To my amazement, I saw that Joyce was carrying the suitcase full of ladies' underwear.

'They can pull us in for breaking and entering,' I protested. 'We are up against the Eighth Commandment, and it's worse on Sunday when the pawnshops are closed.'

He brooded awhile and said, 'If there were no pawnshops there would be no need for an Eighth Commandment.'

'There are no pawnshops in the Bible,' I objected.

'There are money changers, usurers and a lot about covetousness.'

'When I think of what went on in the Bible, it's just a miracle that there are only ten commandments. Never let me hear you say that I don't believe in miracles!'

'It is a miracle to believe in anything,' he said.

I looked at him sharply. Was this one of his jokes? But the thin lips did not cream or wrinkle.

'What do you intend to do with them?' I said.

'I intend to present them to our lady friends with the compliments of the Hermetic Society.'

I thought this over. 'Give me a few dozen for Jenny.'

Jenny was an acrobat and a friend of Sweeney, the greengrocer. Any little act of kindness done to Jenny (provided that it was not of love) would not be lost on Sweeney, as it certainly would not be on Jenny.

Joyce suggested that we call on Jenny with my gift, and we took a cab to Mountjoy Street. Jenney was, as always, charmed to see us. After some desultory but unedifying conversation, we opened 'Maunsell's manager's travelling bag,' and Joyce advanced with what should have been my present. As he bowed over its recipient his toe struck a night jar, which rang sonorously like a gong.

Jenny sat up and, as a little voluntary act of recompense, proceeded to try the undies on. The display was so edifying that Joyce threw in the rest, suitcase and all.

Later, as we sat in the last train back to Sandycove, the sea and the clear air, Joyce, who had been in a brown study, announced abruptly, 'At last I've got a title for my collection of lyrics.'

'What is it?' I inquired.

'*Chamber Music*,' he said.

One term when I came down from Oxford, I brought to the tower a friend, a Balliol man, Samuel Chevenix Trench, an enthusiastic Gaelic speaker and, in his spare time, an amateur teacher of Gaelic, in Oxford of all places. It was with him I learned the few sentences I know. I thought that it would be an enjoyable thing for him to come to Ireland and meet the galaxy of Gaels and those who were working for a renewed Ireland: Horace Plunkett[4] and his pet editor, George Russell, and the men who were quoting Dean Swift, 'Burn everything English but her coal', in their efforts to revive Irish industries. The effect on Trench was astonishing. First of all, he applied to the courts for permission to change his name by deed poll. He became Diarmuid instead of Samuel. He grew so zealous for things made in Ireland that he went about with his shoe leather all green for want of blacking made in Ireland. He removed the shades of our lamps and filled the tower with smoke until Irish glass should appear to take their places. He upset Joyce literally and metaphorically. Joyce courteously offered his place by the door for Trench's bed and went over to the right under the large shelf with his bed.

All went well for some weeks, for we were using the tower only to sleep in, except on weekends. Trench tried but failed to convert Joyce to Gaelic, so he becomes the Englishman, Haines, in *Ulysses*, where Joyce betrays a hidden respect for what is derisively called 'The Ascendancy'. As for me, he makes me open *Ulysses* as Buck Mulligan shaving before a cracked mirror (by which he is supposed to symbolise Ireland) on the tower: another 'buck' like Whaley.

One summer night, when it was too hot to sleep although the door was open, shortly after midnight Trench, who had been dozing, awoke suddenly and screamed, 'The black panther!'

He produced a revolver and fired two or three shots in the direction of the grate. Then, exhausted, he subsided into sleep. I gently removed the gun. Joyce sat up on his elbow, overcome by consternation. Soon again, as I had guessed he would, Trench awoke and saw the black panther again.

'Leave him to me,' I said and shot down all the tin cans on the top of Joyce. This was too much for that sensitive soul who rose, pulled on his frayed trousers and shirt, took his ash plant with the handle at right angles to the shaft, and in silence left the tower forever. This will explain the rather obscure reference to the black panther in *Ulysses*. But I am sure that the scholiasts can explain it more obscurely.

Apparently he bore me no resentment. He may have thought that Trench had done the shooting, for he makes some comments on my visitor from Oxford. To this day I am sorry for that thoughtless horseplay on such a hypersensitive and difficult friend. But, if he had not pawned my rifle, he would have been less gun-shy. Trench fell in love with a titled Irish enthusiast and shot himself, being crossed in love.

In September 1912, some years after Joyce walked out of the tower, I received in the mail from Flushing, Holland, a long strip of paper which looked like a galley proof and contained a poem of about one hundred lines. It was from Joyce, and was called 'Gas From a Burner', obviously a reference to the burner in AE's Hermetic Society room. Of all the self-revelations, 'epiphanies', or portraits of the artists he ever wrote, this was the most revealing. It was all revolt, all bitterness. . . .

Twelve years or so later, Joyce called on me in Ely Place.[5] I shook the lank hand. He ignored the offer of a chair.

He stared about the room, then he looked out of the bay window and inspected the garden.

'Is this your revenge?' he inquired.

'Revenge on what?' I asked, puzzled.

'On the public.'

And with that cryptic remark he left. I never saw that contrary man again.

NOTES

Oliver St John Gogarty (1878–1957), Irish poet, surgeon and wit. He was a close friend of Joyce for a while, and is featured in *Ulysses* as 'stately plump Buck Mulligan'. His relationship with Joyce is described in J. B. Lyons, *James Joyce and Medicine* (Dublin: Dolmen Press, 1973); and in James F. Carens, 'Joyce and Gogarty', in *New Light on Joyce from the Dublin Symposium*, ed. Fritz Senn (Bloomington, Ind.: Indiana University Press, 1972) pp. 28–45.

1. The Clifton School in Dalkey.

2. Arthur Rimbaud (1854–91), French poet who has become one of the high-priests of the Symbolist movement in poetry.

3. Hermes Trismegistus, supposed author of ancient works on mysticism, the so-called hermetic books. There was in fact no such person, although the

tradition was real enough. Gogarty, by identifying Hermes with AE, mocks the latter's philosophy.

4. Sir Horace Plunkett (1854–1932), author of *Ireland in the New Century* (1904), was the leading exponent of agricultural co-operation in Ireland, and supporter of two journals which AE edited, *The Irish Homestead* and *The Irish Statesman*. In 1904, Joyce published – under the pseudonym Stephen Daedalus – three stories in *The Irish Homestead*, and these later became part of *Dubliners* (1914).

5. This visit took place in 1909.

The Beginnings of Joyce*

WILLIAM K. MAGEE [JOHN EGLINTON]

As I think of Joyce a haunting figure rises up in my memory. A pair of burning dark-blue eyes, serious and questioning, is fixed on me from under the peak of a nautical cap; the face is long, with a slight flush suggestive of dissipation, and an incipient beard is permitted to straggle over a very pronounced chin, under which the open shirt-collar leaves bare a full womanish throat. The figure is fairly tall and very erect, and gives a general impression of a kind of seedy hauteur; and every passer-by glances with a smile at the white tennis shoes (borrowed, as I gather from a mention of them in *Ulysses*). It was while walking homeward one night across Dublin that I was joined by this young man, whose appearance was already familiar to me; and although I cannot remember any of the strange sententious talk in which he instantly engaged, I have only to open the *Portrait of the Artist as a Young Man* to hear it again. 'When we come to the phenomena of artistic conception, artistic gestation and artistic reproduction I require a new terminology and a new personal experience.' I have never felt much interest in literary aesthetics, and he seemed to set a good deal of store by his system, referring, I recollect, to some remark made to him by 'one of his disciples', but I liked listening to his careful intonation and full vowel sounds, and as he recited some of his verses, 'My love is in a light attire', I remember noticing the apple in his throat, the throat of a singer; for Mr Joyce has turned out to be an exception to a sweeping rule laid down by the late Sir J. P. Mahaffy,[1] who used to say that he had never known a young man with a good tenor voice who did not go to the devil. Some ladies of the pavement shrieked at us as we crossed over O'Connell Bridge. I remember that we talked of

* Extracted from *Irish Literary Portraits* (London: Macmillan, 1935) pp. 131–40.

serious matters, and at one point he impressed me by saying: 'If I knew I were to drop dead before I reached that lamp-post, it would mean no more to me than it will mean to walk past it'. Why did this young man seek out my acquaintance? Well, writing folk are interested in one another, and there were peculiarities in the occasion of the present writer's inglorious attempts at authorship about which it may be well to say something, as the relation may help indirectly to define the nature of Joyce's own portentous contribution to Irish literature.

James Joyce was one of a group of lively and eager-minded young men in the University College (a Jesuit house), amongst whom he had attained a sudden ascendancy by the publication in the *Fortnightly Review*, when he was only nineteen, of an article on Ibsen's play, *When we Dead Awaken*. The talk of these young men, their ribald wit and reckless manner of life, their interest in everything new in literature and philosophy (in this respect they far surpassed the students of Trinity College) are all reproduced in Joyce's writings; for his art seems to have found in this period the materials on which it was henceforth to work. Dublin was certainly at this moment a centre of vigorous potentialities. The older culture was still represented with dignity by Dowden,[2] Mahaffy and others; political agitation was holding back its energies for a favourable opportunity, while the organisation of Sinn Fein was secretly ramifying throughout the country; the language movement was arrogant in its claims; the Irish Literary Theatre was already famous; and besides Yeats and Synge, AE and George Moore, there were numerous young writers, and even more numerous talkers, of incalculable individuality. There was hardly anyone at that time who did not believe that Ireland was on the point of some decisive transformation. What, then, was wanting to this movement? For it has passed away, leaving Ireland more intensely what it has always been, a more or less disaffected member of the British Commonwealth of Nations. That Ireland should achieve political greatness appeared then to most of us to be an idle dream; but in the things of the mind and of the spirit it seemed not a folly to think that Ireland might turn its necessity of political eclipse to glorious gains. A regenerate and thoughtful Ireland, an Ireland turned inwards upon itself in reverie, might recover inexhaustible sources of happiness and energy in its own beauty and aloofness, through a generous uprush of wisdom and melody in its poets and thinkers. It was not in the interest of the constituted spiritual authorities in Ireland that such a dream should ever be realised: a new movement of the human mind in Ireland was indeed precisely what was feared; the noisy language movement, the recrudescence of political agitation, outrage, assassination – anything was preferable to that! There was a moment nevertheless when it seemed possible that this might be the turn events would take. Among other hopeful indications, a little magazine was started, under the editorship of the present writer, and AE boldly recommended 'The Heretic' for a title, but the somewhat less compromising name, *Dana, A Magazine of Independent Thought*, was chosen. The fruitfulness of the moment was revealed in the number of eminent writers who contributed freely to its pages (Shaw and Chesterton promised contributions): Joyce, who chortled as he pocketed half a sovereign for a poem,[3] was the only one to receive remuneration. Yeats held aloof, talking cuttingly of 'Fleet Street atheism'.

Joyce is, as all his writings show, Roman in mind and soul; for, generally speaking, to the Romanised mind the quest of truth, when it is not impious, is witless. What he seemed at this period I have attempted to describe, but what he really was is revealed in his *Portrait of the Artist as a Young Man*, a work completed in Trieste just ten years later. Religion had been with him a profound adolescent experience, torturing the sensitiveness which it awakened; all its floods had gone over him. He had now recovered, and had no objection to 'Fleet Street atheism', but 'independent thought' appeared to him an amusing disguise of the proselytising spirit, and one night as we walked across town he endeavoured, with a certain earnestness, to bring home to me the extreme futility of ideals represented in *Dana*, by describing to me the solemn ceremonial of High Mass. (Dost thou remember these things, O Joyce, thou man of meticulous remembrance?) The little magazine laboured through a year, and the chief interest of the volume formed by its twelve numbers[4] is now, no doubt, that it contains the series of sketches by George Moore, *Moods and Memories*, afterwards embodied in *Memoirs of my Dead Life*. It might have had a rare value now in the book market if I had been better advised one evening in the National Library, when Joyce came in with the manuscript of a serial story[5] which he offered for publication. He observed me silently as I read, and when I handed it back to him with the timid observation that I did not care to publish what was to myself incomprehensible, he replaced it silently in his pocket.

I imagine that what he showed me was some early attempt in fiction, and that I was not really guilty of rejecting any work of his which has become famous. Joyce at this time was in the making, as is shown by the fact that the friends and incidents of this period have remained his principal subject matter. Chief among these friends was the incomparable 'Buck Mulligan', Joyce's name for a now famous Dublin doctor[6] – wit, poet, mocker, enthusiast, and, unlike most of his companions, blest with means to gratify his romantic caprices. He had a fancy for living in towers, and when I first heard of him had the notion of establishing himself at the top of the Round Tower at Clondalkin; afterwards he rented from the Admiralty the Martello

Tower at Sandycove, which presently became the resort of poets and revolutionaries, something between one of the 'Hell-Fire Clubs' of the eighteenth century and the Mermaid Tavern. Joyce was certainly very unhappy, proud and impecunious: no one took him at his own valuation, yet he held his own by his unfailing 'recollectedness' and by his sententious and pedantic wit, shown especially in the limericks on the various figures in the literary movement, with which from time to time he regaled that company of roysterers and midnight bathers. Buck Mulligan's conversation, or rather his vehement and whimsical oratory, is reproduced with such exactness in *Ulysses* that one is driven to conclude that Joyce even then was 'taking notes'; as to Joyce himself, he was exactly like his own hero Stephen Dedalus, who announced to his private circle of disciples that 'Ireland was of importance because it belonged to him'. He had made up his mind at this period, no doubt with vast undisclosed purposes of authorship, to make the personal acquaintance of everyone in Dublin of repute in literature. With Yeats he amused himself by delivering the sentence of the new generation, and 'Never,' said Yeats, 'have I encountered so much pretension with so little to show for it'. He was told that Lady Gregory, who was giving a literary party at her hotel, had refused to invite himself, and he vowed he would be there. We were all a little uneasy, and I can still see Joyce, with his air of half-timid effrontery, advancing toward his unwilling hostess and turning away from her to watch the company. Withal, there was something lovable in Joyce, as there is in every man of genius: I was sensible of the mute appeal of his liquid-burning gaze, though it was long afterwards that I was constrained to recognise his genius.

As already noted, Nature had endowed him with one remarkable advantage, an excellent tenor voice, and there is still, I have read, in existence a copy of the programme of a Dublin concert, in which the names of the singers appear thus, perhaps only in alphabetical order:

1. Mr James A. Joyce
2. Mr John M'Cormack. [*sic*]

He had persuaded himself to enter as a competitor in the Irish Musical Festival, the Feis Ceoil, but when a test-piece was handed to him, he looked at it, guffawed, and marched off the platform. Who but Joyce himself could have surmised at this moment the inhibition of his daemon, or the struggle that may have been enacted in his dauntless and resourceful spirit? Perhaps it was then that he slipped past the Sirens' Rock on the road to his destiny. Our daemon, as Socrates pointed out, will only tell us what *not* to do, and if Joyce's daemon had made the mistake of saying to him in so many words, 'Thou shalt be the Dante of Dublin, a Dante with a difference, it is true, as the Liffey is a more prosaic stream than the Arno: still, Dublin's Dante!' he might quite likely (for who is altogether satisfied with the destiny meted out to him?) have drawn back and 'gone to the devil' with his fine tenor voice. He chose, what was for him no doubt the better part, his old vagabond impecunious life. One morning, just as the National Library opened, Joyce was announced; he seemed to wish for somebody to talk to, and related quite ingenuously how in the early hours of the morning he had been thrown out of the tower, and had walked into town from Sandycove. In reading the early chapters of *Ulysses* I was reminded of this incident, for this day, at least in its early portion, must have been for Joyce very like the day celebrated in that work, and I could not help wondering whether the idea of it may not have dawned upon him as he walked along the sands that morning.

Certain it is that he had now had his draught of experience: all the life which he describes in his writings now lay behind him. Suddenly we heard that he had married,[7] was a father, and had gone off to Trieste to become a teacher in the Berlitz School there. It must have been two or three years later that he looked into the National Library for a few minutes, marvellously smartened up and with a short trim beard. The business which had brought him back had some connection, curiously enough, with the first introduction into Dublin of the cinema. The mission was a failure, and he was also much disgusted by the scruples of a Dublin publisher in reprinting a volume of short stories, of which all the copies had been destroyed in a fire. (It was not until 1914 that *Dubliners* was published in London.) 'I am going back to civilisation' were the last words I heard from him. He has not, I believe, been in Dublin since.[8]

NOTES

William Kirkpatrick Magee [pseud. John Eglington] (1868–1961), Irish essayist. He appears in the Scylla and Charibdys chapter of *Ulysses*, which is set in the National Library of Ireland where Magee worked; and is treated with more respect than Joyce usually accorded his real-life subjects.

1. Sir John Pentland Mahaffy (1839–1919), scholar, wit and Provost of Trinity College Dublin.

2. Edward Dowden (1843–1913), man of letters.

3. 'My love is in a light attire' was published in the August 1904 issue of *Dana*.

4. *Dana* appeared twelve times from May 1904 to April 1905.

5. An early draft of *A Portrait of the Artist*.

6. Oliver St John Gogarty.

7. Of course Magee knew well that Joyce and Nora had *not* married. This is an example of the Dublin prudery Joyce found so laughable. Cf. his sister Eileen's remark, p. 62.

8. Here Magee seems to confuse or conflate the two visits Joyce made to Dublin in 1909 and 1912.

James Joyce as a Young Man*

PADRAIC COLUM

James Joyce was very noticeable amongst the crowd of students who frequented the National Library or who sauntered along the streets between Nelson's Pillar and Stephens' [*sic*] Green. He was tall and slender when I knew him first, with a Dantesque face and steely blue eyes. The costume I see him in as I look back includes a peaked cap and tennis shoes more or less white. He used to swing along the street carrying in his hand an ash-plant by way of a cane (that ash-plant is celebrated in *Ulysses*, Stephen Dedalus carries it through that tremendous day and frequently addresses it). He spoke harshly in conversation, with a marked accent, and using many words of the purlieus. Stories were told about his arrogance. Did not this youth say to Yeats, 'We have met too late: you are too old to be influenced by me?' Back in 1901 – he was just twenty then – he reproved the promoters of the Irish Literary Theatre, writing in 'The Day of the Rabblement' –

> No man, said the Nolan, can be a lover of the true or the good unless he abhors the multitude; and the artist, though he may employ the crowd, is very careful to isolate himself. This radical principle of artistic economy applies specially to a time of crisis, and to-day when the highest form of art has been preserved by desperate sacrifices, it is strange to see the artist making terms with the rabblement. . . . The Irish Literary Theatre gave out that it was the champion of progress, and proclaimed war against commercialism and vulgarity. It had partly made good its word and was expelling the old devil when after the first encounter it surrendered to the popular will. Now your popular devil is more dangerous than your vulgar devil. Bulk and lungs count for something, and he can gild his speech

* *The Road Round Ireland* (New York: Macmillan, 1926) pp. 313–19.

aptly. He has prevailed once more, and the Irish Literary Theatre must now be considered the property of the rabblement of the most belated race in Europe. . . . The official organ of the movement spoke of producing European masterpieces, but the matter went no further. Such a project was absolutely necessary. The censorship is powerless in Dublin, and the directors could have produced *Ghosts* or *The Dominion of Darkness* if they chose. Nothing can be done until the forces that dictate public judgment are calmly confronted. . . . Accordingly, the rabblement, placid and intensely moral, is enthroned in boxes and galleries amid a hum of approval, and those who think that Echegaray is 'morbid', and titter coyly when Melisande lets down her hair, are not sure but they are the trustees of every intellectual and poetic treasure. . . . Meanwhile, what of the artists? It is equally unsafe at present to say of Mr Yeats that he has or has not genius. In aim and form *The Wind Among the Reeds* is poetry of the highest order, and 'The Adoration of the Magi' (a story which one of the great Russians might have written) shows what Mr Yeats can do when he breaks with the half-gods. But an æsthete has a floating will, and Mr Yeats's treacherous instinct of adaptability must be blamed for his recent association with a platform from which even self-respect should have urged him to refrain.

We, the fry swimming about in the National Library, looked with some reverence on the youth who already had an article published in the *Fortnightly Review*. He had taught himself whatever Scandinavian language Ibsen wrote in – he used to repeat Ibsen's lyrics in the original – and when *When We Dead Awaken* was published in English his essay on it came out in the *Fortnightly*; William Archer had it published as a sort of preface to his translation. He took part in an amateur production of *Hedda Gabler*, taking the part of Lovberg. I did not see the production, but I imagine he did well in it.

He talked of Ibsen on the night I first spoke to him. We met coming out of the National Library and we walked towards his home in the north side of the city. For most of the way he listened, rather ironically, to what I had to say for myself. The Irish Revival had no allegiance from him – he distrusted all enthusiasm, he said. The prospect of creating a national theatre was already discounted by him. He talked of Ibsen with the greatest admiration. *A Doll's House* had just been given by some amateur company, but Joyce in conversation dismissed this play. It was interesting, he said, just as a letter written by Ibsen would be interesting, but it had no relation to such great plays as *Hedda Gabler* and *The Wild Duck*. I contrasted Joyce's remarks with George Moore's whom I had heard speak of the same production a night or two before. 'Sophocles, Raphael, Shelley,' George Moore had cried, running his hands through his blond hair, 'What have they done compared with *A Doll's House?*'

He gave me his poems to read in a beautiful manuscript. He used to speak arrogantly about these poems of his, but I remember his saying something that made me know how precious these beautifully-wrought lyrics were to him – he spoke about walking through the streets of Paris, poor and tormented, and about the peace the repetition of his poems had brought him. They were perfect in their form. But could one who expressed himself so perfectly at twenty-three really go far? Yeats had said to him 'I do not know whether you are a fountain or a cistern', and AE had remarked, 'I do not see in your beginnings enough chaos to make a world'.

He went to Paris for a while and then returned to Dublin. It was then that he began to write the stories that are in *Dubliners* and began the writing of *A Portrait of the Artist as a Young Man* (its beginning is dated Dublin 1904). After he had begun this book he went abroad to take a place as a teacher of English in a Berlitz School. I saw him back in Dublin a few years later. He was glad, he told me then, to be away from a place where 'the reformed conscience' had left its fetter, and away from the fog of Anglo-Saxon civilisation. His boy went to the operas in the city where they lived – Trieste, I think it was – delighted in the airs, and was already singing them. It seemed to me that Joyce was pleased that musical expression which Dublin had not permitted to flower in himself was coming to his son freely. He would not have this boy brought up as an Englishman nor as a modern Irishman.

He was in Dublin then on business. The Cinematograph had come in, and an Italian company had theatres in many European cities. Joyce had come over to open one in Dublin. That was in the foredawn of the movies. His 'Volta' Theatre was opened, but I never heard that it was successful.

As I think over this episode in his career I am reminded that Joyce had schemes of making a business that would bring him wealth. In the days when I first knew him he projected a great daily newspaper. He elaborated a scheme; he would tell us about the organisation it would have and the sort of articles that would appear in it. It would be along the lines of a Continental newspaper, and it would cost twenty thousand or a hundred thousand pounds to produce. I have forgotten the amount,[1] but Joyce was exact about the figures. He took the trouble to have its title registered – 'The Goblin' it was to be called. It seems incredible, but this penniless and jobless young man tried to raise the capital – an amount that in Dublin would be almost fabulous.

And while I am looking back on this business scheme of his I am reminded of an incident that might find a place in *Dubliners* – an incident that seems a parody on the plans that now and again occurred to him. He came to me one day with a request for that which was very rare with student Dubliners – a golden half-sovereign. By a miracle I had one. A financial scheme was involved in its use.

Joyce has been given a pawn-ticket by a medical student. Now, to any one else a pawn-ticket would be a minus quantity, but to Joyce it was realisable. The ticket was for books, and six shillings was the amount they were in for. They were medical books, for a certainty, and valuable. And we would take them to our friend, George Webb on the Quays, and sell them, and make fifty or even a hundred per cent on the transaction.

So we handed seven shillings, and the books came across Terence Kelly's counter to us. Hastily we undid the wrappings. And, behold! the books were Walter Scott's, an unsalable edition of the Waverley novels, with one volume missing.

There was wan hope in going to Webb's. That most knowing of all booksellers, sitting outside his shop, with his one closed and his one open eye, received Joyce cordially. 'Some of your Italian books, Mr Joyce?' 'No, Webb; these are special.' We opened the parcel and exhibited the wretched, papier-mâché bound set! Very loftily indeed did Joyce talk to the incredulous Webb. 'But you have brought some Italian books with you, haven't you, Mr Joyce?' the bookseller kept on saying, for he had his eye on the Italian collection that Joyce was then selling. When he gathered that Joyce really wanted to sell him the books in the parcel, and that he had released them from Terence Kelly's on the prospect of selling them, he had them wrapped up for us. 'There is only one thing for you to do about it, boys. Take the books back to Terence Kelly; maybe you can get him to let you have six shillings on them again.' We took them back and managed to get our six shillings.

NOTES

Padraic Colum (1881–1972), Irish poet and dramatist. He was the last living link with Yeats, Synge, Lady Gregory and the early days of the Irish literary revival.

1. £2000.

Joyce Among the Journalists*

PIARAS BÉASLAÍ

In 1909 George Bernard Shaw wrote a one-act play, *The Shewing-up of Blanco Posnet*, which he described as 'a sermon in crude melodrama'. The play was to be produced in a West-End (London) theatre when the Censor of Plays banned it. Certain references by Blanco Posnet to the Deity, which sounded disrespectful, were objected to. Shaw refused to alter them.

At this time Ireland was under English rule, but by some legal oversight the authority of the Censor, derived from the Lord Chamberlain, did not apply to this country. It occurred to the directors of the Abbey to offer Shaw the first production of his uncensored play. The offer was accepted.

The Lord Lieutenant, Aberdeen, who had power to revoke the Abbey licence, made a protest but did not proceed to extremes. *Blanco Posnet* got its first production in the Abbey on 25 August 1909, the Thursday of Horse Show Week – a curious time of the week.

I attended the first night as drama critic of the *Evening Telegraph*. A good many English dramatic critics had crossed to Dublin for the occasion. A great many English visitors to the Horse Show were among the crowded audience. As Shaw's play was not long enough for a whole night's performance it was preceded by another, Yeats's *Kathleen Ni Houlihan*. This play, which has such an immediate appeal to patriotic Irishmen, caused bewilderment to the English visitors. I heard them whispering among themselves during the interval, wondering what it meant, what it was all about, who was the mysterious old woman – played, I think, by Sara Allgood.

Then I got into conversation with a tallish, thin young man, of agreeable manners and address, who told me he had come all the way from Trieste to see Shaw's play. I told him that I was a journalist, and he told me he was one also, on the staff of *Piccolo della Sera* of Trieste.

He seemed to imply that *Piccolo* had sent him to Dublin to criticise the play. This made me wonder, as I knew that Italian newspapers were not financially strong. Some time before I had been appointed

* Extracted from 'I Introduced Joyce to a Dublin Newspaper Office', *Irish Independent* (Dublin), 4 July 1962, p. 5. Condensed as 'Joyce Among the Journalists', *Irish Digest* (Dublin), 75 (September 1962) 71–3.

correspondent of a Roman daily. I had written a weekly letter in English which they translated into Italian and published over my name – but they never paid me. When I had sent in a bill several times in vain and ascertained that they were not financially sound, I stopped my letters.

The agreeable stranger said his name was Joyce and he was a Dublin man. I invited him to meet his fellow-journalists in the *Evening Telegraph* office next day.

Next day he called on us, and the editor, Pat Meade, who had evidently already met him, introduced him to the others as a journalist from Trieste. He stayed a long time and out of that and subsequent visits he derived the material for a large portion of *Ulysses*, which consists of conversation and incidents in the *Evening Telegraph* office. In his narrative the editor appears as 'Myles Crawford' and Hugh MacNeill (father of Major-General MacNeill, at that time a teacher at Maynooth College) is 'Professor MacHugh', and John Wyse-Power is 'Wyse Nolan'. Some other journalists figure under their real names.

In *Ulysses* Stephen Dedalus (Joyce himself) plays a leading part in the conversation in the office, but in reality he was very quiet and reserved on this occasion. When those who were at liberty adjourned to a neighbouring bar, Joyce went with them, but drank only lemon soda.

He paid several visits to the *Telegraph* office and I met him in the street a couple of times. On both occasions he stopped me and asked me to have a drink, but again drank only lemon soda. Not foreseeing his future fame, I kept no record of our conversation, but I remember we discussed literary subjects and contemporary writers and that our opinions largely coincided. He was never aggressive or dogmatic in stating his views, but always courteous and considerate.

Those who formed their idea of Joyce from his own portrayal of the character of Stephen Dedalus in *A Portrait of the Artist as a Young Man* and *Ulysses* probably pictured him as an arrogant, supercilious, self-assertive type of young man, who lectures a Jesuit priest on St Thomas Aquinas, and the Chief Librarian of the National Library on Shakespeare and *Hamlet*. Nothing could be more unlike this portrait than the man I met.

Miss Sylvia Beach,[1] in opening the Joyce Museum recently,[2] must have surprised many of her hearers by asserting that Joyce was a shy, sensitive, retiring sort of man; but she did not surprise me. I would say Joyce was a man whose inhibitions were strong, so strong as to be troublesome to him; and that he sought release from them in his writing and tried to express his subconscious self. If he drank heavily at times it was as an escape from his inhibitions. At the time I met him his inhibitions would be at their strongest because of his abstinence from alcohol.

I felt attracted to him and remembered our meetings with pleasure, and when somebody later showed me his father, whom he has made famous in his story, I surveyed the old gentleman with interest. He was a familiar figure, a real 'man about town' with his monocle, spats and air of faded gentility. He seemed to be treated with respect by everyone who knew him. I never spoke to him and James I never saw again, though he paid another visit to Dublin.[3]

NOTES

Piaras Béaslaí (1881–1965), journalist, revolutionary (he fought in the 1916 Rebellion and in the civil war) and Gaelic scholar and playwright.

1. For a note on Sylvia Beach and her recollections of Joyce see p. 79.
2. The Joyce Museum was opened in June 1962 in the Martello Tower in Sandycove, where Joyce and Gogarty had briefly lived in 1904.
3. Actually, two visits: in October 1909 and in July 1912.

A Recollection of James Joyce*

JOSEPH HONE

It was in 1908 – the summer, I think – that I read Joyce's *Dubliners* in manuscript.[1] The stories were written out in cheap notebooks in a copperplate hand that would have won for a schoolboy a prize in calligraphy. They were handed to me by George Roberts, the managing-director of Maunsel & Co., a publishing firm of which I was then a member. Roberts was a very good judge of a book, besides being a fine printer; but one, at least, of the stories gave him pause: such is my recollection. This was 'Ivy Day in the Committee Room', in which Dublin's grave councillors are depicted in discussing, among other matters, the private life of King Edward VII. As I look back, it occurs to me that the firm's hesitation, so far as this particular story was concerned, may have been due to a desire not to prejudice itself with

* *Envoy* (Dublin), 5 (May 1951) 44–5.

Lady Aberdeen, the then Lord Lieutenant's wife, by whom it had been commissioned to publish tracts relative to her anti-tuberculosis campaign. But of this I am not certain. I took the manuscript home, the issue still undecided, and I am ashamed to think of the length of time I had it in my possession. A month or two at least. It visited with me the house of a friend near Bray, Victor Le Fanu, a nephew of the novelist, Joseph Sheridan Le Fanu, the agent for Lord Meath's estates, and in my mind's eye I can still see it lying open on the table of his book-room, for I had invited his opinion upon it. Le Fanu, formerly a famous rugby international, was a good classical scholar, and in the midst of his country pursuits he found time to read a great deal. Kipling, Meredith and Stevenson were his favourite novelists, and I did not expect that he would take very kindly to *Dubliners*. Nor did he; the life described was off his beat. But he read the stories carefully, and recognising their remarkable quality, took more interest in them than in the usual Maunsel publications.

Apparently, Joyce learned that I had been given it to read, and on my way home, while stopping at Marseilles, I had a letter of complaint from him, dated Trieste, and forwarded to me from Dublin. In my reply I may have asked him whether he would assent to the exclusion of 'Ivy Day' from the collection;[2] but, at all events, whatever it was that I said, it furnished him with a pretext for submitting the story in the next year, after King Edward's death, to his successor, George V. Subsequently, he published an account of his grievance against Maunsel and of his appeal to Caesar (which of course was abortive) in a communication to Arthur Griffith's *Sinn Féin*; but I was out of Ireland then, and only heard of this long afterwards, when someone told me, or I read somewhere, that he had quoted 'A Mr Hone writing from Marseilles'[3] in his covering letter to the King. I have never consulted his version of the episode, and I must confess that I feel a disinclination to do so now, though my memory might be thereby refreshed.

On reference to the bibliography of Joyce in the London edition of *Ulysses*, I find that the letter to *Sinn Féin* appeared in August 1911. It was a year or two after this that I had my one and only encounter with the author.[4] I was then living in London and had ceased to be a partner of Maunsel & Co., but I used to call at an agency which the firm had opened in the Bloomsbury district. On my way there one morning, I met a young man, leading a small boy by the hand, who introduced himself as the author of *Dubliners*. I can still point to the spot where we stood and talked; but I remember nothing of what passed between us except his saying that he had 'crossed Europe' to see me. From this it may be concluded that he was still in communication with Maunsels about *Dubliners*. I fancy, however, that it was at the instance of Ezra Pound, who had heard of him from Yeats, that he had come to London. And it was through Pound's good offices that he at last found a publisher for *Dubliners*.

NOTES

Joseph Maunsel Hone (1882–1959), biographer of Yeats and George Moore, and one of the founders of the publishing house of Maunsel and Company.

1. In February 1908, Hone wrote asking formally to see the manuscript, but Joyce did not send it until April 1909.

2. Joyce agreed to make certain alterations.

3. *The Letters of James Joyce*, ed. Richard Ellmann (New York: Viking, 1966) II, p. 228, refer to Hone from Maunsel's on 13 February 1909, re: *Dubliners*.

4. In July 1912, during Joyce's brief visit to London on his way to Dublin. Actually, Hone had already met Joyce once before in 1909, during Joyce's first visit to Dublin. In a letter to his brother Stanislaus dated 21 August 1909, Joyce informed him that his meeting with Hone and George Roberts had been successful. On 19 August 1909, Joyce signed the contract for *Dubliners*.

James Joyce in Trieste*

ITALO SVEVO

In appearance Jim has not changed much from what he was when he arrived in Trieste. He is over forty. Lean, lithe, tall, he might almost seem a sportsman if he had not the negligent gait of a person who does not care what he does with his limbs.

I believe I am right in thinking that those limbs have been very much neglected and that they have never known either sport or gymnastics. What I mean is that from near he does not give the impression of being the tough fighter that his courageous work would lead you to expect. He is very shortsighted and wears strong glasses that make his eyes look enlarged. It is a blue eye and very notable even without the glasses, and it has a look of ceaseless curiosity matched with supreme coldness. I cannot help imagining that Joyce's eye would rest no less curiously and no less coldly on any adversary with whom he might have an encounter. It must be because I see him so seldom and think of him so much.

* Extracted from *James Joyce: A Lecture Delivered in Milan in 1927*, trans. Stanislaus Joyce (Norfolk, Conn.: New Directions, 1950). Editor's title.

After reading *Ulysses* there can be no doubt that his nose is not very good, but his ear is that of a poet and musician. I know that when Joyce has written a page of prose he thinks that he has paralleled some page of music that he delights in. This feeling – I cannot say whether it accompanies his inspiration because I only know that it follows it – proves his desire. In regard to music he is oddly fastidious. He understands the German classics, old Italian music, popular music where Richard Wagner found it, even our composers of operas from Spontini down, and the Frenchmen as far as Debussy. He possesses a magnificent tenor voice; and one who loves him hoped for a long time to see him tread the boards triumphantly, made up as Faust or Manrico. Even now Mrs Joyce regrets that her husband preferred the art that has made him one of the best known and most hated men in that Anglo-Saxon world to which he unwillingly belongs.

His fastidious taste in music leads him to throw his arms wide open to the future. Last year Mlle Monnier[1] of the *Navire d'Argent* gathered some cultured musicians together one evening to hear the latest thing in modern music by an American composer, Anthil or Antheil.[2] After a quarter of an hour of it many of the guests rose and went away, protesting and shouting. But Joyce declared, 'He reminds me of Mozart'. I cannot doubt Joyce's sincerity. He had attempted, and perhaps succeeded in the attempt, to superimpose on music some literary dream of his own. Of course the connection between literature and music can not be wholly musical because it is also literary.

Joyce's outward life at Trieste can be summed up as a spirited struggle to support his family. His inner life was complex but already clear-cut: the elaboration of the subject matter offered him by his childhood and youth. A piece of Ireland was ripening under our sun. But he had to pay for it; for the life of a gerundmonger is not an easy one.

It was not until after the war that success relieved him of every preoccupation. Sometimes he strove to make his life at Trieste easier either by seeking advancement in his profession or by changing it. On one occasion he sat for an examination to compete for a professorship in English. I do not know how it came about, but what is certain is that he did not get the job, and I shall never forget his disappointment. On another occasion he learned that in his native city Dublin there was not a single motion picture theatre while Trieste was swarming with them. He persuaded a cinema proprietor to open a branch in Dublin, and even went over himself to help the foreigners find their way around in John Bull's other island. He was to have shared in the profits. Unfortunately there were no profits, and the whole group came home again a little out of pocket. Joyce also contributed articles to a newspaper and was English correspondent in a bank. He did not lack friends in Trieste. The little foreign poet with his culture, his originality and his wit, brought into our group an agreeable note which was very surprising and charming. . . .

Everybody who knows Joyce knows that the Joyce who washes himself every day is not Stephen Dedalus, the unwashed bard, who thinks when he sees others washing and scratching themselves: 'They are trying to get at their consciences'. Dedalus is loose-spoken, while Joyce one day called me to task because I allowed myself to make a rather free joke. 'I never say that kind of thing,' said he, 'though I write it.' So it seems that his own books cannot be read in his presence. Perhaps some other personage has stolen into Dedalus; but it is all so welded together, so much of a piece, that as in cabinet-making it is impossible to see the juncture of the added piece. It is, however, the autobiography of Joyce the artist. If it were not, it would be necessary to believe that at that time Dublin hatched another artist of the same calibre, which I doubt very much. In fact, it is part of the novelty of the work that it makes the reader feel he is watching the evolution of an artist, and of an artist of importance. The tragedy of the book lies in the doubt whether in such circumstances the artist will succeed in emitting his lusty breath or die strangled. For the rest, Joyce signed his first published writings with the name Stephen Dedalus. It is a confession.

NOTES

Italo Svevo [pseudonym of Ettore Schmitz] (1861–1928), Italian novelist who became a friend of young Joyce when the latter set up as a private tutor at Trieste and had him for a pupil for English lessons. It was Joyce who introduced him to French critics and in this way his much-neglected work came to the light. On the relationship between the two writers see P. N. Furbank, 'Svevo and James Joyce', in *Italo Svevo: The Man and the Writer* (Berkeley and Los Angeles: University of California Press, 1966) pp. 78–91.

1. Adrienne Monnier.
2. George Antheil.

James Joyce: Two Reminiscences*

ANTONIO FONDA SAVIO and LETIZIA FONDA SAVIO

I am really embarrassed to speak about the great Irish writer, James Joyce, I was personally acquainted with him before the first World War, but I saw him only a very few times. I remember him as a tall young man, awkward in his gait, with bright, almost watery eyes peculiarly magnified by his glasses.

One day when I was about eighteen I saw him briefly in Piazza della Borsa, here in Trieste, and that meeting is still vivid in my memory. I was participating in a benefit begging together with Italo Svevo's daughter, who at that time was already my fiancée. We stopped Joyce, who gave us money and stayed a moment to chat with us. He spoke good Italian as well as our dialect, and it would not have been necessary for us to speak English, but of course I wanted to show off the two or three English words I knew.

I continued to be very much aware of Joyce because I lived with my father-in-law who always talked about Joyce, recollecting and appreciating him. I admired *Ulysses* because of its ingenious new literary scheme and narrative technique, and also because, since I am a Triestine with a strong attachment to my town. I was pleased to think that Joyce's masterpiece had been conceived here and that its author had perhaps drawn some inspiration for his work from Trieste and its people.

I must confess, however, that my admiration for Joyce was slightly diminished by a small disappointment. When he was asked to suggest a title for the English translation of Svevo's novel, *Senilità*, he recommended *As a Man Grows Older*. My father-in-law accepted this title without any hesitation, for he was very grateful to Joyce for returning him to literary life like a new Lazarus. However, I think Joyce misinterpreted the real sense of the title. The book's main character, Emilio Brentani, is described by Svevo as a man with many doubts, sorrows and inner hesitations, but he is not simply a man who is getting on in years. The sense of the novel is in the precocious moral aging of Brentani, so that

* *James Joyce Quarterly*, 9 (Spring 1972) 320–2.

he becomes a man lacking in will power, almost a good-for-nothing, full of good intentions that he can never realise.

Perhaps I have gone beyond the limits of my task which was to talk about my memories of James Joyce. I have spoken without knowing that subject very well, and yet I have pretended to be a critic. But at bottom what I have said has been my most vital recollection of the man.

AFS

During my life I have had to bear deep sorrows, but I have been cheered too by meeting remarkable people. One of them was James Joyce.

I should be able to write a great deal about my remembrances of Joyce, but I shall be content to mention some anecdotes partly derived from my personal experience and partly from my parents' remembrances.

One day I went to Joyce's apartment, when he was living in via Bramante, and was surprised to see the dining room completely filled with chairs. It was almost impossible for anyone to move. Joyce was fond of this arrangement because he could sit on one chair while using four others to rest his arms and long legs. His wife, Nora, was in despair because, as she said with reason, they needed their money to buy necessities.

Another personal remembrance springs from the time of the First World War when I lived in Zürich. Joyce also lived there at that time, and I took English lessons from him. Of course nobody could forget the war. I was from Trieste, sided with Italy, and hoped the English would win, while Joyce, as an Irishman, hoped the English would lose. He began reading an article from a newspaper to me in order to persuade me he was right. As I listened to him I grew depressed because I thought I could no longer understand English. But the argument ended in a burst of laughter when I realized that Joyce, excited as he was, was reading the German *Züricher Zeitung* with an English pronunciation.

My parents told me other anecdotes like this: Joyce was afraid of thunder and used to hide himself under a mattress during thunder-storms.

One day Joyce went to my parents' house, gave them their usual English lesson, and told them with pleasure that his wife and daughter were leaving for Ireland and that he and Giorgio would be happy to live alone like two single men. After some days he went again to my father and asked him for a loan because he could not live without Nora.

I also remember Joyce's fine voice. He could sing very well and interpret a melody with taste, a gift he shared with his brother Stannie and his sister Eileen. He sang only in Italian; in fact, he said that our language was the only one fit for singing because the stresses fall on the next to last syllables of most words.

In writing *Finnegans Wake*, Joyce drew inspiration for 'Anna Livia Plurabelle' from my mother's blond hair. This is the one chapter from the *Wake* that Joyce translated into Italian with the help of some friends.

In closing, I think that the Italian translation of a portion of this highly complex work is a moving achievement. For these memories and for your devotion to our language, I thank you, James Joyce.

LFS

Recollections of Joyce*

ALESSANDRO FRANCINI BRUNI

We met in Pola in 1904. Joyce had come from Ireland and I from Florence, both for the same purpose – to teach at the Berlitz School, he, English and I, Italian.

In Pola, as Grabriele d'Annunzio once said, the air was filled with the languages of Babel. For us the Babel outside simply was a continuation of the Babel inside. Nearly everyone knows about the Berlitz School. We taught practically all the languages of Europe: French, English, German, Spanish, Hungarian, Russian, Serbo-Croatian and Slavic. We also had exceptional students, among whom the most illustrious, I recall, was Lord Horthy, the ex-regent of Hungary. There was a group of us, each teaching the language of his native country. We were all moderately friendly with each other, according to our inclinations. I was the director.

Because of certain affinities, Joyce and I became friends, setting ourselves apart from our colleagues, who were a mixed lot. Our two families led a communal, bohemian life. Joyce's first child, Giorgio, was born in Pola,[1] not exactly on a straw bed, but certainly naked.

Do ut des [I give so that you will give], we used to say. Joyce made

* *James Joyce Quarterly*, 14 (Winter 1977) 160–8.

much more progress learning Italian from me than I in learning English from him. This was not due to laziness on my part. Joyce grabbed but did not give. Although he made sure of my *do* in Italian, I never got his *des* in English. Unable to be his student, I adapted myself to being his teacher, and what I lost in the exchange I recovered in authority. In fact, Joyce was not a beginner in the study of Italian. His progress up the scale of Italian phonetics had gone beyond the simple '*do*'. He had started studying Italian in Dublin. He could understand everything and read everything, though he had spent most of his time learning critical trifles and philological esoterica. He could quote Dante and Dino Campagni[2] from memory. But if he had to speak the language, he got nowhere. His syntax was so garbled that he sounded like an escapee from a madhouse; however, he was an intelligent student and made progress. In one year he learned so well that I had to put the brakes on his linguistic enthusiasm to leave time for my own programme to keep from being pushed too far into the dark labyrinth of linguistic curiosities and improprieties.

In the summer of 1905, we left Pola, he forced to go and I after him, expelled as an undesirable alien. We drifted toward Trieste, where once again the Berlitz School rescued us. For six months we returned to living together. We shared a house half-and-half, in fact among three, since, in the meantime, Joyce's brother Stanislaus had arrived from Ireland. He stayed in Trieste and for twenty years taught English at the University. It was the most tormented period of our communal life. Joyce had begun to bend the elbow.

One day when he was drunker than usual, I said to him sharply, 'My old Bacchus, have you gone mad?'

He answered meekly as an unweaned calf, 'No, I am developing myself'. He was glassy-eyed and thick-tongued. That kind of development pleased me little and it pleased his brother even less, who showered him with invective enough to crush him. It was a comic scene, these Irishmen exchanging insults in Italian! Apparently they found English a less effective instrument than Italian for venting their emotions.

As long as the verbal blast continued, Joyce's tactic was to fold himself up completely and become silent and passive. That way he allowed the storm to pass, and soon returned on his course towards – the bottle. Then little by little he crept out from under the incubus of rebuffs and launched into some discourse, his tongue oiled by a certain little wine from Lissa. Later on his exuberance was broken by periods of moderation, but that summer he reached the summit of his Bacchic indulgence. A litre of Opollo wine, and later a flask of Tuscan, had a place of honour on his work table.

In these circumstances he preserved a lucid subconscious, kept his imagination alive, and even planned the overall design of his works.

However ironically he may have treated it, Ireland was his agony. His spirit, particularly when he was depressed, would always return to Ireland. And if you were to ask him then what was on his mind, you would have heard a man discuss the torment of his country, showering it with mockery, while drowning his grimaces in a flow of unrestrainable tears.

One day we decided to go our own ways. Joyce went to live on via Donato Bramante in the new district between St Giusto and Montrizza in an apartment which he fitted out with custom-made furniture, constructed according to designs found in a Danish catalogue. This expenditure reflected not only his devotion to Ibsen but also a rise in his standard of living. Even after our separation we saw each other often, passing our free time together, usually at the Joyces'. He was as astute in his reasoning as he was amiable in his conversation. We discussed a variety of subjects – literature, art and religion. We used to sing together. Religion and music were of equal interest to us. Born with a musical talent, Joyce had an inclination for liturgical chants. He had a tenor voice that seemed naturally suited to this kind of music. We frequently listened in astonishment as he sang parts in the traditional Georgian style.

Joyce's interest in art was limited to the work of Meštrović.[3] He had an unbounded admiration for this Serbian sculptor, whom I believe he had come to know in Rome. He had gathered various reproductions, cut out from here and there, assigning entirely subjective interpretations to their meanings and to the artist's intentions.[4]

Among Italian poets he preferred Prati,[5] whose Ruello and Azzarellina had become mythic characters in his repertoire of universal poetry. He set Azzarellina to music.

One year, in honour of our suffering fatherlands, we arranged to celebrate together the festival of St Patrick, the national saint of Ireland. My family and I approached the occasion with patient curiosity – the Joyce family almost with solemnity. The most serious part of the festivities was the preparation of the plum pudding, which, according to Irish tradition, required nine days to perfect. Joyce had to go from shop to shop, searching for the ingredients. The entire family, including the writer himself, zealously joined in the preparation, disproving the proverb that 'too many cooks spoil the broth.' The pudding was exquisite. My family, of course, was invited; but in order not to appear simply as a freeloader and to give the impression of helping with this dish, I went each day at the same hour, like a doctor visiting a patient, to receive the tidings.

'How is the lump? Is it swelling? Has it begun to suppurate? Is a scab forming?' I would ask.

'Fine, fine,' one or the other of the Joyces would answer from the top of the lighted stairway.

The ninth day found us, nine devoted souls, punctually at dinner on St Patrick's Day. The coincidence of the prophetic number nine was immediately noted, of course. The pudding, which was brought to the table on a large serving plate resembling the shield of Achilles, was of colossal proportions, sinuous and eroded, with cavities like the moon. One would have thought that it could never be eaten or that, as it had required nine days to create, so it would take at least nine to consume. This proved only an illusion – the saffron-colored planet disappeared in a flash.

In June 1906, I joined the staff of the *Piccolo*, while Joyce went his own way. Restless and discontented with his situation, he left the Berlitz School to devote his time to private teaching. Soon, however, he decided to leave Trieste for Padua and Rome.[6]

In Padua, Joyce, who already had a doctorate in letters from the University of Dublin,[7] was awarded the diploma of *Abilitazione*, qualifying him to teach English in the Italian schools.[8] But he did not make use of his diploma. In Rome he became a bank clerk. It was a diversion for him to see the city, but the year was also one of great hardship for his family. Feeling himself free and unrestrained, Joyce resumed his senseless wine drinking with the *vino de li castelli*. Because of his overindulgence and loss of interest in his work, he hastily returned to 'his' Trieste, where he renewed his old acquaintances and pattern of life. Later he was invited to occupy the Chair of English Literature in the secondary school, Scuola Superiore di Commercio Revoltella, now a university. He remained there until the end of his stay in Trieste.

It was during these years that the *Piccolo della Sera* published a number of Joyce's articles, written in his usual densely-packed and vigorous style. Though veiled in a steely coldness, they are intense pieces treating various burning issues related to his native Ireland. I recall well such titles as 'The Last Fenian', 'Home Rule Comes of Age' and 'Ireland at the Bar'.

In August 1914, the war erupted, and ten months later I returned to Italy for the mobilisation. Joyce, physically unsuited for soldiering, an English subject, and a friend of Prince Hohenlohe, whose sons were his former students, obtained a visa to enter Switzerland, although he was considered at that time an enemy alien. He chose to settle in Zürich and remained there until the end of the war, while his brother Stanislaus was confined to a concentration camp in Moravia. When Joyce left for Switzerland, we separated with tears in our eyes and a heartfelt handshake.

Joyce's sojourn in Switzerland marked the beginning of his recognition as a writer. This favourable turn brought an improvement in his domestic and financial affairs. His acquaintances in Zürich, especially among wealthy Americans who were safe from the scourge of the war, opened important doors of editors in England and America – doors which until then had been implacably closed to him.

After the war Joyce reappeared in Trieste, having returned to complete his *Ulysses*. In fact, some Triestines served as models for certain characters in his novel. Then we saw each other again and relived some of those hours that we had shared in the past. However, times had changed, and Joyce was obviously no longer the same man. He seemed serious, almost conventional now.

Here the memoirs of my personal contact with Joyce end. He remained in Trieste until 1922,[9] the year in which we separated forever. He moved on to Paris, and I returned to Florence to assume a newspaper position. For a while we heard of one another by way of friends and occasionally letters. But Joyce rarely wrote. Suffering from an eye ailment, he now required the services of a secretary.

It is difficult indeed to assess the personality of the Irish writer, even for me, who observed him during his formative years. He had the temperament of an incoherent sophisticate, who was discriminative, destructive, and contradictory in all speculations concerning metaphysics, morality, esthetics. . . .

It is not true, as the carelessly improvised biographies assert, that Joyce knew seventeen languages. That's a joke! He did not know even Irish, the language of his fathers. He spoke and wrote French and Italian, as well as English, with great skill, but his knowledge of other languages was limited. Joyce used English with the precision of an expert craftsman. His stylistic innovations and way of treating his material have never been attempted by another writer.

English speakers may live in Italy as long as they like, but they will never be able to mask the hissing 's' which is typical of their language and of others. Joyce pronounced Italian in a way that would deceive others about his foreign origin. He knew Latin but not very well. I was convinced that he knew just enough about Ciceronian Latin to satisfy his general cultural needs. Never did I hear him claim to know Greek. It is possible that he learned it as an old man, as did Cato, though this does not seem likely. Most linguists are well aware that one lifetime is not enough to master the classical languages. On the other hand, it is possible not to know Homer's language and still to have a profound knowledge of Greek literature. So it was with Joyce. There is considerable difference between making this assertion and claiming that he knew so many living and dead languages. One cannot find in the history of European literature and language many examples of great linguistic achievement. Pico della Mirandolas and Cardinal Centofantis are rare.

In his judgements of Italian literature, Joyce was eccentric and paradoxical. His attitude was consistent, but his knowledge of the literature itself was noticeably superficial. Italian literature interested him until the fifteenth century, but the world beyond these 'pillars of Hercules' was unknown to him.

One pleasing trait of Joyce was his genuine love for Italy, an obvious, luminous and conscious love. His Catholic education and training was the real force that brought him irresistibly to our country. It is impossible to measure the increased admiration and respect for Italy that Joyce and his fame created wherever he lived, especially in those countries whose people and governments had previously looked upon Italy and her people with contempt. All the writers who have spoken of Joyce before and since his death have testified to his deep love for Italy. Even in Paris where his family had settled, Joyce never forgot that his children were born in Italy. In family conversations, which had become polyglot through necessity, Joyce often initiated long discourses in Italian because he did not want the language to be forgotten. Although he allowed his guests to select their own language for conversation, there were two words that he never permitted to be translated – the names of his children. For Joyce they were always to be 'Giorgio' and 'Lucia'. He used to say that the language of family affection could only be Italian. He understood Dante very well and could explicate him with the insight of a genius, not as the sterile and mummified commentators do. I saw him many times with tears in his eyes after such a reading.

Who could avoid noticing this eccentric during the years that he strolled the streets of Trieste? Agile and lean, his rigid legs like the poles of a compass, he went about with an abstracted look. In summer he wore a Panama hat of indescribable colour and old shoes, in winter, a shabby overcoat with raised fur collar.

James Joyce was born a gentleman. He descended from a noble family in Western Ireland, a section which carries the name of his ancestors – the Joyce Country. He was proud of his birth and his family, as one could easily see from the many ancestral portraits that hung on a wall of his apartment.

What is left from all the turmoil? What became of the comfortable life that he had earned so laboriously? The family seems to have become victims of a tragedy. The large and stately Paris apartment with its valuable library and its many manuscripts was abandoned, perhaps destroyed. The other apartment at Vichy also was abandoned, under threat of the German advance. Joyce died in Zürich – the alpha and omega of his cycle of glory. His wife and son Giorgio, thus parted from him, were crushed.

The tragedy of his daughter Lucia was even more distressing. A lovely girl, with a promising intellect, wise and caustic like her father, she was later committed to a sanitarium in Paris and there abandoned.[10]

Although we were poles apart in our religious beliefs, we were always friends. Joyce tenaciously held to his ideas, and I remained steadfast in my opposition to them.

Joyce had a personable and good-natured disposition. So far as his genius was concerned, one could say he was sovereign. In the more worldly and less significant matters, however, Joyce was naive and almost childlike. A sort of hysterical man with a morbid hypersensibility, he was insanely frightened by electrical storms. On occasion, during such storms, he would lose control of himself, becoming completely irresponsible and cowardly, like a child or a foolish woman. Overcome by terror, he would clap his hands over his ears, run and hide in a small darkened room or hurl himself into bed in order not to see or hear. Each time he would say that Italy was a country of cosmic revolutions and that he wanted to go away. But he stayed.

NOTES

1. Giorgio Joyce was born in Trieste.
2. Dino Compagni (1255?–1324), Italian prose-writer and close friend of Dante.
3. Ivan Meštrović (1883–1962).
4. In his room Joyce kept three photographs of sculptures by Meštrović.
5. Giovanni Prati (1815–1884).
6. Joyce left for Rome in July 1906, returning to Trieste in March 1907. The trip to Padua was in the spring of 1912 to take an examination qualifying him to teach in the public schools.
7. Joyce had a BA from the Royal University, later (1909) the National University of Ireland. The University of Dublin is Trinity College, Dublin.
8. The Italian officials did not award Joyce the diploma.
9. Actually 1920.
10. Lucia Joyce began to show serious signs of mental illness around 1930. Until her death in December 1982, she was at St Andrew's Hospital, Northampton, England.

My First English Teacher*

MARIO NORDIO

James Joyce was my first English teacher. Many years have gone by since then. Almost sixty. And what years! But although it was a long time ago, the memory of that regrettably brief meeting with James Joyce has remained vividly in my mind.

It was somebody working at *Il Piccolo* who called my attention to a young English teacher who had lately made his name in Trieste. As I wished to know that language, I sent word to Joyce asking if he could give me private lessons.

Joyce then lived in one of the many modest houses built in via Bramante for the lower middle class people. It stood in a slight depression between the hill of San Vito and that of San Giusto, a piece of ground overwhelmed by buildings.

The impression I gained of Joyce during that first meeting is still alive. I had in front of me a young man of about thirty, blondish, tall, slim and without a beard, just the man described by Silvio Benco. Italo Svevo also remembered him thus.

One day Joyce defined himself as 'belonging to the family of giraffes', for his sarcastic wit did not spare even himself. He looked like a boy grown in a rather irregular way, especially with his bony structure. Everyone was struck at once by his blue eyes. Although he was nearsighted, his eyes were very sharp and keen, flashing with a deep, intelligent light under his spectacles. His hand was cold and inert, and he never shook hands properly. As he walked the streets, his legs looked like a pair of rigid compasses.

What a great difference between the two brothers! While Stanislaus, who also taught English, always looked like a typically stiff, decorous teacher, Jim was just the opposite. His mind was nimble and open to every problem of that time and to broad questions of any sort. His conversation was always vivid, incisive, and so varied that nobody could foresee its subjects. It was often full of humour and ironic hidden thoughts. As he passed from one subject to another, he would season his speech with anecdotes in his favourite form of apologues. Aphorisms and paradoxes expressed with shrewd wit were often repeated in his talks. What he said was spontaneously witty. His was the caustic

* *James Joyce Quarterly*, 9 (Spring 1972) 323–5.

humour typical of Irish people, ending almost always with a slight, malicious smile and sometimes with a laugh.

I have said that Joyce was my first English teacher. And what a teacher! He could not conceal his dislike for the job, which he held only to stave off poverty. If I could have then imagined that the world of culture would some years later exalt him as one of the most considerable writers of our time, I would have been very proud of it. My progress, instead, was so slow that after a certain point my lessons became less and less frequent and then ceased altogether. I remember that our meetings were sometimes interrupted by Joyce's two noisy children while Mrs Joyce tried without success to make them be silent in a room close to ours.

As a very young journalist at the beginning of my career, I was eager to know everything in whatever field of culture, and during those meetings we frequently discussed everyday events, politics, literature and music. In short, we talked about everything except English, which was the main reason I went there. Joyce spoke fluent, correct Italian, but he often inserted some characteristic Triestine sentences into his speech. Our conversations grew increasingly friendly in that small apartment, and I came to know his wife and his sister Eileen.

One evening when Joyce was in a mood to reveal another side of himself, he sat at his piano and sang in a fine tenor voice, giving out some trills. He confessed that if it depended on him singing would be the most important occupation in his life. During the hours of his nightly escapes, it was easy to find him in some of the wine shops in the old part of town, where he carefully emptied glasses of a generous Dalmatian wine and sang in chorus with the wharf porters.

During this period, from 1905 to 1914, there occurred one of the most singular and little known episodes of his stay in Trieste. It is the adventure of a certain James Joyce who in 1909 became an Italian pioneer of movies in his faraway Ireland. At that time Italy was the most important producer in Europe of spectacular films drawn from episodes of Roman history. Jim was immediately an ardent admirer of the new technique and foresaw its great artistic and economic development from the very beginning. No films escaped him, and one day he decided to take movies to Dublin, where almost no one knew of them. He was convinced it would be a succees, and he succeeded in persuading a small group of people who managed the first cinemas in Trieste to finance a sort of society of moving pictures. It was then that he opened a cinema in Dublin.

His partners were an upholsterer who had built a new type of divan bed, a leather dealer, a draper and a bicycle seller. I saw them all and remember their names. They went to Dublin with Joyce and opened the first cinema in Mary Street. Joyce himself chose the Italian name,

'Cinema Volta', in memory of his favourite Trieste cinema. They formed a regular partnership with that name, but after a short period the partners broke off and lost interest in the firm. Ireland was too far and too foggy, and of course *la bora* at home was better. Joyce had to resign himself to that failure. He was not a businessman. This was his last attempt to be directly involved with Irish life.

When the First World War broke out, Joyce remarked with his usual irony that 'the Irishman at war with England had become a British subject at war with Austria'. He was compelled to move to Zürich with his family, and in order to gild the pill he said that he was going away because now he had taught all the Triestine people the English language. Before leaving he promised his dearest friends that he would come back as soon as the political situation allowed it. He kept this promise in 1919. A few years before, he had left Trieste as a stranger, but he came back to our freed town as a famous man. However, he did not give himself airs more than before. He looked a little older, but he was still caustic and witty. His second stay in Trieste was brief. Finally he took Ezra Pound's advice, carried all his belongings to Paris, and from that time I did not see him again.

James Joyce: an Occasion of Remembrance*

NORA FRANCA POLIAGHI

I was a child when Joyce lived in Trieste, and my father was one of his pupils. Now I find that many scattered and insignificant memories of that time spring to mind when I read *Ulysses*.

Joyce's milkwoman reminds me of her Triestine counterpart, who carried with her tin and zinc vessels and a small measure for pouring milk; who spoke in a scrubby, mixed-up way and always brought the scent of fresh country air into the houses of the town. The blind piano tuner from *Ulysses* also reminds me of the man who used to come to set in order for our small black piano of good quality which had been ruined by the damp air of Friuli, where it was built.

One also recalls the funeral of a young man who suddenly died like Dignam. A young relative of the deceased was present wearing a pair of tan shoes – Boylan's tan shoes, walking happily through the town.

* *James Joyce Quarterly*, 9 (Spring 1972) 326–7.

In *Ulysses*, too, we find a beach, a church and some cliffs reminiscent of Barcola; a lighthouse like our Lanterna; fireworks recalling those which burst on our gulf every 18 August in honour of the birthday of Emperor Franz Joseph; and restless, malicious girls like those one could meet trooping out of school or walking down via Cavana to the main street, il Corso.

I am also reminded in various ways of the processions of state officials, conceited and superb, filing through the streets of the town when the ships were launched, with a lot of people around, noisy and caustic as Joyce described them. There was Seltz water or, to speak more correctly, Seltzer, kept in earthen bottles to add to hot milk. It was a great cure for children's disorders when taken with castor oil and followed by a bit of toasted sweet bread. There were the small pills a Chinaman was selling, opening in the water and becoming a ship, a house, or flowers, as the sailor recalls in 'Eumacus'. These came with steamers from the Far East and were a delightful present for us children eager of novelties and fanciful things.

There were also the books of Rénan and Gorky, which were published in Naples in 1905 by Ferdinando Bideri. They probably had a large circulation in our town, for I remember them lying in the modest library of my family, and Joyce apparently believed that the Italians loved these authors more than any others.

Finally, 'The really appetising fragrance of our daily bread, the first of all the articles of wide consumption and more necessary than the others' (*Ulysses*, p. 614) reminds me of the excellent scent coming from the bakehouses in via Machiavelli and via Ponterosso, both standing near the piazza where Joyce lived for a short period. I always liked to go there with the woman who went to those shops every day to fetch our bread.

Nobody can say for certain which details of Trieste influenced Joyce. But I suspect that many of the 'bricks' in his great works bear a Triestine mark.

Pappy Never Spoke of Jim's Books*

EILEEN JOYCE SCHAUREK

CURTAYNE. Mrs Schaurek, all I know about Joyce is derived from

---

* *Evening Herald* (Dublin), 15 July 1963, p. 7; 16 July 1963, p. 6. Interviewed by Alice Curtayne.

books, especially of course Richard Ellmann's *Life*.[1] Did you read that, by the way, and do you think it is a fair presentation of your brother?

SCHAUREK. No, I didn't read it – only dipped into it here and there. I'm not a literary person at all, you know. I don't read many books. I have never read *Ulysses*. But this I do know, that Ellmann wasn't in a position to understand Jim as I knew him.

CURTAYNE. Yes I know from my reading that there was a close bond between you and Joyce, closer than between any other two members of the family. That is what I want to talk about. What kind of a man was Joyce in the intimacy of his family?

SCHAUREK. Jim was always my favourite out of a very large family. He was seven years older than me and I looked up to him as a child. I never changed my affection. He gave me no reason to change.

Dependence on Mother

CURTAYNE. Of course I know you gave Ellmann a great deal of information on most points, but I would like you to add to that now if you can. I think it was you who saw Joyce saying his rosary on the way to school when he was attending Belvedere. Shall we start there?

SCHAUREK. Yes, and that is still the way I always think of him. People have told me since that I am devout. If I am, I got it from him. You can imagine how impressed I was by his example at that age.

CURTAYNE. Tell me something about his relationship with his mother. I know from his own writings that he was very attached to her.

SCHAUREK. He was her favourite, too. Jim completely depended on her, not only for the usual sort of care, but even more for her moral support. He wanted her to believe that he would do well as a writer.

CURTAYNE. I know from what he has told us himself that her death was a great crisis in his life.

SCHAUREK. He was called home from Paris when we thought she was dying. Actually she lingered for months after that and he stayed on with us. We were very glad to have him as he was the only one who could cheer her up. He used to sing for her, accompanying himself on the piano and leaving the doors open so that she could hear him. She liked that. It soothed her. When she died, we had an awful time with Baby. I mean Mabel – she was the youngest, only a very small girl then. She was distracted. Jim used to tell her that the only thing that could spoil Mother's happiness in heaven was to see Baby cry and that used to make her stop.

CURTAYNE. And his own grief was very real?

SCHAUREK. Oh, years later in Trieste, he was still deploring her death. You see, Mother was wonderfully understanding with Jim. She always wanted him to go on with his studies and his writing. There was no money at all, and all the relations were saying that Jim should get a job and help on with the big family – he being the eldest, but Mother never took that point of view. She always did everything in her power to help him follow his bent.

Father and Son

CURTAYNE. And Joyce was your father's favourite, too?

SCHAUREK. Yes, and that used to drive the others mad. I really think that Jim understood my father even better than my mother did. He never blamed him like the others used to; Stannie, for instance, was hard on my father. You know all about Pappy retiring when he was only forty and so on?

CURTAYNE. Yes. Was your father proud of Joyce's fame as a writer?

SCHAUREK. No, I don't think so. Although Jim used to consult him and send him bits to read, Pappy never spoke of Jim's books. He didn't read them when they were published and I don't think he liked what he heard of them. The bond between Jim and Pappy was the love between father and son. Nothing that happened could change it.

CURTAYNE. Was there never a quarrel?

SCHAUREK. Never a serious one, oh no, never anything that you could call a quarrel. There was a sort of coolness after Jim ran away with Nora, his wife, but that was all forgotten when Jim brought home his little son. My father adored Giorgio. They always kept in touch by letter. My father gave the family portraits to Jim and in his will made him sole heir, although by that time Jim was quite well off. He was terribly upset at my father's death. I suppose you know the poem he wrote about it?

CURTAYNE. Yes. Ellmann gives it. What other memories have you about Jim in the family?

SCHAUREK. Well, when my mother died, Aunt Josephine kept a sort of an eye on us, and Jim went all out in his affection for her. That's the kind he was. We used to laugh at him about Aunt Josephine. He had to have someone. It wasn't long after my mother's death before he met Nora Barnacle and married her a few months later [*sic*]. After that, of course, Nora was the only woman in his life.

CURTAYNE. And then you went out to Trieste?

SCHAUREK. Jim took me out there. On his first visit home after his marriage, there was a sort of crisis on. My eldest sister, Poppie, had

been doing the house keeping and she was leaving to become a nun.
That meant four girls still with Pappy, so Jim said he would take
Eva and myself back with him. I needn't tell you we were overjoyed
to go.

CURTAYNE. It was a great adventure?

SCHAUREK. Yes, oh more than that. It was a new life opening out.
Pappy never took much interest in us – he lived his own kind of
life – so Jim was like a father to us. He said Eva should have her
tonsils out because of the way she was speaking and he paid for that
to be done. Then I used to sing with him – there was always music
going on in our house – and he praised my voice and said I should
have it trained. I thought that marvellous. He said it could be trained
in Trieste. And he bought us new clothes for the journey. It was
very exciting.

CURTAYNE. Did you have your voice trained in Trieste?

SCHAUREK. Oh, yes, and I enjoyed that very much.

CURTAYNE. Did you go far in your career as a singer?

SCHAUREK. I sang in opera. Of course, my marriage more or less put an
end to that. Anyway I don't think I had enough voice for it. But when
I came back to Ireland as a widow, I sang too in the Dublin Opera.

CURTAYNE. How long did you live with the Joyces in Trieste?

SCHAUREK. Six years.

Happiest Years of All

CURTAYNE. Were you happy there?

SCHAUREK. I loved it. Looking back on it now, I see that those were
the happiest years of my life. You see, I was twenty when I went
out and that's a lovely age to travel for the first time. There had
been a lot of sadness at home and one could forget it all in Trieste,
which was a gay little city then.

CURTAYNE. What did you do there besides having your voice trained?

SCHAUREK. Well, I did most of the housekeeping and I took care of
Jim's two children, Giorgio and Lucia, and I learned to speak Italian.
Jim helped me there, too, by talking Italian to me. He was a very
good linguist.

CURTAYNE. I got the impression from Ellmann that you were the good
angel of the Joyce household. Do you agree?

SCHAUREK. I wouldn't quite claim that. You know they were an awfully
happy couple, Jim and Nora. She was a lucky woman. Jim was so
devoted to her. Talk about being faithful – he couldn't bear to be
separated from her even for the shortest time. I told you, there was
never another woman in his life. He was always one for giving her a

good time, taking her out to dinner and to every kind of amusement.

CURTAYNE. Would you say that it was Joyce's devotion to Nora made their home so happy?

SCHAUREK. Oh, Jim was a wonderful father too. He used to play by the hour with Giorgio and Lucia. He adored them. Then we were all young people together. We had great parties in the flat, when we'd all sing and play musical instruments. We were lighthearted.

Enjoyed Shocking People

CURTAYNE. Didn't it ever trouble you that Joyce had given up his religion?

SCHAUREK. No, because he was going on like that in Dublin too, and I always thought he'd come round again. You know all this business that he was an enemy of the Church has never convinced me. I don't believe he ever gave it up in his heart. He was sort of mischevious and enjoyed shocking people. He was always trying to make out that he was an awful fellow. It was a kind of – oh, I don't know ...

CURTAYNE. Self-defence, or a pose, would you call it?

SCHAUREK. Yes, yes, something like that. He hated people finding out what he was really like, but I knew.

CURTAYNE. What was Joyce really like?

SCHAUREK. Soft-hearted, sentimental, full of affection ...

CURTAYNE. What else do you remember about his attitude to the Church?

SCHAUREK. Well, Eva used to be at him to go to Mass on Sundays, but I used to tell her it was useless to take that line with Jim. It only made him more stubborn.

CURTAYNE. He never went to Mass?

SCHAUREK. Oh, indeed, he did – often. He used to go to the Greek Orthodox Church because he said he liked the ceremonies better there. But in Holy Week he always went to the Catholic Church. He said that Catholics were the only people who knew how to keep Holy Week.

CURTAYNE. Did he go with you?

SCHAUREK. No, he went there and came home by himself. I don't think he liked sitting with his sisters, or something like that. I saw him there often, standing in a corner by himself. You know Italian men mostly stand during Mass and he had taken on that fashion.

Mass in Paris

CURTAYNE. It must have been after Trieste, then, that he gave up the practice of religion?

SCHAUREK. I don't know. Did he ever give it up? He took Nora's sister to Mass in England. Years and years after, when I stayed with them in Paris, he went to Mass too, but always by himself. I saw him there.

CURTAYNE. So you think he remained always a Catholic in his heart?

SCHAUREK. I'm certain of it. He wouldn't let people talk against the Church, always shut them up. I often used to go to daily Mass in Trieste; it is a habit I have all my life. Jim was very pleased that I did that. Of course he'd never say it, but I knew. He'd ask me nearly every night whether I was going or not in the morning. I'd know by the very look he'd give me – sort of anxious, what was in his mind. You know the kind of play that goes on between brother and sister? When I'd say something cheeky, like 'What's it to you where I go?', he'd pretend it was only because he wanted the paper brought in early – I could pick it up on my way back. As a matter of fact, some days he'd never look at the paper if he was taken up with the writing. I knew well he liked me to go to daily Mass.

CURTAYNE. So there was a good deal of happiness in Trieste even though money was scarce?

SCHAUREK. I have told you they were the happiest years of my life. It is true that money was scarce. Jim was teaching English and that's not well paid. Most of the housekeeping money was given by Stannie, who lived with us too. He used to get mad at Jim's extravagance and was always preaching economy. I'd make peace between them.

CURTAYNE. There, I told you you were the good angel of the household.

SCHAUREK. Well if you put it that way . . . I often made peace between Jim and Nora too. Although it was such a happy marriage they had their rows of course, they were only human. Nora was completely different from Jim. In those days she was always at him to teach more and spend less time at the silly writing, so as to earn more money. One day I heard them arguing in very loud voices and I went in. Just as I opened the door, Jim was saying 'Very well, I'll give up the writing'. And he stuffed into the stove the original of *Stephen Hero*. Nora was only laughing and she said to me. 'He's mad! He's mad!' I dashed forward and pulled the copy out of the stove, but not before some of the pages got burned, and I burned my hand too. Next day, when Jim had cooled down, he gave me a present to show how thankful he was. He said it was the only copy he had and that he could't have written it all again.

Some Got Burned

CURTAYNE. Yes. I remember Ellmann describes that scene too. But I thought it was an open fire like we have here.

SCHAUREK. Oh, no, it was a wood stove like they use in Italy. He had to lift off the cover to stuff in the pages; that's why some of them got burned.

CURTAYNE. So you respected the writing even if you didn't read it?

SCHAUREK. Oh, yes. I told you I'm not a literary person myself and I wasn't really interested in the literary people who were always thronging around Jim. I suppose I felt like my mother about the writing. As Jim was so mad to write, he should be left at it and perhaps he would make good some day. Of course I made my mistakes too. I don't want to make out that I was a great person in those days.

CURTAYNE. What kind of mistakes?

SCHAUREK. Well, I remember Jim once bought a very modern picture and he was immensely pleased about it – came home telling us all about the grand picture. I forget the name of the painter. The picture was delivered one day when he was out and Nora and myself decided to hang it, so as to give him a nice surprise when he came back. We spent some time getting it up on the wall and when Jim came home, he looked furious. We had hung it upside down! Even when he explained the whole thing to us, we still couldn't see any difference which way you looked at it.

Missed the Children

CURTAYNE. Did your marriage mean a big separation from Joyce?

SCHAUREK. Oh, awful, the way things turned out. Although I was greatly in love with Frantisek,[2] I was kind of broken-hearted going away. I think I missed the children more than anything. You see, I had really reared Giorgio and Lucia. I used to do everything for them and we were always together. Frantisek was in a bank and he was moved to Prague. Then came World War I, which cut us off completely. Jim couldn't stay in Trieste; he moved to Zürich. It was years before I saw them again.

CURTAYNE. When did you all meet again?

SCHAUREK. Not until after the war. Stannie had been interned and he joined up with us again after Frantisek got another transfer back to Trieste. Jim never liked Zürich as much as Trieste and when he heard we were all together there again, he immediately wanted to bring his family back to us and all of us to live together again like we used. Neither Stannie nor Frantisek wanted Jim back. I had a family of my own by this time and they thought the two familes too much of a crowd. But I held out for Jim against both of them. I said that if he wanted to come, he should come and that was that. I won that little battle. But then I found that Stannie had changed towards Jim during the long separation of the war. Things were never the same again between the two of them. Before he had spent a year with us, Jim had to go to Paris on business, meaning to stay only a few days. But he liked it and made his home there until World War II.

Sent a Telegram

CURTAYNE. After that you didn't see much of Joyce?

SCHAUREK. I always wrote to him. About a year later, I stayed with the Joyces in Paris on my way home to Ireland, and I stayed with them again after my husband's death. Jim is my eldest daughter's godfather. He was always very good to her, never forgetting her on her birthday, and buying little presents for her. All my three children loved him. They were always asking me why he was so sad. Isn't that funny? When Lucia got mentally ill – that was some years later of course – Jim sent me a telegram. 'Come at once. Lucia calling for you.' The poor thing remembered how I used to nurse her in Trieste. The telegram came from Zürich where Jim had taken her to see a specialist. I took charge of the poor child with the help of a nurse. We seemed to be getting on so well that Jim left again for Paris, taking his own family with him. That was the biggest sacrifice I ever made for him. I was terribly torn because I had left my own children in boarding-school in Dublin and I was dying to get back to them. Of course Jim was pathetic; he was so sure it was only a passing thing with Lucia and that she would be better in no time. Then Miss Weaver[3] invited Lucia to London so I took her there and saw her settled in before going back to Dublin. But this arrangement didn't last either. Lucia got upset when I left her and Miss Weaver couldn't manage her. I got another SOS. The only thing I could do was take Lucia to Bray and mind her there. Jim was delighted with this plan. He couldn't take Lucia himself because she had turned against Nora so much that he couldn't have that. Much as he loved Lucia, he always put Nora first. Anyway, I kept Lucia with me in Ireland for quite a long time before she became restless again and Jim had to make other plans for her. That was the last thing I did for him. He died early on in the second year.

CURTAYNE. When they opened the Joyce Tower in Dublin last year, weren't you pleased to see your brother receive so much honour in his own country?

SCHAUREK. Oh I had very mixed feelings, there was such an awful lot written about him then that I hated.

CURTAYNE. What did you hate about it?

SCHAUREK. All the people boasting how they had helped Jim in the past. A lot of it wasn't even true. And even if it was . . . would you like it if someone helped you financially and then boasted about it in print.

CURTAYNE. No.

His Younger Days

SCHAUREK. You'd think by the way they wrote that Jim was nothing but a scrounger. I hated that, it was so one-sided. It was only in his younger days he borrowed from anyone. Nobody said how generous he was later on when he had money. He shared it out with everyone. I wrote to him for money whenever I needed it, even after my marriage, and he always sent it. Nobody said about all the people he helped. I knew him to empty his pockets in Trieste and Paris for fellows trying to make a career; Dujardin,[4] and you know that Italian who used the pen-name 'Svevo'[5] – I forget his other name; and Sullivan,[6] the singer. He was ridiculous – I mean poor Jim – all he did for Sullivan; and for Silvestri,[7] the painter, and I don't know how many more. He even raised money for some of these people.

CURTAYNE. Didn't you like anything about the Joyce Festival last year when the Tower was opened?

SCHAUREK. I can't remember reading anything I liked. Then so many people turned up on the day of the opening who weren't sincere at all. They were just cashing in on Jim. They had nothing but abuse for him until he became famous. If only they had been a bit more friendly when he needed help. Jim suffered, you know. What's the use of all the applause now?

CURTAYNE. I am sorry you felt like that on what should have been a great day for you.

SCHAUREK. Ah, but I'll tell you something really marvellous that happened to me not so long before that. I was making a retreat in the convent at Perpetual Adoration in Merrion Square, given by a very nice priest, young and an excellent speaker. I enjoyed his talks. He was preaching on devotion to Our Lady and he was listing all the ways we should spread that devotion and the great writers who had made her better known. And then he said: 'And now I'm going to add a name that will surprise you, the name of a great writer and a great Irishman, who made Our Lady known to hundreds of thousands but for him would never have heard of her. He was James Joyce.' I nearly jumped out of my seat. I could hardly wait for Benediction to end before running round to the sacristy to thank him and tell him who I was. He was delighted to hear that Joyce's sister was in the congregation and he shook hands with me and said he had only spoken the truth. I went home that night walking on air. I had never heard Jim praised from the pulpit before. I never thought I would. But I heard many, many people saying he was damned.

CURTAYNE. I wouldn't let that trouble me if I were you. We're good at handing out damnation in Ireland. I'm sure you'll meet Joyce again some day.

SCHAUREK. Oh, wouldn't that be wonderful – at the end of it all. Wouldn't that be wonderful?

NOTES

Eileen Joyce Schaurek (1889–1963), Joyce's sister who left Dublin in January 1910 to live with him in Trieste.

1. Richard Ellmann, *James Joyce* (London and New York: Oxford University Press, 1959).

2. Eileen got married to Frantisek Schaurek, a Czech bank cashier in Trieste, in April 1915, with Joyce as best man. They later named their first child Beatrice Bertha, after the two women in *Exiles*.

3. Miss Harriet Shaw Weaver, editor of the *Egoist* who settled a bounty on Joyce.

4. Edouard Dujardin (1861–1949), French journalist and writer.

5. Italo Svevo, pseudonym of Ettore Schmitz.

6. John Sullivan.

7. Tullio Silvestri, who painted Joyce and Nora.

Recollections of James Joyce*

FRANK BUDGEN

One afternoon in the early summer of 1918 I was sitting at my work table in the commercial department of the British Consulate in Zürich. Taylor[1] stood by the window. He had just come in.

'I met James Joyce today,' he said.

I looked past the dark blue silhouette and profile of King George V

* *James Joyce and the Making of 'Ulysses'* (London: Grayson & Grayson; New York: Harrison Smith & Robert Haas, 1934) pp. 9–22. Editor's title.

at the yellow, white and blue sky, green lime trees, trickling Sihl and dark railway sheds.

'Yes,' I said.

'Yes. It was in the Stadttheater. Kerridge[2] is chorus master there, you know. Joyce came in to ask Kerridge something and then he sat at the piano and sang to us.'

Taylor stretched out hands to a keyboard and turned his head to an audience.

'He has a fine tenor voice and he knows it.'

Taylor sings and is a judge of singing.

'But who is James Joyce?' I asked.

'He's a writer,' Taylor said. 'You've never heard of him? People think an awful lot of his book, *A Portrait of the Artist as a Young Man*. Do you never read? Anything but newspapers, I mean?'

He waved his hand in the direction of the office newspaper files.

'Very little,' I said. 'And that little not English. What do you expect? I haven't even time to paint.'

'It doesn't matter,' said Taylor. 'I want you to meet Joyce.'

'Why?'

'Because I think you'd get on well together. Of course he's Irish. You can tell that by his name. And somehow he hasn't hit it off with the CG.'

I tried without much success to make some sort of shape out of the material Taylor had given me: well-known writer, tenor singer, Irishman who couldn't get on with the Consulate-General. Still, there was friend Blaise Cendrars, also a well-known writer. August Suter and I stood godfathers to his son Odilon in the Mairie of the 14th arrondisment. His polychrome *Transsibirien*. Now he has lost an arm in the war. One mustn't label people in advance. Taylor must have read something negative in the pause. He broke in on my image building.

'Don't be lazy and standoffish,'' he said. 'Joyce is dining with me at my pension the day after to-morrow. You can manage that, can't you?'

'I don't see what I have to do with well-known writers,' I said, 'or they with me. Still, I'm free, and if you think . . .'

'I do,' said Taylor. 'Half past seven, if we don't go up together.'

Taylor was in Zürich on a cultural mission. Enemy countries were being bombarded with shot and shell, neutral countries with propaganda of all sorts designed to prove that it was both interesting and agreeable to be friends with the triple entente and its allies. A collection of modern British pictures had been got together for exhibition in the principal towns in Switzerland and Taylor was in charge of it. The show was good enough of its kind, but in the matter of painting the French and Germans had already queered the pitch. The French had shown some of the dazzling best of their nineteenth-century masters, and the Germans had sent a less brilliant, but vastly interesting collection, covering the efforts of a century. On account of transport dangers and difficulties, the British collection was limited to the work of living painters, so that those who expected to see Constables and Turners were disappointed. Both Taylor and myself were painters and both of us were working for the Ministry of Information. My own job was to survey the Swiss press, translate letters and make myself generally useful.

Taylor's pension was high up on the Zürichberg beyond the Fluntern tram terminus. That his guest was delayed was of no consequence. We sat in the gravelled garden under a tree, drinking our aperitif and occasionally striking too short at wasps. The daylight began to fail. In the restaurant they switched on the lights. Taylor broke off a sentence with: 'Ah, here's Joyce'.

Following Taylor's look I saw a tall slender man come into the garden through the restaurant. Swinging a thin cane he walked deliberately down the steps to the gravelled garden path. He was a dark mass against the orange light of the restaurant glass door, but he carried his head with the chin uptilted so that his face collected cool light from the sky. His walk as he came slowly across to us suggested that of a wading heron. The studied deliberateness of a latecomer, I thought at first. But then as he came nearer I saw his heavily glassed eyes and realised that the transition from light interior to darkening garden had made him unsure of a space beset with iron chairs and tables and other obstacles.

Joyce's greeting to us is of elaborate European politeness, but his manner I think is distant, his handshake cool. Close up he looks not so tall though he is well above average height. The deception is due to his slender build, his buttoned coat and narrow cut trousers. Then he listens to, not looks at, his man. The form of his head is the long oval of heads of the Norman race. His hair is dark enough to look black in this light. His beard is much lighter, orangey-brown and cut to a point – Elizabethan. Behind the powerful lenses of his spectacles his eyes are a clear, strong blue, but uncertain in shape and masked in expression. I notice later that in a moment of suspicion or apprehension they become a skyblue glare: The colour of his face is a bricky red, evenly distributed. The high forehead has a forward thrust as it issues from under the front rank of hair. His jaw is firm and square, his lips thin and tight, set in a straight line. Something in Joyce's head suggests to me an alchemist. It is easy to imagine him moving around in a room full of furnaces, retorts and books full of diagrams. And something in his poise suggests a tall marshfowl, watchful, preoccupied. But I feel reassured. What I had imagined under a well-known writer is not there. He might easily be a painter.

At dinner Joyce told us of his departure from the Habsburg Empire after Italy's entrance into the war and praised the generosity of the Austrian authorities, who had allowed him to leave the country and who had even taken his word for the contents of his luggage. The war itself and its progress were left alone by common consent, but war literature was mentioned, and in this connection Joyce said that the only poem on the subject that at all interested him was one by the Viennese poet, Felix Beran, a friend of his in Zürich.

> Und nun ist kommen der Krieg der Krieg
> Und nun ist kommen der Krieg der Krieg
> Und nun ist kommen der Krieg
> Krieg
> Nun sind sie alle Soldaten
> Nun sind sie alle Soldaten
> Nun sind sie alle Soldaten
> Soldaten
> Soldaten müssen sterben
> Soldaten müssen sterben
> Soldaten müssen sterben
> Sterben müssen sie
> Wer wird nun küssen
> Wer wird nun küssen
> Wer wird nun küssen
> Mein weisses Leib

The word *Leib* (body) moved him to enthusiasm. It was a sound that created the image of a body in one unbroken mass. From liquid beginning it passes over the rich shining double vowel till the lips close on the final consonant with nothing to break its blond unity. He spoke of the plastic monosyllable as a scultpor speaks about a stone.

He asked us if we knew the painting of Wyndham Lewis. He had read some of Lewis's writings and seen some of his drawings. Neither Taylor nor myself knew Lewis's work sufficiently well to talk about it with assurance. Joyce said he had read a story of Lewis's that had pleased him. It was the story 'Cantelman's Spring Mate'. One of us, it must have been myself, referred to Shelley's *Prometheus Unbound*.

'That seems to me to be the *Schwärmerei*[3] of a young Jew,' Joyce declared bluntly.

And when I, apropos of some love affair or other, used the conventional word, heart, he said in the same tone:

'The seat of the affections lies lower down, I think.'

His meaning, I thought, was clear. He objected to the sentimental convenient cliché. The allusion that prompted his remark I learned

only some time later when, at his insistence, I read Phineas Fletcher's
Purple Island or the Isle of Man. The Norfolk Rector in describing the
provinces of the human body says the following:

> The sixt and last town in this region,
> With largest stretcht precincts, and compass wide,
> Is that where Venus and her wanton sonne
> (Her wanton Cupid) will in youth reside.
>   For though his arrows and his golden bow
>   On other hills he friendly doth bestow,
> Yet here he hides the fire with which each heart doth glow.

So far, in spite of all politeness and conventional amiability, I had felt
aware of something watchful and defensive in Joyce's attitude. But on
leaving our host we walked down the hill together to the
Universitätstrasse where Joyce lived, and I experienced a sense of
relief, due I feel sure to a sudden expansiveness and cordiality on
Joyce's part. He asked about my work, my stay in Zürich, and suggested
future meetings. Some time afterwards he said to me:
   'You remember that evening at Taylor's pension on the Zürichberg?'
   'Yes,' I said, 'of course I do.'
   'Well, I went up to Taylor's to dinner with a mind completely made
up that you were to be a spy sent by the British Consulate to report
on me in connection with my dispute with them.'
   Joyce laughed a clear long laugh of full enjoyment at his mistake. A
laugh is a significant gesture. Joyce's laughter is free and spontaneous.
It is the kind of laughter called forth by the solemn incongruities, the
monkeyish trickeries and odd mistakes of social life, but there was no
malice in it or real *Schadenfreude*. His is the kind of laugh one would
expect to hear if the president of the republic took the wrong hat, but
not if an old man's hat blew off into the gutter.
   'And what good reason had you,' I asked, 'for coming to the
conclusion that I wasn't a spy?'
   'Because,' said Joyce, 'you looked like an English cricketer out of
the W. G. Grace[4] period. Yes, Arthur Shrewsbury. He was a great bat,
but an awkward-looking tradesman at the wicket.'
   It was shortly after our meeting at Taylor's pension that I again met
Joyce, by chance this time, and we strolled through the double avenue
of trees on the Utoquai from Bellevue towards Zürich Horn. To the
left of us were the solid houses of Zürich burgesses, on our right the
lake and on the far shore of the lake the green slopes and elegant
contours of the Uetliberg ridge.
   'I am now writing a book,' said Joyce, 'based on the wanderings of
Ulysses. The Odyssey, that is to say, serves me as a ground plan. Only

my time is recent time and all my hero's wanderings take no more than eighteen hours.'

A train of vague thoughts arose in my mind, but failed to take shape definite enough for any comment. I drew with them in silence the shape of the Uetliberg-Albis line of hills. The Odyssey for me was just a long poem that might at any moment be illustrated by some Royal Academician. I could see his water-colour Greek heroes, book-opened, in an Oxford Street bookshop window.

Joyce spoke again more briskly:

'You seem to have read a lot, Mr Budgen. Do you know of any complete all-round character presented by any writer?'

With quick interest I summoned up a whole population of invented persons. Of the fiction writers Balzac, perhaps, might supply him? No. Flaubert? No. Dostoevski or Tolstoi then? Their people are exciting, wonderful, but not complete. Shakespeare surely. But no, again. The footlights, the proscenium arch, the fatal curtain are all there to present to us not complete, all-round beings, but only three hours of passionate conflict. I came to rest on Goethe.

'What about Faust?' I said. And then, as a second shot, 'Or Hamlet?'

'Faust!' said Joyce. 'Far from being a complete man, he isn't a man at all. Is he an old man or a young man? Where are his home and family? We don't know. And he can't be complete because he's never alone. Mephistopheles is always hanging round him at his side or heels.* We see a lot of him, that's all.'

It was easy to see the answer in Joyce's mind to his own question.

'Your complete man in literature is, I suppose, Ulysses?'

'Yes,' said Joyce. 'No-age Faust isn't a man. But you mentioned Hamlet. Hamlet is a human being, but he is a son only. Ulysses is son to Laertes, but he is father to Telemachus, husband to Penelope, lover of Calypso, companion in arms of the Greek warriors around Troy and King of Ithaca. He was subjected to many trials, but with wisdom and courage came through them all. Don't forget that he was a war dodger who tried to evade military service by simulating madness. He might never have taken up arms and gone to Troy, but the Greek recruiting sergeant was too clever for him and, while he was ploughing the sands, placed young Telemachus in front of his plough. But once at the war the conscientious objector became a *jusqu'auboutist*. When the others wanted to abandon the siege he insisted on staying till Troy should fall.'

* This sentiment is apparently shared on the other side of the footlights. Many years afterwards I asked Joyce why his friend Sullivan, the Paris–Kerry tenor, was so loth to sing in an opera that has become the standby of the Academie Nationale, and he replied: 'That Samson of the land of Dan has told me that what bothers him is not so much the damnation of Faust as the domination of Mephistopheles.'

I laughed at Ulysses as a leadswinger and Joyce continued:

'Another thing, the history of Ulysses did not come to an end when the Trojan war was over. It began just when the other Greek heroes went back to live the rest of their lives in peace. And then' – Joyce laughed – 'he was the first gentleman in Europe. When he advanced, naked, to meet the young princess he hid from her maidenly eyes the parts that mattered of his brine-soaked, barnacle-encrusted body. He was an inventor too. The tank is his creation. Wooden horse or iron box – it doesn't matter. They are both shells containing armed warriors.'

History repeats itself. The inventor of the tank also found his Ajax at the War Office in the shape of Lord Kitchener.

It seems to me to be significant that Joyce should talk to me first of the principal character in his book and only later of the manifold devices through which he presented him. If the two elements of character and material can be separated this is the order in which he would put them. On the home stretch back to Bellevue a question grew in my mind.

'What do you mean,' I said, 'by a complete man? For example, if a sculptor makes a figure of a man then that man is all-round, three-dimensional, but not necessarily complete in the sense of being ideal. All human bodies are imperfect, limited in some way, human beings too. Now your Ulysses . . .'

'He is both,' said Joyce. 'I see him from all sides, and therefore he is all-round in the sense of your sculptor's figure. But he is a complete man as well – a good man. At any rate, that is what I intend that he shall be.'

The talk turned on music, and I mentioned that Taylor had heard him singing in the Stadttheater.

'Yes, I remember,' said Joyce. 'I went there to ask Kerridge something about the disposition of the instruments in the orchestra, and to put him up to some of the commoner mistakes his chorus was likely to make in singing Italian. What I sang was the tenor Romanza 'Amor Ti Vieta' from Giordano's *Fedora*. I wanted to show the vocal necessity for putting an atonic vowel between two consonants. Listen.'

And he began to sing:

'Amor ti vieta di non amar la man tua lieve che mi respinge.'

He turned to me again:

'You hear', he said. 'It would be impossible to sing that "*respinge*" without interpolating a vowel breath between the "n" and the "g".'

When I first called on Joyce and his family they were living at No. 38 Universitätsstrasse. There were two guests beside myself. It was after these had gone and Joyce had asked me to stay for a final half-hour's chat that we fell to talking about religion. Being an orthodox agnostic I saw nothing illogical in admitting that what are called miracles might occur. I had no satisfactory evidence that any ever had occurred, but on my limited experience I felt I couldn't rule them out. Perhaps I didn't succeed in defining my position too well, for when I rose to go Joyce laughed and said:

'You are really more a believer than is many a good Catholic.'

The next day I found a packet and a letter awaiting me in my little room in the Schipfe. The packet contained a copy of *A Portrait of the Artist as a Young Man* and the letter extracts from press notices of *A Portrait of the Artist, Dubliners* and *Exiles*. I read the book and then the praises of Ezra Pound, H. G. Wells and others, quoted on the many-coloured leaflets. H. G. Wells wrote:

> Its claim to be literature is as good as the claim of the last book of *Gulliver's Travels*. . . . Like Swift and another living Irish writer, Mr Joyce has a cloacal obsession. . . . Like some of the best novels in the world, it is the story of an education. . . . One conversation in this book is a superb success. I write with all due deliberation that Sterne himself could not have done it better.

And Ezra Pound and a dozen others to the same purpose, each in his own way, I remember very well my own impression. The affirmative young man, the terror-stricken and suffering adolescent were but timebound phases of a personality the essence of which was revealed in the boy Stephen Dedalus. He is like a young inquisitive cat taking stock of the world and of himself: climbing, hiding, testing his claws. This bold, sensitive, tenacious, clear-seeing boy is the essential artist. There comes a moment when hostile forces – cramping poverty and the tyrannies of Church, nation and family – threaten him with loss of freedom, with extinction as an artist, and he must mobilise all his forces of defence and attack to save himself. 'Silence, exile and cunning,' says Stephen himself, and he uses those arms and more besides before the battle is won.

A cold wind was blowing when I met Joyce one evening on the Bahnhofstrasse. The brown overcoat buttoned up to his chin lent him a somewhat military appearance.

'I'm glad you liked the *Portrait*,' said Joyce. I had returned the book with a letter recording some of my impressions of it.

'That simile of yours, "a young cat sharpening his claws on the tree of life," seems to me to be very just applied to young Stephen.'

I enquired about *Ulysses*. Was it progressing?

'I have been working hard on it all day,' said Joyce.

'Does that mean that you have written a great deal?' I said.

'Two sentences,' said Joyce.

I looked sideways but Joyce was not smiling. I thought of Flaubert.

'You have been seeking the *mot juste?*' I said.

'No,' said Joyce. 'I have the words already. What I am seeking is the perfect order of words in the sentence. There is an order in every way appropriate. I think I have it.'

'What are the words?' I asked.

'I believe I told you,' said Joyce, 'that my book is a modern Odyssey. Every episode in it corresponds to an adventure of Ulysses. I am now writing the Lestrygonians episode, which corresponds to the adventure of Ulysses with the cannibals. My hero is going to lunch. But there is a seduction motive in the Odyssey, the cannibal king's daughter. Seduction appears in my book as women's silk petticoats hanging in a shop window. The words through which I express the effect of it on my hungry hero are: "Perfume of embraces all him assailed. With hungered flesh obscurely, he mutely craved to adore." You can see for yourself in how many different ways they might be arranged.'

A painter is, perhaps, more originality proof than any other artist, seeing that all recent experimental innovations in the arts have first been tried out on his own. And many a painter can labour for a day or for many days on one or two square inches of canvas so that labour expended on achieving precious material is not likely to surprise him. What impressed me, I remember, when Joyce repeated the words of Bloom's hungrily abject amorousness to me, was neither the originality of the words themselves nor the labour expended on composing them. It was the sense they gave me that a new province of material had been found. Where that province lay I could not guess, but as our talk proceeded Joyce spoke of it himself without question of mine. We were by this time sitting in the Astoria Café.

'Among other things,' he said, 'my book is the epic of the human body. The only man I know who has attempted the same thing is Phineas Fletcher. But then his *Purple Island* is purely descriptive, a kind of coloured anatomical chart of the human body. In my book the body lives in and moves through space and is the home of a full human personality. The words I write are adapted to express first one of its functions then another. In 'Lestrygonians' the stomach dominates and the rhythm of the episodes is that of the peristaltic movement.'

'But the minds, the thoughts of the characters,' I began.

'If they had no body they would have no mind,' said Joyce. 'It's all one. Walking towards his lunch my hero, Leopold Bloom, thinks of his wife, and says to himself, "Molly's legs are out of plumb". At another time of day he might have expressed the same thought without any underthought of food. But I want the reader to understand always through suggestion rather than direct statement.'

'That's the painter's form of leverage,' I said.

We talked of words again, and I mentioned one that had always pleased me in its shape and colour. It was Chatterton's 'acale' for freeze.

'It is a good word,' said Joyce. 'I shall probably use it.'

He does use it. The word occurs in 'The Oxen of the Sun' episode of *Ulysses* in a passage written in early English, describing the death and burial of Bloom's son Rudolph: '. . . and he was minded of his good lady Marion that had borne him an only manchild which on his eleventh day on live had died and no man of art could save so dark is destiny and she was wondrous stricken of heart for that evil hap and for his burial did him on a corselet of lambswool the flower of the flock, lest he might perish utterly and lie akeled. . . .'

In leaving the café I asked Joyce how long he had been working on *Ulysses*.

'About five years,' he said. 'But in a sense all my life.'

'Some of your contemporaries,' I said, 'think two books a year an average output.'

'Yes,' said Joyce, 'But how do they do it? They talk them into a typewriter. I feel quite capable of doing that if I wanted to do it. But what's the use? It isn't worth doing.'

NOTES

Frank Budgen (1882–1972), English painter with whom Joyce became more intimate than with any friend in his life except J. F. Bryne.

1. Horace Taylor, English painter at whose house Joyce first met Budgen.
2. W. H. Kerridge.
3. Enthusiasm.
4. W. G. Grace (1848–1915), one of the most famous of English cricketers.

How I Published *Ulysses**

SYLVIA BEACH

My father was a Presbyterian Minister in Priceton, New Jersey, and he sent me over to Paris during the 1914 war to study.

My studies brought me in contact with Adrienne Monnier, a very interesting woman, famous in literary history in France, who had a bookshop in rue de l'Odéon where all the French writers went in and out. I used to frequent this bookshop – perhaps the only foreigner during the 1914 war who went there.

I was first going to have a bookshop in New York – a French bookshop. But I did not have the capital to do this: it would have been too expensive. So, when I was talking this over with Adrienne Monnier, she suggested having an American one in Paris.

The young American writers had not arrived in Paris when I opened my bookshop. But I had confidence that they would come. I did not realise that there was going to be an exodus from America. But the opening of my bookshop coincided with the arrival of all these writers – these 'big-timers' as my generation called them – who came to make Paris their home.

At the house of the French poet André Spire I met James Joyce. Ezra Pound and his wife Dorothy Pound were there too. They had brought the Joyces, and I met Mrs Joyce. Joyce seemed interested in my bookshop and became a daily visitor.

At the time his *Ulysses* was appearing in the *Little Review* in New York.[1] And he told me about his troubles with *Ulysses*. It was being suppressed regularly in the *Little Review*. They suppressed it four times in all and finally altogether. And the editresses, Margaret Anderson and Jane Heap, were hauled off to court: they escaped with a fine of 100 dollars, and their fingerprints and thumbprints were taken and then *Ulysses* was finished in America.

This was the winter of 1920. James Joyce came to tell me this sad news. He was very downcast, and he said: 'My book will never appear.'

I knew that in England an effort had been made by Miss Harriet Weaver. She had published *A Portrait of the Artist* in her review the

* Extracted from 'Shakespeare and Co., Paris', *Listener* (London), 2 July 1959, pp. 27–8. Condensed as 'How I Published *Ulysses*,' *Irish Digest* (Dublin), 67 (December 1959) 39–41.

Egoist, but she was not able to publish *Ulysses*. She first tried in her review, and the subscribers said it was not suitable for a family paper; so then she suppressed her review herself and opened a publishing house, the Egoist Press, in order to publish Joyce's work.

She was still not able to publish *Ulysses*. So that is where I came in. I, who was not a publisher at all, but just a little bookseller with no capital and no experience, offered to publish *Ulysses* and Joyce accepted. I went ahead and found a printer who was willing to accept the risk, and I said: 'Your bills won't be paid unless we get the subscriptions, but we'll get the subscriptions.'

Then Miss Weaver sent me a big mailing list from England; and in Paris, Ezra Pound and Hemingway and [Robert] McAlmon and everybody turned in and brought me subscriptions very nicely. Colonel Lawrence subscribed and he kept complaining that the book was not out yet.

Joyce was working on the Circe episode at the time. He had not finished *Ulysses* yet and he was having serious trouble with his eyes. The manuscript was very illegible, as he could not see. Nine stenographers tried to tackle the copying of the Circe episode and gave it up.

One of them, Joyce told me, wanted to throw herself out of the window, and another one – the last one – threw her copy in the doorway where Joyce lived at the time, in the Boulevard Raspail, and rushed away down the street. Finally, two friends copied, and each in turn had to give it up for one reason or another: my sister Siprian who was taking part in a film worked on it for a while, then her film went elsewhere and she could not continue. Then an English friend at the British Embassy was very interested in *Ulysses* and she said she would copy it. But her husband saw it and threw the manuscript and copy into the fire.

We were faced with a dreadful dilemma: the manuscript had been sent over to America and there was no other copy in Paris. John Quinn, the Irish-American lawyer, had this manuscript, which he was purchasing bit by bit. We tried to get him to return the part that had been destroyed, and finally he had it photo-copied and sent us this piece.

I had a bet with Joyce that Shaw would subscribe. I said: 'I'm going to send him a prospectus. He's always so interested in his fellow-Irishmen, and in anything like a suppressed book, I'm sure he will.'

Joyce burst out laughing. He said: 'He will *not* subscribe.'

So we bet on that, and I said I would give Joyce a box of his favourite cigars and he was to give me a silk handkerchief to dry my eyes on.

Bernard Shaw wrote a letter explaining on a whole page why he could not subscribe: and he ended by saying that I did not know his fellow-countrymen if I thought that an elderly Irish gentleman could afford to pay as much as 150 francs for a book. But there were French subscribers – André Gide was one of them; and there were other subscribers everywhere.

When *Ulysses* appeared I had no trouble getting it into England. I got in all the copies specially, though an article had appeared in the *Pink 'Un* and posters were up in London saying 'This scandal of *Ulysses*', and the *Sporting Times* seemed very much shocked.[2] But immediately I got a great many letters from Colonels, asking me to send it to their clubs in London.

I did not get the copies into America. They were all seized at the port of New York. I told Ernest Hemingway about this and asked what I should do to get the copies to the American subscribers. Hemingway had a splendid scheme of getting it in through Canada. A man used to cross over on a ferry boat carrying a copy of *Ulysses* in his trousers, day by day until he got them all in. In the end, when he had to hurry, he took a friend with him, and they each took two and looked like prospective mothers.

NOTES

Sylvia Beach (1887–1962). Born in Baltimore, Md., she became best known for her small bookshop on the Left Bank in Paris, which she called Shakespeare and Co. It was a centre for literary and artistic activities in the 1920s and 1930s. She published her recollections, *Shakespeare and Company* (New York) in 1960. In June 1962 she visited Dublin to open the Joyce Museum at Sandycove.

1. The *Little Review* began to serialise *Ulysses* in March 1918.
2. 'Aramis', 'The Scandal of *Ulysses*', *Sporting Times*, no. 34 (1 April 1912) 4.

The Joyce I Knew*

ARTHUR POWER

On the evening in question I had gone there[1] to meet a party which, however, did not materialise; and I wandered about the hall watching the couples dancing thinking perhaps I might meet someone I knew to

---

* Extracted from *From the Old Waterford House* (Waterford: Carthage Press, 1940) pp. 148–50, 153–5. Editor's title.

dance with. I saw a group of people at the far end of the hall I knew, but I did not want to get in with them, I wanted to dance, life is too short to talk it away. However, towards the end, one of the ladies hailed me over, and introducing her friends who sat at the table, presented me to James Joyce. The meeting was unexpected, and gave me rather a shock. I had read a couple of his early books and had disliked them intensely. As an author you either admire Joyce without reserve: or you hate him: I had done the latter. But I rather liked the man: slightly and gracefully built, with a rather Shakespearian head, he wore strong glasses, which greatly magnified one eye, a small goatee beard covered a thin lipped, curiously shaped mouth. His hands were noticeably fine, and slight fingered. Every movement of his proclaimed a poet – everything except his mouth. His manner was sympathetic rather than friendly – because Joyce's social manner is not easy. He surrounds himself normally with a kind of mental barbed wire – but his exquisite manners reminiscent of the Dublin of the Grand Days – that remarkable Irish courtliness – he always has. And the more difficult the position is the more perfect his manner. It has the detachment and nobility to it of a grandee, and is as superior as a diamond is to glass to what passes for manners among provincial gentry and nobility. It is the outward sign of inward refinement: and like all remarkable men he has no conceit: no boorish arrogance.

He asked me if I was 'a man of letters?' The question 'man of letters' had a curiously old-fashioned nineteenth century tang to it, in the rough and tumble of a popular dance hall it sounded like an invitation to a minuet if only an intellectual one. I told him I was interested but did little myself.

'What are you trying to write?' he asked.

I told him that I was interested in the eighteenth century French satirists, and I wanted to write like them.

'You'll never do it,' he said, 'never – you are an Irishman – you must write in an Irish tradition: write what is in your blood, and not what is in your head.'

I told him I was tired of nationality, I wanted to become international – all great writers were international.

'Yes – but they were national first – if you are sufficiently national you will be international.'

We rose to go out, and I gathered that the party was to celebrate the fact that an American publisher, a Miss Beach, had agreed to publish his new book, *Ulysses*. He had spent seven years writing it, in Rome, in Geneva, in Paris; and having it written, he had had no idea who would undertake its publication. Now Miss Beach had agreed to do it. We stopped for a while at the 'Café des Lilas', and drank 'tilleals' before returning home, on the high terrace facing the miniature wood which fills that corner of the boulevard. Joyce spoke of the power of language; and he compared the English language to an organ for its sonorous wealth. But several of us protested that we preferred the French language for its precision and musical quality. But he would not agree, and to support his argument he quoted passages of the English Bible and then quoted corresponding passages out of the French text.

Joyce has a marvellous memory, and he can quote stanzas of poetry on end. To support his argument now he quoted passages from the Authorised Version. . . ..

One day Joyce asked me if I would like to read his new work. I told him I would, and I met him at a cafe in Rue du Bac, near where he was living at the time, and he handed over to me the manuscript, a voluminous affair. As I returned home carrying it I was conscious that I was probably carrying the original manuscript of a book which, when it came to be published, would cause a tremendous literary revolution, for I had already read excerpts of it in American magazines – enough to guess at its import. However, when I sat down to read it I was baffled by its intricacies, and I annoyed him afterwards by saying I liked the description where such and such a scene 'happened'. 'But,' exclaimed Joyce in an irritated voice, 'it didn't happen at all – it was all in Bloom's imagination.' So except for telling him that I was certain that his book would cause as big a revolution in literature as Cezanne works has done in painting, I held my peace about it. In truth, I did not care for it very much. Language to me is a definite thing, and cannot be played about with, as Form can be, for it is a coin used constantly in every-day life, and has a definite value which cannot be changed. Trying to twist and contort words into made-up words and expressions to suit emotional exigencies is a fantastical pastime.

During the printing and subsequently the publication of *Ulysses*, which caused a world-wide reaction, I used to see a good deal of Joyce. At that time he was suffering a good deal from his eyes, and was subject to attacks of iritis, which might have ended in blindness. He lived in a flat opposite the Eiffel Tower, and it was a common thing to walk in and find him lying full length on his bed stuping his eye. Indeed he lived under a continual threat of blindness in one eye, and in the evening on his way to the oculist he used to count the number of lights in the Place de la Concorde to test his vision, for he knew the total number – though for me I had always looked on them as countless like those of some constellation. Indeed stories of his bad sight became so prevalent that an American paper gave as news that Joyce was working on a new book, and lived in a room in the Eiffel Tower describing huge characters on white black-board.

It was an excellent piece of journalism, but far from the truth, for

Joyce is a man who lives without exaggeration or excess. Like most creators, he is shy of people and sensitive.

He has a charming family to which he is devoted and seldom moves outside its circle. His favourite entertainment is to make cheer in his own home, and after dinner to sit down at the piano and sing Irish songs. He has an excellent tenor voice: and he tells himself once how he sang in a concert in competition with John McCormack in their early Dublin days, and how the first prize was awarded to him but when his name was called he had already left the hall in disgust at his performance. This interest in singing he has never lost, and the family talent has shown itself again in the son, who has been trained as a singer.

NOTES

Arthur Power (1891–1985), Irish painter. After the First World War he went to live in Paris, where he became friends with Joyce.

1. To Bal Bullier, a famous dance-hall opposite the Café of the 'Closerie des Lilas'. It had been for a number of years a meeting-place for all manner of writers and painters in Paris.

First Meeting with James Joyce*

WYNDHAM LEWIS

James Joyce had come to Paris from Zürich. In the summer of 1920 I went there with Thomas Stearns Eliot. We went there on our way to the Bay of Quiberon for a summer holiday, which his wife said would do him good. We descended at a small hotel, upon the left bank of the River Seine. It was there I met, in his company, James Joyce for the first time. And it was the first time that Eliot had seen him, too. Joyce was the last of my prominent friends to be encountered; last but not least.

It had been agreed before we left London that we should contrive to

* *Blasting and Bombardiering*, 2nd edn (Berkeley and Los Angeles: University of California Press, 1967) pp. 265–70.

see Joyce in Paris. And Eliot had been entrusted with a parcel by Ezra Pound (as a more responsible person than myself), which he was to hand to Joyce when he got there. We did not know at all what it contained. It was rather a heavy parcel and Eliot had carried it under his arm, upon his lap, as it was too big to go in a suitcase.

At that time I knew very little indeed about Joyce. He 'conveyed nothing' to me, I was in the same position as the white-coated doctor I mentioned in my introductory remarks – except that I did not, in my person, resemble James Joyce in any way, whereas certainly the doctor did, and yet had not even heard of his double.

Beyond what Ezra Pound had told me, which was mostly apologetic (the good Ezra assuming that I should laugh at him for his over-literary respects and genuflexions) I knew nothing. That was the situation. It was in consequence of this that in our subsequent intercourse Joyce and myself were often talking at cross-purposes.

I had not read *The* [*sic*] *Portrait of the Artist* nor *Dubliners*. *Exiles* and *Chamber Music* I had never heard of, *Ulysses* had not, of course, yet made its appearance.[1] But Joyce, on the other hand, had, I am persuaded, read everything I had ever written. He pretended however not to have done so.

In very marked contrast with Joyce I was indifferent as to whether he had followed the fortunes of Tarr and Kreisler or not. There was no arrogance at all in my indifference. But, as it is easy to suppose, since their author assumed I had read all his books (*Ulysses* included although it had not been published) but was pretending like himself to have forgotten, things were at first very involved. Bad jams occurred in the dialogue, in both directions.

It does not follow that a couple of authors, when they come face to face need meet as 'authors'. But aside from everything else, James Joyce was in a superlative degree the writer of books, the champion Penman, and breathed, though and felt as such. We had been starred together on many occasions. He saw me as a Penman, too, and as a champion – one I expect he thought he could easily 'put-to-sleep'. It was quite impossible, under these circumstances, to encounter Joyce otherwise than as one of a pair of figures in the biography of a big Penman – I, of course being the interloper. For the biography would be one devoted to *him*, not to me. And finally why I on my side was indifferent was of course because I had no feeling for history. I was in fact a chronological idiot. A burlesque situation!

But this light comedy was sufficiently curious for it to be worth while to go into yet more detail. *Some* pages of the *Portrait* I had read, when it first appeared as a serial in the *Egoist*, a paper edited by Miss Harriet Weaver. But I took very little interest. At that time, it was of far too tenuous an elegance for my taste. Its flavour was altogether too literary.

And as to its emotional content, that I condemned at once as sentimental Irish. Even now, for that matter, I feel much the same about *The Portrait of the Artist*, with the important difference that I have obliged myself to read a great many more books, in the meanwhile, many of which suffer from the same shortcomings, as I see it. So I do recognise the *Portrait of the Artist as a Young Man* to be one only of a large class, and of its kind a very excellent example.

On my side my first meeting with James Joyce was (at first) devoid of any particular interest. I found an oddity, in patent-leather shoes, large powerful spectacles, and a small gingerbread beard; speaking half in voluble Italian to a scowling school-boy: playing the Irishman a little overmuch perhaps, but in amusingly mannered technique. Soon I was prepared to be interested in Joyce for his own sake. I took a great fancy to him for his wit, for the agreeable humanity of which he possessed such stores, for his unaffected love of alcohol, and all good things to eat and drink.

What should have been a momentous encounter, then, turned out to be as matter-of-fact a social clash as the coming together of two navvies, or the brusque *how do you do* of a couple of dogs out for a walk. The reason: just my inveterate obtuseness where all that is historic and chronological is concerned. It is because I cannot see things as *biography*. I have not got the Barretts of Wimpole Street mind. My insensitiveness in this respect is to blame if all this part of my narrative is literally *flat*, like a Chinese or a Japanese picture.

I have gone ahead like this, outrunning the physical, to take all surprise out of these happenings, as a preliminary disinfection. Also I have hoped to drive home the fact that I have nothing up my sleeve, in these harmless exercises.

Returning, however, to my narrative of the physical encounter. T. S. Eliot – need I say the premier poet of Anglo-Saxony? – T. S. Eliot and myself descended at a small hotel. The Eliot fan will appreciate this way of putting it. He will see I know my Eliot. The hotel was nearer to the quays of the Seine than to the central artery of the Saint Germain quarter. It was the rue des Saints Pères, or it may be the rue Bonaparte: no matter, they are all the same. Our rooms were the sort of lofty, dirtily parquetted, frowsily-curtained, faded apartments that the swarms of small hotels in Paris provide, upon their floors of honour. These small hotels still abound.

T. S. Eliot ringing for the chasseur, dispatched a *petit bleu*[2] to James Joyce. He suggested that Joyce should come to the hotel, because he had a parcel, entrusted to him by Ezra Pound, and which that gentleman had particularly enjoined upon him to deliver personally to the addressee; but that it would likewise be a great pleasure to meet him. This was accompanied by an invitation to dinner.

An invitation to dinner! I laugh as I write this. But at the time I did not know the empty nature of this hospitable message, seeing to whom it was directed!

The parcel was then placed in the middle of a large Second Empire marble table, standing upon gilt eagles' claws in the centre of the apartment. About six in the evening James Joyce arrived, and the Punch and Judy show began.

Joyce was accompanied by a tallish youth, whom he introduced to Eliot as his son. Eliot then introduced me to Joyce. We stood collected about the shoddily-ornamented french table, in the décor of the cheap dignity of the red-curtained apartment, as if we had been people out of a scene in an 1870 gazette, resuscitated by Max Ernst, to amuse the tired intelligentsia – bowing in a cosmopolitan manner to each other across Ezra's prize-packet, which was the proximate cause of this solemn occasion.

When Joyce heard my name he started in a very flattering fashion. Politely he was galvanized by his historic scene, and then collapsed. It was as if he had been gently pricked with the ghost of a hat-pin of a corsetted demirep out of the Police Gazette, and had given a highly well-bred exhibition of *stimulus–response*. Suppose this exhibition to have been undertaken for a lecture (with demonstrations) on 'Behaviour', and you have the whole picture. He raised his eyebrows to denote surprise and satisfaction at the auspicious occasion; he said *Ah! Wyndham Lewis* civilly under his breath, and I bowed again in acknowledgement, at the repetition of my name. He then with a courteous haste looked around for his son, who was heavily scowling in the background, and effected an introduction. His son stiffened, and, still scowling, bowed towards me with ceremony. Bringing my heels together, unintentionally with a noticeable report, I returned the salute. We all then sat down. But only for a moment.

Joyce lay back in the stiff chair he had taken from behind him, crossed his leg, the lifted leg laid out horizontally upon the one in support like an artificial limb, an arm flung back over the summit of the sumptuous chair. He dangled negligently his straw hat, a regulation 'boater'. We were on either side of the table, the visitors and ourselves, upon which stood the enigmatical parcel.

Eliot now rose to his feet. He approached the table, and with one eyebrow drawn up, and a finger pointing, announced to James Joyce that *this* was that parcel, to which he had referred in his wire, and which had been given into his care, and he formally delivered it, thus acquitting himself of his commission.

'Ah! Is this the parcel you mentioned in your note?' enquired Joyce, overcoming the elegant reluctance of a certain undisguised fatigue in his person. And Eliot admitted that it was, and resumed his seat.

I stood up: and, turning my back upon the others, arranged my tie in the cracked Paris mirror – whose irrelevant imperfections, happening to bisect my image, bestowed upon me the mask of a syphilitic Creole. I was a little startled: but I stared out of countenance this unmannerly distortion, and then turned about, remaining standing.

James Joyce was by now attempting to untie the crafty housewifely knots of the cunning old Ezra. After a little he asked his son crossly in Italian for a penknife. Still more crossly his son informed him that he had no penknife. But Eliot got up, saying 'You want a knife? I have not got a knife, I think!' We were able, ultimately, to provide a pair of nail scissors.

At last the strings were cut. A little gingerly Joyce unrolled the slovenly swaddlings of damp British brown paper in which the good-hearted American had packed up what he had put inside. Thereupon, along with some nondescript garments for the trunk – there were no trousers I believe – a fairly presentable pair of *old brown shoes* stood revealed, in the centre of the bourgeois French table.

As the meaning of this scene flashed upon my listless understanding, I saw in my mind's eye the phantom of the little enigmatic Ezra standing there (provided by our actions, and the position of his footgear at this moment, with a dominating stature which otherwise he scarcely could have attained) silently surveying his handiwork.

James Joyce, exclaiming very faintly 'Oh!' looked up, and we all gazed at the old shoes for a moment. 'Oh!' I echoed and laughed, and Joyce left the shoes where they were, disclosed as the matrix of the disturbed leaves of the parcel. He turned away and sat down again, placing his left ankle upon his right knee, and squeezing, and then releasing, the horizontal limb.

With a smile even slower in materialising than his still-trailing Bostonian voice (a handsome young United States President, to give you an idea – adding a Gioconda smile to the other charms of this office) Eliot asked our visitor if he would have dinner with us. Joyce turned to his son, and speaking very rapidly in Italian, the language always employed by him, so it seemed, in his family circle, he told him to go home: he would inform his mother that his father would not be home to dinner after all. Yes, his father had accepted an invitation to dinner, and would not be back after all, for the evening meal! Did he understand? To tell his mother that his father – But the son very hotly answered his father back, at this, after but a moment's hesitation on account of the company: evidently he did not by any means relish being entrusted with messages. It was, however, with greater hotness, in yet more resonant Italian, that the son expressed his rebellious sensations when the imperturbable Jimmie handed him the parcel of disreputable footwear. That was the last straw – this revolting, this unbecoming packet. Having exchanged a good number of stormy words, in a series of passionate asides – in a good imitation of an altercation between a couple of neapolitan touts, of the better order – Joyce, *père et fils*, separated, the latter rushing away with the shoes beneath his arm, his face crimson and his eyes blazing with a truly southern ferocity – first having mastered himself for a moment sufficiently to bow to me from the hips, and to shake hands with heroic punctilio. This scene took place as we were about to leave the small hotel.

NOTES

Wyndham Lewis (1884–1957), British artist, novelist and critic. On the relationship between Joyce and Lewis see Geoffrey Wagner, *Wyndham Lewis: A Portrait of the Artist as the Enemy* (New Haven, Conn.: Yale University Press, 1957) pp. 168–88.

1. *Ulysses* was published as a book in 1922, but had started to appear as a serial in the *Little Review* in March 1918.

2. Telegraphic letter card.

Visits with James Joyce*

P. BEAUMONT WADSWORTH

My 'pilgrimage' to see Joyce took place during the first weekend in August, a British national holiday, in 1921. It was my first trip to Paris, my second visit to France. The boat was packed with holiday-makers; the Channel crossing rough; myself violently seasick.

At that time Joyce was without a proper permanent home; he was still living in rented apartments. When I got to Paris, feeling half-dead that hot August morning, I made my way immediately to 71 rue du Cardinal Lemione where Joyce and his wife occupied the flat lent them by the French writer, Valery Larbaud, who was away on holiday. It was a short narrow street on the Left Bank, behind Notre Dame and near to the river.

In my eagerness to make the call, I had completely forgotten that it was far too early in the morning. I had also forgotten to obtain a

* Extracted from *James Joyce Quarterly*, 1 (Summer 1964) 15–16.

proper letter of introduction, and to bring a Joyce book to be autographed. First of all, I took a room in a small hotel at the corner of the street. Then I made my way to No. 71.

When I had crossed the inner courtyard to reach the flat, the door was opened by Mrs Joyce whose wide-eyed face wore a questioning look. I told her that I had come specially from London to see Mr Joyce and mentioned the names of Ezra Pound and Miss Weaver. She asked me to return in an hour.

When I went back at the appointed time, it was James Joyce himself who opened the door and welcomed me inside with a warm friendly smile.

Unfortunately, I did not make any notes about my talk. I don't think Joyce had ever given an interview at that time. And, in any case, he made me talk far more than he did. In the back study where we sat, the shutters were half closed to keep out the August heat and the dazzling sunshine. I had not heard that Joyce was having serious trouble with his eyes.

With his back to the window Joyce lounged easily on a lowish couch in the semi-gloom and began to question me very closely about my own life. When he discovered that I had recently returned from 18 months in Calcutta he began to work that vein. What kind of meat and vegetables did we eat there, what hours did we have meals? Were there barmaids in the hotels and bars? Not a word about literature or about his own work. So there I sat on my chair opposite to him chattering away about myself and awed all the time by his overwhelming genius.

It was a strange situation, but I didn't realise that then. I merely regarded Joyce as being very curious about all human beings.

The only time we got near to the subject of books was when I was about to take my departure. 'There,' he said, pointing at some proof pages lying in orderly fashion on a desk, 'are the first proof pages of my book, *Ulysses*', but he did not volunteer any more information. Later, I learned that he was engaged in the laborious work of reading through those proofs sent from the French printer, Darantière.

Out in the glare of the Paris sun I looked at my watch and was surprised that I had been in the flat for two whole hours; time had passed so quickly.

James Joyce in the Twenties*

MORRILL CODY

Once in Paris I looked up the bird-like Sylvia and she received me most enthusiastically. One could not help admiring this little dynamo and her unique bookshop. 'No one has ever written us up before,' she told me, which was surprising even though the popular cult of the Left Bank had not yet begun.

And then, one day, when I was browsing around her shop, she asked me if I would like to interview James Joyce.

'Yes,' I replied at once. 'But will he do it?'

'Probably not. He never has, but we can try.'

Joyce was already a big name in those days to the writers and intellectuals of the Left Bank including the French as well as the British and Americans, but little had been written about him as a person. *Ulysses* had only recently been published by Sylvia and a few copies had yet filtered through the censorship which guarded the morals of the British and American peoples. But in our group his prestige as a master craftsman was very high indeed. He certainly exerted more influence on the important writers of the first half of the twenties than any other man, though many of them would have been reluctant to admit it. And there is no doubt about the respect in which he was held. He was always *Mister* Joyce even to some of his best friends, like Sylvia, for instance. This was partly because he kept a certain distance from those around him, aloof always from familiarities of name or spirit. He liked a joke and particularly puns, but they must not be personal. And then his formal politeness kept people at arms' length.

Joyce agreed to the interview, although reluctantly. I think that Sylvia persuaded him with the argument that I was young and needed help, an appeal that always met with sympathy with Joyce, and that I could be trusted not to exaggerate or distort what he said to me. Even so, he cancelled the appointment twice before he actually received me.

During my interview with Joyce that day toward the end of 1923, he slowly relaxed, slowly warmed to me as a person I suppose, and began to talk about the years he had spent in writing *Ulysses*. It had been a long seven years in Trieste where he earned a very modest living at Berlitz teaching languages of which he spoke quite a number,

* Extracted from *Connecticut Review*, 5 (April 1972) 12–13.

such as German, French, Italian, Spanish, Swedish, Yiddish and Hebrew, as well as having a fine classical knowledge of Latin, Sanscrit and Greek. When not teaching, he had worked doggedly at *Ulysses*, sometimes as much as ten hours a day.

'So precious was my time,' he told me, 'that I would make notes on scraps of paper, menus, bus tickets and the margins of newspapers. To sort out these ideas for future reference, I made them in pencils of various coloured leads. The red represented philosophical ideas, for instance, the blue religious concepts. I carried some ten pencils of different colours in my pocket.' He showed me some of the scraps of paper which he had saved in an envelope. I could not read them for his writing with thick, stubby pencils was almost illegible. But it was crystal clear to him.

Joyce was a man of great organisation of mind, phenomenal memory, profound scholarship, immense philosophical understanding of human nature, but basically of little human warmth as his thin lips clearly indicated. He was a good family man. He was seemingly devoted to his attractive red-haired wife, Nora, and to his children, but his relationship with them was not an intellectual affair. Nora, for instance, refused to read *Ulysses* and told everyone that she was simply not interested. The real centre of Joyce's being was his own ego, focused on his mastery of the written word and engulfed in a big white cloud of shyness.

Joyce, who had valiant moral courage and remarkable bravery in facing difficulties of practical living, had at the same time a great fear of people, dogs, thunderstorms, sudden noises, heights and all physical phenomena of an unusual character. He wrote *Ulysses* in Trieste because the statistics showed there were fewer thunderstorms in Italy than in other European countries. The nearness of a dog, however harmless, would cause him to turn white with fear and if he saw one at a party, he would rush away without a word to his hostess even when he was the guest of honour. He was also full of superstitions, particularly about the number thirteen, but curiously, he was very fond of cats.

When my interview with him had come to a close, he asked if he might see my article before I sent it to New York. I agreed because this had been part of the original bargain with Sylvia. In it I described Joyce's work methods, his character, his idiosyncrasies, the elements of *Ulysses* which so shocked many of the critics. I talked of his early training by the Jesuits and his study of medicine. I portrayed him as the misunderstood writer of great sincerity. When I brought it to him, he made some useful suggestions but generally agreed with what I had written. 'That is a good article,' he said very seriously. Clearly he was pleased by my description of his enigmatic character. Because he liked it, we became friends and I was invited to after-dinner drinking sessions with him and his friends and sometimes to dinners at a restaurant.

Joyce's Way of Life*

SYLVIA BEACH

Most of the letters I got from Joyce were, of course, written during my summer holidays or in the course of his own travels. And of course he always demanded replies by 'tomorrow', 'by express', 'by return of post'. As a rule, he would be in need of funds, and when I was away, he usually managed to get something through Myrsine, who was left in charge of Shakespeare and Company. As she well knew, whether anything was left in his account or not, we had to look after the author of *Ulysses*.

Joyce's expenses were heavy, naturally, with a family of four, and, besides, he enjoyed spending the way some people enjoy hoarding. A visiting publisher said to me, after dining out with Joyce, 'He spends money like a drunken sailor'. A funny thing to say, even if it were true, when you had been someone's guest.

Joyce and his family, when they travelled, usually went to places connected with the work he was engaged on at the time. From Belgium, he sent me a series of postcards, reproductions of the mural paintings at the post office. He wrote me that he was making progress in Flemish – he had had his fortieth lesson – and that he had perfected his Dutch. The Joyces crossed the Channel to see Miss Weaver, Mr Eliot and Joyce's brother Charles and his old friend from the Zürich days, Frank Budgen. Sometimes the Joyces were accompanied by the Stuart Gilberts, who, however, would never stay with them at the local Palace Hotel. Mr Gilbert said he couldn't afford to. Neither could the Joyces.

Adrienne[1] and I just managed to make ends meet by living in the simplest style. But Joyce liked to live among the well to do – he wanted to get away as far as he could, no doubt, from the sordidness of the surroundings of his youth. Also, he considered, and rightly, that, with his reputation and achievements, he was entitled to certain material ease, and he spent money freely, loved to throw it away – on others, not himself. Nothing was too good for Nora and the children, and when they travelled, it must be in first-class style.

When you think of Joyce's labours, he was certainly underpaid. And his idea that years of poverty should be followed by many prosperous

* *Shakespeare and Company* (New York: Harcourt, Brace, 1959) pp. 196–200.

ones was right; but, then, he should have been a different kind of author.

In Paris, Joyce and his family dined out every evening. His particular restaurant – this was in the early twenties – was the one opposite the Gare Montparnasse, Les Trianons.[2] The proprietor and the entire personnel were devoted to Joyce. They were at the door of his taxi before he alighted and they escorted him to a table reserved for him at the back, where he could be more or less unmolested by people who came to stare at him as he dined, or brought copies of his works to be autographed.

The headwaiter would read to him the items on the bill of fare so that he would be spared the trouble of getting out several pairs of glasses and perhaps a magnifying glass. Joyce pretended to take an interest in fine dishes, but food meant nothing to him, unless it was something to do with his work. He urged his family and the friends who might be dining with him to choose the best food on the menu. He liked to have them eat a hearty meal and persuaded them to try such and such a wine. He himself ate scarcely anything, and was satisfied with the most ordinary white wine just as long as there was plenty of it. As he never drank a drop all day long, he was pretty thirsty by dinnertime. The waiter kept his glass filled. Joyce would have sat there with his family and friends and his white wine till all hours if at a certain moment Nora hadn't decided it was time to go. He ended by obeying her – it was according to an understanding between them, one of the many understandings between this couple who understood each other so well.

Wherever Joyce went, he was received like royalty, such was his personal charm, his consideration for others. When he started on his way downstairs to the men's room, several waiters came hurrying to escort him. His blindness drew people to him a great deal.

Joyce's tips were famous; the waiters, the boy who fetched him a taxi, all those who served him, must have retired with a fortune. I never grudged tips, but, knowing the circumstances, it seemed to me that Joyce overtipped.

All of us who have been guests at Joyce's parties know how hospitable and how amusing he was as host. A most elaborate supper was supplied by one of the best caterers, and a waiter to serve it. Joyce piled food on your plate and filled your glass with his Saint Patrick wine – Clos Saint Patrice, of which once he sent me a crate. Another of his favourites was the Pope's wine – Châteauneuf du Pape; all, of course, on account of the associations. But on the sideboard he kept bottles of his own white wine, and from time to time replenished his glass.

After supper, we would insist that George, or Georgio [*sic*], as he used to be called, sing for us. Georgio had inherited the family gift, the Voice, to the great satisfaction of his father. He would sing one of his favourites, such as 'Il mio Tesoro', which was one of my favourites, too.

In the first years, among the few guests invited to these parties were two American couples, great friends of the Joyces: Mr and Mrs Richard Wallace and Mr and Mrs Myron Nutting. Nutting was an artist, and I wonder what has become of the portrait he drew of Joyce, which I always liked. A friend of Goerge's, Fernandez, whose sister Yva was one of the translators of *Dubliners*, was also one of the guests at the parties in the early period.

In the mid-twenties, when Eugene and Maria Jolas came on the scene, they helped to make Joyce's parties very lively. With her fine voice, Maria Jolas might have had a singer's career, and Joyce was enraptured with her American repertory, particularly with a song he always requested. This was 'Farewell Titanic', a rather gruesome but fascinating ditty that, in Maria's dramatic soprano, was most impressive. I noticed that Joyce was quite taken with another of her songs, about someone named 'Shy Ann', a character he associated, probably, with his Anna Livia.

Not until the end of the party would Joyce himself be persuaded to wind up the program with some of his Irish songs. He would seat himself at the piano, drooping over the keys, and the old songs, his particular way of singing them in his sweet tenor voice, and the expression on his face – these were things one can never forget.

Joyce never failed to remember people's birthdays, and on all occasions such as Christmas huge floral offerings turned up, flowers and colours referring to the work he was engaged on at the moment. Adrienne received from him after her publication of 'Anna Livia Plurabelle' in the *Navire d'Argent*[3] a magnificently dressed, gigantic cold salmon from Potel and Chabot. Even his gifts to Nora were always related to his books.

NOTES

1. Adrienne Monnier.
2. Les Trianons (now l'Auberge d'Armor) at 5 place de Rennes (now called 18 juin 1940).
3. On 1 October 1925.

Afternoon with James Joyce*

FANNY BUTCHER

I had heard that James Joyce, if he were ever to be encountered anywhere, would be found in Sylvia Beach's bookshop, so I dashed there hoping to get a look at him, maybe to manage an interview, though feeling that was probably a vain hope. The walls of the shop were almost papered with pictures of the sacrosanct circle, but mainly of Joyce, the man whose novel had become internationally famous – not because it was widely read but because it couldn't be read at all except illegally. (All of the smugglers of *Ulysses* didn't risk a scrimmage with customs out of high literary curiosity. There was a profitable black market in copies, and I heard of one compulsive yearner for its contents who paid five hundred dollars for a copy.)

Sylvia Beach couldn't have been kinder to an *ex-confrère* than she was to me. I was discovering Paris on proceeds from the sale of my own bookshop, and she had heard of it, I was pleased to find. She showed me around hers, and when I looked at a picture of Joyce and said, 'I suppose I'll never see that particular Shelley plain,'[1] she just smiled, which I interpreted to mean 'not a chance'. I wasn't surprised, because I had been told that he never saw anyone except his few cronies, with whom he could comfortably – and often did – get roaring drunk, that he never gave interviews period, and that he was really a sick man and could not waste what strength he had on curiosity seekers. I was resigned to missing him. Or maybe it was just a premonition of what trying to talk to him would be.

To my surprise, a couple of days later a note came from Sylvia Beach, saying that Mr Joyce would very much like to see me if I would be at his apartment in the rue de Grenelle at three o'clock that very day. Not to miss the unexpected boon I spent the morning juggling engagements, and I was Jenny on the spot as the clock struck thrice. Mr Joyce opened the door, a smallish man, his head and face moulded in planes. There wasn't a curve anywhere about him. Even his hands seemed to move in angles, and they were nervously not still. I knew, as did everyone, that he was nearly blind. He was always photographed with a patch over one eye, the left as I remember, but that day he was

---

* Extracted from *Many Lives – One Love* (New York: Harper & Row, 1972) pp. 269–72. Editor's title.

not wearing either the patch or glasses. He led me into a room so darkened that I couldn't make out whether it was late Victorian, sometime Irish, or *bon marché* French in decor. He had not smiled at me in welcome, and the first words he spoke were an emphatic statement that he never gave interviews and I must promise not to write anything about him for any American newspaper or magazine.

He sat with his back to the light, what little there was, and after swallowing a huge gulp of silence, I asked him if he were soon coming to the United States, where his books had first been published, where he had received critical praise, and where eager admirers of his work awaited him. 'No,' was his expansive reply, and when I continued with a question as to whether he weren't curious about what was happening in our yeasty young land, and if he wouldn't like to meet some of the people who had had faith in his work, his answer was again of the simplest: 'Why should I be?' And that avenue of conversation was closed to traffic.

Even a trained newspaper person runs out of questions that can be answered only with 'Yes,' or 'No,' and I had exhausted my supply. I had heard, for instance, that Mrs Rockefeller McCormick of Chicago had given his work financial help,[2] and I asked him if he had ever seen her in Zürich when he was living there and she was studying with the great psychologist and psychiatrist, Carl Jung. He answered merely, 'Yes'. . . .

My afternoon with James Joyce was a unique and painful experience. It was like having deposited your last dime in a public telephone and getting a dial tone, but no response to your dialling – thoroughly frustrating. A couple of times I had a moment of hope, because when I made that gesture of clutching the handbag that signals departure, Mr Joyce would say a whole sentence. But immediately I settled back he would sink into his pet yeses and nos. Finally after about an hour and a half of the torture, I looked at my watch and said, in what I hoped was a convincing voice, that the time had passed so quickly that I was already late for an appointment. I assured him again that I would remember my promise to him and write nothing, absolutely nothing, about my conversation with him. (I hadn't achieved anything to write, anyway.)

Mr Joyce accompanied me to the door with his first smile and with these bombshell words: 'I have really enjoyed this afternoon greatly. Do be sure, please, the next time you are in Paris to let me know and let me see you.' The next time I was in Paris, a couple of years later, he wasn't there, and then he wasn't anywhere, so I never knew whether or not he was really as bored as he seemed, and I was.

NOTES

1. A reference to the lines by Browning in *Memorabilia*:

> Ah, did you once see Shelley plain,
> And did he stop and speak to you
> And did you speak to him again?
> How strange it seems, and new!

2. Mrs Harold McCormick (Edith Rockefeller) began patronage of Joyce in March 1918.

I Met James Joyce*

NINA HAMNETT

I met James Joyce one day; Ford[1] introduced me to him. He was a most charming man and had a most beautifully proportioned head. I asked him if I could do a painting of him. He said that I could, but I sent telegrams to him and he sent telegrams to me, and all of them arrived too late or too early and so I never painted him at all. He dined every evening at the Trianon and one evening I did a drawing of him when I was sitting at another table and he did not know that I was doing it. It was a very good likeness and I believe was reproduced in an American paper. The drawing is unfortunately lost and I never got paid for it. I met him and his wife whenever I went to the Trianon which, alas, was not often as it was rather expensive. Joyce is the most respectable and old-fashioned man that I have ever met. He also has the most beautiful manners, which is a pleasant change from most of the modern young men. He has a most charming voice and occasionally will sing. I think he is a little older than I am, but we were discussing old-fashioned songs one evening, 'Daisy, Daisy, give me your answer, do', and others of the same kind and I said, 'Did you see many years ago a show that was a kind of Magic Lantern show with a ship going down? The ship was attached to the screen and heaved up and down and voices sang a song, called, "I'll stick to the ship, boys, you save your lives"?' It was a tragic story of a ship that sank and the Captain stuck to his ship because he was a bachelor and the crew had wives and families. Joyce remembered it and knew the whole song. I

---

* *Laughing Torso: Reminiscences* (London: Constable, 1932) pp. 341–2. Editor's title.

remembered only the chorus and we sang that together. I went to the show (it was called somebody's 'Diorama') with my Grandmother, who wept, as she always did, at the sight of a ship. Joyce, I have heard since, paid me a very nice compliment and said I was one of the few vital women that he had ever met. I don't know if that is true, but I have very big lungs and can make a great deal of noise if encouraged. Joyce spoke with the most charming accent. His wife was fair and extremely nice; he had two children, a son and a daughter, who did not speak very much.

NOTE

1. Ford Madox Ford (1873–1939), English author.

Joyce's Birthday Parties*

SISLEY HUDDLESTON

Those birthday parties of Joyce, in his apartment on the Left Bank, were memorable occasions; but they were memorable not because they were highly intellectual, but because they were remarkably respectable. The host and hostess were anxious to please their guests neither in an esoteric nor a bohemian manner, but by the adequate provision of food and drink. At one end of the double salon a long table was covered with a white cloth; and on it were sandwiches and cakes galore and jugs of lemonade, bottles of champagne, liqueurs and Irish whisky. The guests could never take enough; food and drink were pressed upon them. Those guests were not selected because they were highbrow, or because they admired Joyce – though I have no doubt most of them did admire Joyce – but because they were friends of the family. There were the young folk, brought by the son and daughter, George and Lucia. There were the older folk, who had been associated in a personal way with Mr and Mrs Joyce. There was a good sprinkling of Irish acquaintants, some of them exiles. The keynote of the assembly was the true note of all family parties. You had not to bring a certificate

* *Back to Montparnasse: Glimpses of Broadway in Bohemia* (Philadelphia, Penn.: Lippincott, 1931) pp. 198–9. Editor's title.

showing that you had read, much less understood, Joyce. You had merely to be *sympathique*.

So while a section of the guests clustered round the white cloth table, and another section of the guests sat in easy chairs at the other end of the room, by the cosy fire, under the family portraits (there was an amazingly good picture of a fierce-looking Irishman – Joyce's father),[1] Joyce would come and go, bringing refreshments and obviously trying to please. He always succeeded in making everybody feel at home, and as the evening wore on in arousing a spirit of gaiety. He required much pressing to sit at the piano, and to accompany himself in one of his amusing Irish ballads. George too was pressed to sing; he had an excellent voice which showed to best effect in the airs of Handel. The general conversation was as general as such conversations are. Occasionally – but only occasionally – it turned on Joyce's own work; and once he was persuaded to read a chapter of that work in his sweet precise tenor voice. It might happen that somebody proposed the toast of the host, and I remember singing lustily in chorus, 'For he's a jolly good fellow'. My point – if it has not yet become clear – is that Joyce is a man of simple tastes who is never happier than in a simple family party.

NOTES

Sisley Huddleston (1883–1952), English journalist and writer. She wrote the first review of *Ulysses* in which she acknowledged Joyce's genius amid much criticism of the book's vulgarity.

1. By the Irish painter Patrick Tuohy (1894–1930). Joyce commissioned this picture of his father in 1923.

At Lloyd Morris's Party*

GLENWAY WESCOTT

Just at the height of Lloyd Morris's[1] party, this humorous personage was to be seen seated in a corner profoundly chatting with the guest we were all proudest of having there with us, namely, Joyce; and one

* Extracted from 'Memories and Opinions', *Prose*, 5 (Fall 1972) 201–2. Editor's title.

of us wandered over close enough to hear what they were chatting about: St Augustine and St Athanasius and Origen, and other patristic theologians. Presently Joyce was heard to inquire, 'How, Mr Richards,[2] have you happened to be so well read in the Fathers of the Church?' And Richards answered, 'I *was* a priest,' emphasising the intransitive verb in the past tense somewhat smugly.

I can still see clearly in my mind's eye the expression on Joyce's face as he rose out of that corner. It was more than theological; at least it visaged forth both sides of theology, the side of the devil as well as the side of the angels. It transcended intolerance and dislike; indeed what it chiefly appeared to signify was a wild self-pity and absolute dread of the consequences.

I had seen him look like that upon one previous occasion, when speaking in a rather matter-of-fact tone, but with uninhibited feeling, of his fear of water. Compelled to travel to England for some reason, he had waited for days in a hotel in Le Havre or Dieppe, until the weather forecast and the astrological situation got to be conjointly favourable. Once he was heard to say, perhaps jokingly, that he even minded crossing the bridge from the Left Bank to the Right Bank of the Seine.

There on the Left Bank at Lloyd Morris's party he rose to his feet. The weak blue of his unhealthy eyes seemed more pitiful than ever. His face turned pale with an almost golden pallor, like one of the fine white wines that he was partial to. His nose came to a point as though someone had whittled it with a jackknife.

'I was a priest,' said Richards.

'Oh,' cried Joyce, 'Oh, it is worth my immortal soul to sit here discussing theology with an unfrocked priest!'

And with impatient gestures of his somewhat stiff-fingered hand adorned with that very large ring which one sees in so many photographs of him, undeterred by soothing apologetic utterances by his host and others, who could scarcely keep a straight face, he was helped into his cape and left the premises.

NOTES

Glenway Wescott (1901–), American fiction writer.
1. The American writer.
2. Edmund Richards.

A Drink with Joyce*

ERNEST HEMINGWAY

One day, much later, I met Joyce who was walking along the Boulevard St Germain after having been to a matinée alone. He liked to listen to the actors, although he could not see them. He asked me to have a drink with him and we went to the Deux-Magots and ordered dry sherry although you will always read that he drank only Swiss white wine.

'How about Walsh?' Joyce said.

'A such and such alive is a such and such dead,' I said.

'Did he promise you that award?' Joyce asked.

'Yes.'

'I thought so,' Joyce said.

'Did he promise it to you?'

'Yes,' Joyce said. After a time he asked, 'Do you think he promised it to Pound?'

'I don't know.'

'Best not to ask him,' Joyce said. We left it at that. I told Joyce of my first meeting with him in Ezra's studio with the girls in the long fur coats and it made him happy to hear the story.[1]

NOTES

Ernest Hemingway (1899–1961), American journalist, novelist and short-story writer.

1. Hemingway met Joyce for the first time in Paris in the spring of 1921, bearing a letter of introduction from Sherwood Anderson (1876–1941), the American poet and novelist.

* *A Moveable Feast* (New York: Charles Scribner's, 1964) pp. 128–9. Editor's title.

With James Joyce*

ROBERT McALMON

In Paris I had a note from Harriet Weaver, publisher of the Egoist Press, to present to James Joyce. His *Dubliners* I much liked. The Stephen Dedalus of his *Portrait of the Artist as a Young Man* struck me as precious, full of noble attitudinisings, and not very admirable in its soulful protestations. He seemed to enjoy his agonies with a self-righteousness which would not let the reader in on his actual ascetic ecstasies. Nevertheless, the short stories made me feel that Joyce would be approachable, as indeed did passages of *Ulysses* which had aleady appeared in the *Little Review*.

At his place on the Boulevard Raspail I was greeted by Mrs Joyce, and although there was a legend that Joyce's eyes were weak, it was evident that he had used eyesight in choosing his wife. She was very pretty, with a great deal of simple dignity and a reassuring manner. Joyce finally appeared, having just got up from bed. Within a few minutes it was obvious that he and I would get on. Neither of us knew anybody much in Paris, and both of us liked companionship. As I was leaving he suggested that we have dinner together that night, and we met at eight for an apéritif and later went to dine.

At that time Joyce was by no means a worldly man, or the man who could later write to the Irish Academy that, living in Paris as he did, it was difficult to realise the importance of their academy. He had come but recently from Zurich, and before that Trieste, in both of which cities he had taught languages at the Berlitz School in order to support his family. He was still a Dublin-Irish provincial, as well as a Jesuit-Catholic provincial, although in revolt. He refused to understand that questions of theology did not disturb or interest me, and never had. When I assured him that instead of the usual 'religious crises' in one's adolescent life I had studied logic and metaphysics and remained agnostic, he did not listen. He would talk about the fine points of religion and ethics as he had been taught by the Jesuits. His favourite authors were Cardinal Newman and St Thomas Aquinas, and I had read neither. He told me some tale of how St Thomas once cracked a woman – possibly a prostitute – over the head with a chair, and

* Extracted from Robert McAlmon and Kay Boyle, *Being Geniuses Together, 1920–1930* (Garden City, N.Y.: Doubleday, 1968) pp. 27–31, 187–8, 279–80. Editor's title.

explained that the Jesuits were clever at logic. They could justify anything if it suited their purposes.

He was working on *Ulysses* at the time and often would make appointments to read rather lengthy extracts of what he had most recently written. Probably he read to me about a third of the book. It was impressive to observe how everything was grist to his mill. He was constantly leaping upon phrases and bits of slang which came naturally from my American lips, and one night, when he was slightly spiffed, he wept a bit while explaining his love or infatuation for words, mere words. Long before this explanation I had recognised that malady in him, as probably every writer has had that disease at some time or other, generally in his younger years. Joyce never recovered. He loved particularly words like 'ineluctable', 'metempsychosis' – grey, clear, abstract, fine-sounding words that are 'ineluctable' a bit themselves. Had I been older and less diffident before him in those days I would have given him *Irene Iddesleigh* to read. Her author also loved words, and flung her work 'upon the oases of futurity' hoping, as did Joyce of *Ulysses*, that it would not be consigned to 'the false bosom of buried scorn'. I don't think I ever did get around to telling Joyce that the high-minded struttings and the word prettifications and the Greek beauty part of his writings palled on me, as did Stephen Dedalus when he grew too noble and forbearing. Stephen's agonies about carnal sin seemed melodramatic, but perhaps they were not so. Several years later a son of Augustus John,[1] Henry, who was studying to be a priest, wrote essays and letters equally intent upon carnal desire and the searing sin of weakening. Mercifully I was not brought up by the Jesuits.

Almost every night Joyce and I met for apéritifs, and although he was working steadily on *Ulysses*, at least one night a week he was ready to stay out all night, and those nights he was never ready to go home at any hour. We talked of the way the free mind can understand the possibility of all things: necrophilia and other weird rites. We agreed in disliking mysticism, particularly the fake and sugared mysticism of many poets and writers. We spoke of what a strange man Robert Burton must have been to have compiled his *Anatomy of Melancholy*, and he didn't know in the end a bit more about it than we did. Sir Thomas Browne, not to speak of Ezra Pound and Eliot and Moore and Shaw, we discussed, but sooner or later Mr Joyce began reciting Dante in sonorous Italian. When that misty and intent look came upon his face and into his eyes I knew that friend Joyce wasn't going home till early morning.

One night he wept in his cups when telling of his forefathers. His father had parented a large family, and his grandfathers before him had been parents of families of from twelve to eighteen children. Joyce would sigh, and then pull himself together and swear that by the grace of God he was still a young man and he would have more children before the end. He didn't detect that I, the youngest of ten children of a poor minister, did not fancy his idea. He would not listen when I suggested that if one is to produce children one had better have the money to educate and care for them in the childhood years.

At the time Valery Larbaud, the French author-critic, was keen about Joyce's work and had written his article noting *Ulysses* as the first Irish book to belong to world literature.[2] He dined with us at times and we generally went later to the Gypsy Bar off the Boul' Mich'. Wyndham Lewis arrived for a stay in Paris and he was a different man from the Lewis of London. He was free and easy and debonair. Indeed, too many Englishmen will do on the Continent what it does not do to do in London. Lewis was intent upon going to the Picasso exhibition; he must meet Picasso and Braque and Derain, although these painters of Paris were cagey and suspicious about English painters of talent. Picasso at the time was doing his pneumatic nudes, which always made me want to stick a pin in them to see if they would deflate.

Lewis was most gracious and jovial and instructed me with a constant flow of theories on abstraction and plastic values. It would not have done to let him know that I had heard most of what he was saying before, in New York, when Marsden Hartley, Alfred Stieglitz and art critics held forth in speech or newspaper articles. Somehow there was no wonder in Lewis' discovery that the engineering demand of structures often gives them an aesthetic value. The Egyptians, Greeks and Mayans seemed to have known that before Lewis.

It was spring, however, and for a time Lewis, Joyce and I met nightly, and upon occasions would stay out till nearly dawn. The Gypsy Bar was usually our late night hangout. The *patron* and the 'girls' knew us well, and knew that we would drink freely and surely stay till four or five in the morning. The girls of the place collected at our table and indulged in their Burgundian and Rabelaisian humours. Jeannette, a big draft horse of a girl from Dijon, pranced about like a mare in heat and restrained no remark or impulse which came to her. Alys, sweet and pretty-blonde, looked fragile and delicate, but led Jeannette to bawdier and altogether earthy vulgarities of speech and action. Joyce, watching, would be amused, but inevitably there came a time when drink so moved his spirit that he began quoting from his own work or reciting long passages of Dante in rolling sonorous Italian. I believed that Joyce might have been a priest upon hearing him recite Dante as though saying mass. Lewis sometimes came through with recitations of Verlaine, but he did not get the owl eyes and mesmerising expression upon his face which was automatically Joyce's. Amid the clink of glasses, jazz music badly played by a French orchestra, the chatter and laughter of the whores, Joyce went on reciting Dante. I danced with Alys, and even sometimes with Jeannette, but she was six foot and buxom, and, dancing, seemed not to realise that I was there at all. In those days, and for some three years later, I didn't have hangovers. Only once, after a particularly mad assortment of drinks, I had to struggle to a lamppost and relieve myself, and Joyce said solicitously, 'I say, McAlmon, your health is rather delicate. Maybe they'll be saying I'm a bad example for you.'. . .

Before Bill and Floss headed for south of France there was a party at the Trianon, which was then the restaurant at which Joyce always dined. Mina Loy, Sylvia Beach, Adrienne Monnier, Kitty Cannell, Laurence Vail and his wife, Peggy Guggenheim, and his sister, Clotilde Vail, were in the party of twenty or more. Bill had perhaps expected Joyce to be more staidly the great man of letters, but Joyce had been having apéritifs before the dinner began, and he dearly loves a party. He wanted there to be singing, preferably of Irish songs and in an Irish tenor voice. He wanted there to be dancing and general hilarity. Bill wanted these, too, but one gathered he also wanted there to be profound discussion. Someone at the table asked Nora Joyce if she read her husband's work.

She answered: 'Sure, why would I bother? It's enough he talks about that book and he's at it all the time. I'd like a bit of life of my own.' She later admitted that she had read the last pages of *Ulysses*, in which Molly Bloom's thoughts are portrayed. Her comment was short but to the point. 'I guess the man's a genius, but what a dirty mind he has, hasn't he?'

I assured Nora that, had it not been for her keeping him down to earth, Joyce would have remained the word-prettifying bard, the martyred sensibility, Stephen Dedalus. But Nora would not have it that he had learned about women from her. 'Go along with you! People say I have helped him to be a genius!' she scoffed. 'What they'll be saying next is that if it hadn't been for that ignoramus of a woman what a man he would have been! But never you mind, I could tell them a thing or two about him after twenty years of putting up with him, and the devil take him when he's off on one of his rampages!'

The party became joyous, as Joyce wished. He sang Irish 'come-all-ye's', and all of us got together for a few like 'Love's Old Sweet Song' and 'Carry Me Back to Ole Virginny'. Clotilde Vail knew a few 'blues' songs, and I recalled some spirituals and cowboy songs. The Trianon stayed open late that night, and it all ended when Nora decided that Jim was going too far and there would be no handling him if she did not get him home. 'It's you who see him in a jolly state,' she said, 'but it's me who has to bear the brunt of it if his eyes get ailing, and what a martyr that man can be, you've no idea!' . . .

Back in Paris I found Joyce feeling alone and deserted. Nora had taken Lucia and Giorgio to London and they were later to visit Dublin for the first time in many years.[3] In the meantime there was political trouble in Dublin, and Joyce fretted constantly. He sent them wires and letters, and he sent me wires and notes to come and talk to him. 'And do you think they're safe, then, really? You don't understand, McAlmon, how this is affecting me. I am worried all of the day, and it does my eye no good. Ah, well.' Joyce would heave a sigh, and my heart sympathised, but my humour told me that friend James has a way of enjoying the martyrdom of his trials and tribulations. Joyce's worry proved justified, however, for Nora, Lucia and Giorgio left Ireland on a train that was constantly bombarded, and they travelled lying flat on the floor of the coach. It struck me as useless to worry with and for Joyce about them, and my ruthless consciousness would recall the closing passage of *Portrait of the Artist*, in which Stephen (Joyce) forswears home, family, friends and native land and goes forth alone into the world to search for beauty, art and freedom – and he intends to have the world understand that he meant 'alone forever'.

How fate tricked him. Joyce is lonely, desolate and an anxious husband, parent, brother and son, if home and family and a degree of loving or admiring friends are not about. He is not his kind of Irish for nothing. Now that he has a grandson,[4] he beams to think that the child recognises him as 'Nono' [*sic*].[5] During these days he missed Nora and his children so much that he generally drank little, and it is doubtful if he did much work. At least he did not talk of it, and when he is working he likes to talk of what he has recently done, and to read it to a listener. Nora and the children returned after a time, however, and Joyce was no longer a lost spirit wailing in the wilderness of Paris.

NOTES

Robert McAlmon (1896–1956), American poet, writer and dilettante publisher.

1. Augustus John (1878–1961), British painter.
2. Valery Larbaud, 'James Joyce', *Nouvelle revue française*, 18 (1922) 385–409.
3. This trip took place in 1922.
4. Stephen Joyce, Giorgio's son, was born on 15 February 1932.
5. Nonno (Ital.) grandfather.

The James Joyce I Knew*

JAMES STEPHENS

The first time that Joyce and I met we disliked each other by what is called instinct, which is always very misleading. We were introduced by a perfect stranger to me. I was walking up Dawson Street, thinking of nothing, which was and is my favourite form of thinking, when I noticed that two men were coming towards me, and that one of them was deliberating upon me as if I were a lifebuoy spotted suddenly in a sea of trouble. Suddenly they stopped, and that one said: 'Stephens, this is Joyce'; and then, turning to his companion, he said: 'I've got to run'. And he ran.

There stood Joyce and I, he stuck with me, and I stuck with him, and the other drowning man was swimming to a reef two streets off. Joyce looked at me without a word in his mouth, and I looked at him with nothing in my mouth except vocabularies. We halted upon each other. We were very different-looking people. Joyce was tall, which I wasn't; he was thin, which I wasn't; he wore specs, which I didn't; he looked down at me, which I couldn't; he rubbed his chin at me, which I wouldn't.

Suddenly I remembered a very cultivated remark which I had once heard a gentleman in a tall hat make to another in a straw hat whom he didn't know what to do with, and I repeated it to Joyce: 'Come and have a drink,' said I. He turned, and we walked back towards Grafton Street, and I regaled him with the gayest remarks that I could think of about what is known as the weather and this and that: 'An American', said I, 'holds that it never rains in Ireland except between the showers'. 'Ah,' said Joyce. 'But a French lady,' I continued 'told me that it rains in Ireland whether there are showers or not'. 'Ah,' said Joyce. 'This is Pat Kinsella's,' I continued, as we halted outside the first tavern that we came to. 'Ah,' said Joyce; and we went in.

The barman brought the refreshment that I ordered. It was called a 'tailor of malt'. It was larger than a single, and it only escaped being a double by the breadth of a tram-ticket, and it cost me threepence. When Joyce had silently dispatched one-third of a tailor into his system he became more human. He looked at me through the spectacles that made his blue eyes look nearly as big as the eyes of a cow – very

* Extracted from *The Listener* (London), 36 (24 October 1946) 565–6.

magnifying they were. 'It takes,' said I brightly, 'seven tailors to make a man, but two of these tailors make twins. Seven of them,' I went on, 'make a clan.'

Here Joyce woke up: he exploded moderately into conversation. He turned his chin and his specs at me, and away down at me, and confided the secret to me that he had read my two books, that, grammatically, I did not know the difference between a semi-colon and a colon: that my knowledge of Irish life was non-Catholic and, so, non-existent, and that I should give up writing and take to a good job like shoe-shining as a more promising profession. I confided back to him that I have never read a word of his, and that, if Heaven preserved to me my protective wits, I never woud read a word of his, unless I was asked to review it destructively.

We stalked out of Pat Kinsella's: that is, he stalked, I trotted. Joyce lifted his hat to me in a very foreign manner, and I remarked: 'You should engrave on your banner and on your notepaper the slogan, "Rejoyce and be exceedingly bad".' 'Ah,' said Joyce, and we went our opposite ways and didn't see one another again for two years.

Our next meeting was in Paris.[2] One evening my concierge told me as I came in that a tall, beautiful, blind gentleman had called and had left a note for me. It was from Joyce, and it asked me to meet him the next day. After that we met several times a week for a long time. I discovered that he approved of me in the most astonishing fashion, but it took me a little time to find out why. Then, as the Dublin newsboys used to yell at customers, the whole discovery was found out.

How Joyce had made this discovery I don't know, but he revealed to me that his name was James and mine was James, that my name was Stephens and the name he had taken for himself in his best book was Stephen: that he and I were born in the same country, in the same city, in the same year, in the same month, on the same day at the same hour, six o'clock in the morning of the second of February. He held, with a certain contained passion, that the second of February, his day and my day, was the day of the bear, the badger and the boar. On the second of February the squirrel lifts his nose out of his tail and surmises lovingly of nuts, the bee blinks and thinks again of the Sleeping Beauty Queen, his queen, the wasp rasps and rustles and thinks that he is Napoleon Bonaparte, the robin twitters and thinks of love and worms. I learned that on that day of days Joyce and I, Adam and Eve, Dublin and the devil all shake a leg and come a-popping and a-hopping, yelling here we are again, we and the world and the moon are new, up the poets, up the rabbits and the spiders and the rats.

Well, I was astonished. I was admired at last! Joyce admired me: I was beloved at last: Joyce loved me. Or did he? Or did he only love his birthday, and was I merely coincident to that? When I spoke about my verse, which was every waking minute of my time, Joyce listened heartily, and said, 'Ah'. He approved of it as second of February verse, but I'm not certain that he really considered it to be better than the verse of Shakespeare and Racine and Dante. And yet, he knew the verse of these three exhaustively!

Now, in order to bring this birthday to an end, let's do it in the proper way. If I were Joyce's twin, which he held, then I had to celebrate this astonishing fact in my own way: so, upon our next birthday, I sent him a small poem of twenty lines:

> As bird to nest, when, moodily,
> The storm-cloud murmurs nigh the tree,
> Thus let him flee,
> Who can to sing,
> Here hath he calm, and sheltering.
>
> As bee to hive, when, with the sun,
> Long honey-gathering is done,
> Who can to sing,
> There let him flee,
> This is his cell, his companie.
>
> As child to mother running, where
> The thunder shudders through the air,
> Thus let him flee,
> Who can to sing,
> Here hath he ward, and cherishing.
>
> Fly to thy talent, to thy charm!
> Thy nest, thine hive, thy sheltering arm!
> Who can to sing
> There let him flee,
> This is, naught else is, certainly.

Joyce reported back to me that he was much obliged. He practically said 'Ah' to my poem, and I could almost see him rubbing his chin at it.

As well as Dublin and the second of February, there were certain things that Joyce loved. There was, for example, a little Swiss wine called Riessler or Reissler,[3] or thereabouts; its name was like that, he loved it; there was another imbibement called champagne *nature*, and he loved that with a critical contentment that he never gave to either prose or verse: and then there was music. Joyce loved music. Perhaps that is not a precise way of putting it: he loved operatic music, the

music that you can sing – Verdi, Puccini, Donizetti. Any opera that
elevated the tenor voice above all other voices was adored by him. He
had himself one of the most musical tenor voices that I have ever
heard, and had he trained to be a singer he might have been renowned
in that art also. He could sing. He also loved folk-song. He took his
hat off to English and German and Italian folk-song, and said 'Ah' at
them, but he adored Irish folk-song, and Reisslers and champagne
natures and Napoleon brandies.

One day we were in that café which is half-way up the Champs-
Elysées, on the left-hand side – very famous, and I can't remember its
name – and he told me at table that he was the only person living who
knew a certain folk-song. He had learned it from his grandfather, and
his grandfather had asserted that it was, one, a lost song and, two,
that it was the best love-song in the world. He sang it to me in his
careful tenor voice, while three devoted waiters listened in and bowed
respectfully at the end of each verse. All waiters loved Joyce: he gave
millionaire tips, and, better, he always asked the waiter's advice. He
would ask a waiter which was better: the *sole chose* or the *gigot quelquechose*,
and would as eagerly ask whether the waiter preferred Racine to
Corneille, or the other way about. They loved him.

NOTES

James Stephens (1882–1950), Irish poet and man of letters. On the relationship
between Joyce and Stephens see Richard J. Finneran, 'James Joyce and James
Stephens', *James Joyce Quarterly*, 11 (1974) 279–92.
  1. This first meeting took place in 1912 during Joyce's visit to Dublin.
  2. In 1927.
  3. Riesling.
  4. Fouquet's.

I Meet, in Time and Space, James Joyce*

ROBERT REID

On the afternoon of 2 July 1928, through the kind persistence of Miss

* Unpublished manuscript in the archives of the James Joyce Museum, Sandycove,
Co. Dublin, Ireland.

Sylvia Beach, I, a down-and-out Pedagogue (*en route* from failure to find work as an English language tutor in Vienna, to unemployment in Dublin) was enabled to have the privilege of talking with Joyce in his Paris flat in the Rue de Grenelle.

The room in which we talked was darkened, due to Joyce's need to protect his eyes from an excess of sunlight, and to increase the protection he wore dark glasses.

I lacked the insight into Joyce's titanic struggle against his eye troubles as well as those other bodily troubles mentioned in 'My Impossible Health' or the case of James Joyce' published by Royal College of Physicians of London, NW1 4LD.

During the greater part of the 'interview', Joyce, who was wearing a house-painter's white coat and navy blue trousers, lay on a couch, and I sat on a chair facing him, wondering what I could find to talk to him about, for I lacked practice in the talk requisite to such an occasion, and I did not know how freely he would talk to me.

Moreover, the only modern Irish writers whose works were known to me in those days were a few by Sean O'Casey and Bernard Shaw. Of Joyce's books I knew, by name only, *Portrait of the Artist as a Young Man*, which I had noticed in a Dublin book-shop.

So our conversation on that Paris afternoon, while it may have run softly, certainly ran neither smoothly nor *rapidamente*. Indeed, I received quite a jolt when he remarked *à propos* of the hesitation I expressed in broaching some topic, now utterly forgotten: 'We may as well talk about that, as about anything else'.

He also surprised me, somewhat, by expressing an interest in accounts of incidents of everyday life, as for example, that of a dog run over by a motor-car.

Points on which Joyce showed interest were the place and date of my birth, my religion and my attitude to teaching; and points on which I expressed interest were his knowledge of Irish, ('I don't know it very well' he said,) and details as to the progress of the sale of his much discussed and objected-to-by-censors *Ulysses*.

On taking my leave of him, I noted that his handshake was unexpectedly limp.

Joyce's gentleness, sensitivity and loneliness of spirit made a deep impression on me. So did his generosity. And when, in reply to my question: 'How do you regard your work, Mr Joyce?', he replied: 'Like carpentry', I was non-plussed by its utter unexpectedness, and later, when I had read *Ulysses* and *The* [*sic*] *Portrait*, was delighted by its rich simplicity. Perhaps he derived the carpentry idea from a suggestion by Remy de Gourmont,[1] more probably perhaps from his own work. Certainly Joyce's application of the carpentry simile – an application of meticulous accuracy – turned out to be revolutionary.

To illustrate the generosity of the 'poet' to a young stranger (I owed, apparently, my meeting with the famous author of *Pomes Penyeach* to Miss Beach's – surprising to me – impression that I resembled Joyce facially), I need only mention that he showed me a sheep-skin-bound, outsize (for those days) edition of *Ulysses* which contained a typewritten synopsis of the story. He also gave me copies of his works, as well as of Gorman's *James Joyce, the First Forty Years* and Paul Jordan Smith's *Key to Ulysses*.

Joyce told me that *Ulysses* dealt with Day, and that *Work in Progress*, then running in 'transition' (and destined to end up as *Finnegans Wake*), dealt with Night.

I asked him if he would be so kind as to autograph *Ulysses* for me, but he declined to do so. I still have two of the other books he gave me. The only one he 'located' and 'dated' for me ['located' and 'dated' – Paris 2 July 1928], namely *Portrait of the Artist as a Young Man*, in the Modern Library Edition, with an introduction by Gorman, I gave to a Cambridge friend, long since dead.

One statement made to me by Joyce that summer afternoon I have never forgotten, for it is by me, at least, unforgettable. It was to the effect that a young French composer, a friend of his, knew *Ulysses* 'off by heart'. Joyce stood up to hand me the big tome, and casually made the remark as I handled it – I didn't drop it.

I received this statement in awed admiration of its maker, and of its musical 'hero'. Later, when I read in *transition* of Joyce's admiration for *Le Ballet Mécanique* I wondered if he, of the prodigious memory, was the gifted young French composer, Georges Anquetil [*sic*].[2] I still wonder, for I have not yet learned the name of this amazing memory-man.

Today, when I reflect on Joyce's sense of humour, and recall that a French equivalent for 'a tall story' is *'une histoire marseillaise'*, I should not be surprised to learn that this statement by Joyce, enshrines one of the briefest tall stories of modern times. The more so, when I recall that Joyce informed me that the maid who answered the door was from Marseilles. Of course, the story, as well as being tall, may also be true! Its truth-value now seems undecidable.

In those far-away days, Joyce had a reputation for unapproachability, especially where journalists were concerned. An example of this is given in Frédéric Lefèvre's book: *Une heure avec . . .*[3] Joyce, according to Lefèvre, answered most of the questions addressed to him by the journalist, with a brief *'Je m'en fous'*.[4]

Incidentally, Joyce's first words to me over the telephone, when I rang him (from Shakespeare & Co.) were: 'Are you a journalist?' Truthfully, I was able to say, 'No'.

To Miss Beach, the world is indebted for the opportunity to read

Ulysses, and I am grateful to her for introducing me to a great writer, and an outstanding Irishman.

NOTES

1. Rémy de Gourmont (1858–1915), French critic.
2. George Antheil (1900–1959), American composer.
3. Reprinted from Fréderic Lefèvre, 'Une heure avec M. Valery Larbaud', *Les Nouvelles littéraires,* 2 (6 October 1923) pp. 1–2 (Larbaud's views on Joyce).
4. 'I couldn't give a damn about it.'

At a Party with James Joyce*

CARESSE CROSBY

It was through Sylvia Beach that my husband and I first heard about James Joyce. She, to her glory, had brought out *Ulysses.* Her 'Shakespeare and Co.' with its Olde Shoppe signboard hanging in the Rue l'Odéon was the gathering place at midday for book-minded Americans – my first encounters with Hemingway, Dos Passos and Eugene Jolas were *chez* Shakespeare and Co.

Harry and I were, of course, as excited as everyone else over the publication of *Ulysses,* and Jolas, then editing *transition,* arranged through Stuart Gilbert, Joyce's amanuensis, that we should meet the great man.

I am pretty sure we were admitted to the Joyce circle because we were Jolas's side partners. Harry and I were launching our Black Sun Press,[1] and we yearned for a piece of the rich Irish cake then baking on the Paris fire.

That afternoon Stuart Gilbert was there and so was Nora, Joyce's wife. The Joyces lived near the Boulevard des Invalides, back of the Gare Montparnasse. The apartment was tidy but unimaginative; we sat in the dining-room.

I think I remember an upright piano and a goldfish bowl. I don't

* *The Passionate Years* (New York: Dial Press, 1953; London: Alvin Redman, 1955) pp. 181–7; (Carbondale and Edwardsville: Southern Illinois University Press, 1968) pp. 191–7.

remember any paintings on the wall; but there was a rug by Marie Monnier depicting the waters of Anna Livia Plurabelle, a bright whirlpool on the floor.

Joyce was uncommunicative and seemed bored with us, retreating behind those thick mysterious lenses until something was said about Sullivan's concert the evening before. Then suddenly he sprang to life. Talking all the while about the great Irish tenor, he led us after him across the hall to his bedroom, where he dropped to his knees beside the iron bedstead and pulled from under it a dilapidated leather suitcase and unlocked it. (I am not sure that the key did not hang around his neck.)

It was stuffed to overflowing with clippings, bits of paper fully scribbled over, larger sheets of typescript-like bulletins that had been five times through the machine, other miscellaneous odds and ends.

'This is my desk,' he said, on all fours, and smiled up at us through magnifying lenses, for the first time that afternoon. 'It is all in here,' and he pulled out one long clipping to carry back to the front parlour.

I was hoping it would be his own poetic creation, but it was merely a journalist's eulogistic report on Sullivan – and Joyce beamed as he passed it around.

Luckily we enthused with him to good purpose, for he asked, in his soft Irish voice, if we'd be liking to join them after the concert the following week.

At that party there was much song and some ribaldry; I think we drank beer. Nora had cooked a special Dublin dish, a huge one, for those tenors' appetites were mighty. I remember Liam O'Flaherty and Seán Ó Faolain; also a young Swede, Hauser, who had just published a best-seller, called *The Island*, and Archie and Ada MacLeish.

Maria Jolas, whose private fortune launched *transition*, took turns with Stuart Gilbert at the piano; the bar-room chords nearly raised the roof. The young Joyces, Giorgio and Lucia, were both there, and a divorcée who later married Giorgio Joyce, and Stuart Gilbert's French wife.

It was several weeks before Harry and I plucked up courage to call on Joyce again, this time to ask him if we might publish part of his *Work in Progress*. Crosby Gaige had just brought out *Anna Livia Plurabelle* in book form and we were determined to emulate it.

'How many pages would you be wanting, now?' asked Joyce.

'It's the meat, not the water, that makes the broth,' I answered, which seemed to please him.

'I'll think it over,' he said. 'I would be getting proof of sheets, would I, and I could make corrections, could I?'

'All you want,' Harry and I quickly answered. We left with a promise from Stuart Gilbert that he would deliver to us whatever manuscript was decided on.

'Mr Gilbert,' said Harry, 'please tell Joyce we will pay him whatever he thinks is right for a single limited edition, and we will pay in advance.'

'I think he knows that,' smiled S.G. 'He's heard about your press, and how beautifully it functions.' We were flattered beyond measure.

Evidently Joyce dumped his suitcase upside down that evening, for the very next day S.G. appeared ready to do business for him – and so we began work on 'The Mookse and the Gripes' and 'The Ondt and the Gracehopper'.[2]

We suggested an introduction and Joyce agreed. He weighed every suggestion we made with the greatest deliberation. Finally, he himself suggested Julian Huxley, because, he said, only a scientist could deal with the material.

I wrote to Mr. Huxley, but he could not give the necessary time just then, and *we* could not be held back! Luckily C. K. Ogden was just as happy a choice for Joyce, and so he was enthusiastically signed up.

Then the portrait. Harry and I wanted Picasso. Joyce seemed to care very much, so I went to see Picasso in the Faubourg St Honoré, where he then lived. My dog, Narcisse Noir, and I climbed two flights of circular stairs. The artist called from over the top banister that I was to come all the way up to his atelier; at that time, he was not the world-shaking figure he is today.

Ulysses had only been published a few years and not in French; Picasso was as indifferent to Joyce as Joyce was not to Picasso – I couldn't strike a spark. To begin with, Picasso said he rarely, if ever, made a portrait and never *sur commande*. I told him he would live to regret it, and I believe he must.

Brancusi was our next choice, but since he was a sculptor, and such an abstract sculptor, the question of likeness bothered us all. Brancusi agreed to do it, Joyce agreed to sit, but it was hard to get them together (and harder to get them apart!).

The artist made several sketches, keeping only one; this one *was* a likeness, but I urged him with Joyce's *appui* to do also an abstract conception, and in this I believe I was wrong, for we decided to use the abstraction in the book instead of the likeness; now to my mind the first drawing proves vastly more interesting.

I did not make the same mistake with Augustus John when I published the *Collected Poems of James Joyce* several years later. Some day, however, I should like to see the two Brancusis published side by side.

The first proofs were ready for Joyce early in November,[3] and he said he would come to the rue de Lille to correct them one afternoon. We waited until dinner time. Just as we were sitting down, a note was handed me; it was from Joyce. He had come as far as our front door, but before Ida could open, he heard Narcisse's watchful bark from within and turned and walked right home again.

He said he was very afraid of small animals, for his eyes were so bad he might run into them – he had to tap his way with a cane and so could easily be tripped by our dog. He asked me if I would tie Narcisse up, then he would come back next day.

I sent the proofs back to him by his messenger, so that when he did appear the following afternoon he had already gone over them, but to my horror they looked like a bookie's score card. I locked Narcisse into my bathroom.

The fire was burning in the library. We went up, cautiously, by the bathroom, because Narcisse had yapped (I promised next time to muzzle him as well). Once ensconced in the biggest chair, Joyce changed his glasses and asked for a stronger light (later I ordered a special 150-watt bulb for these sessions). He picked up 'The Mookse and the Gripes' and read the opening line, already rewritten beyond recognition.

'Now, Mr and Mrs Crosby,' Joyce said, 'I wonder if you understand why I made that change.' All this in a blarney-Irish key.

'No, why?' we chorused, and there ensued one of the most intricate and erudite twenty minutes of explanation that it has ever been my luck to hear; but unfortunately I hardly understood a word, his references were far too esoteric.

Harry fared a bit better, but afterwards we both regretted that we did not have a dictaphone behind the lamp so that later we could have studied all that had escaped us.

Joyce stayed three hours; he didn't want a drink, and by eight he hadn't got through with a page and a half. It was illuminating. When he left, Harry guided him down the slippery stairs – Narcisse was happily eating rabbit in the kitchen – and I started to mix some very dry martinis.

A final, unexpected incident occurred after Harry's death in 1929, for, regrettably, *Tales told of Shem and Shaun* did not appear until the spring of 1930.[4] The pages were on the press and Roger Lescaret, my printer, pedalled over to the rue de Lille to show me, to my horror, that on the final forme, due to a slight error in his calculations, only two lines would fall *en plaine page* – this from the typographer's point of view was a heinous offence to good taste.

What could be done at this late date! *Nothing*; the other formes had all been printed and the type distributed (we only had enough type for four pages at a time).

Then Lescaret asked me if I wouldn't beg Mr Joyce to add another eight lines to help us out. I laughed scornfully at the little man. What a ludicrous idea. When a great writer has composed each line of his prose as carefully as a sonnet, you don't ask him to inflate a masterpiece to help out the printer!

'We will just have to let it go,' I groaned, and Lescaret turned and pedalled sadly away – but the next noon when I arrived at 2 rue Cardinale joy seemed to ooze from the doorway of the Black Sun Press. Lescaret bounced out and handed me that final page. To my consternation eight lines *had* been added.

'Where did you get these?' I accused him.

'Madame, I hope will forgive me,' he beamed. 'I went to see Mr Joyce personally to tell him our troubles. He was very nice – he gave me the text right away – he told me he had been wanting to add more, but was too frightened of you, Madame, to do so.'

NOTES

1. The Black Sun Press was founded in Paris in 1927.
2. Joyce arranged with the Crosbys for *Tales Told of Shem and Shaun*, to include 'The Mookse and the Gripes', 'The Muddest Thick Ever was Dumped' and 'The Ondt and the Gracehoper'.
3. 1928.
4. The book was published in August 1929.

James Joyce in Paris*

ALDOUS HUXLEY

ALDOUS. He was a *very* strange man. I used to see him sometimes in Paris. His – what one might call – magic view of words – I shall never forget sitting next to him once at dinner and mentioning to him, which I thought would give him pleasure – and it *did* – that

* Quoted in Sybille Bedford, *Aldous Huxley*, vol. I (London: Chatto & Windus, 1973) p. 216. Editor's title.

I'd just been re-reading the *Odyssey*. And his immediate response was – he said to me, 'Now do you realise what the derivation of Odysseus, the name Odysseus is?' I said [*sotto voce*] 'No, I don't.' And he said, 'Well, it really comes from the words Udyce, meaning nobody, and Zeus, meaning God, the Odysseus is really a symbol of creation of God out of nothing.' Well, I mean this is exactly the sort of etymology which would have been made by Albertus Magnus in the thirteenth century – with no relation of course to anything we would regard as realistic. But this completely *satisfied* Joyce's mind.

CHANDOS. But he was enormously a man of words.

ALDOUS. Absolutely a man of words.

CHANDOS. This was the lovable thing about him – I love words in my own way.

ALDOUS [with much determination]. Yes, but I mean, surely one has to realise the limitations of words. Joyce – seemed to think that words were omnipotent. They are *not* omnipotent.

NOTE

Aldous Huxley (1894–1963), English novelist and critic. This piece is extracted from an interview he gave in London in 1961.

We Established No Intimacy*

RICHARD ALDINGTON

I saw [Joyce] from time to time. Unfortunately I have little of interest to report, since we established no intimacy, and I soon limited myself to a formal visit of respect on reaching and before leaving Paris. Mr Joyce struck me as a man of great personal dignity with a fine ascetic face, but thrown back on himself by partial or complete blindness. He was very much the vogue at the time, and surrounded by followers who, I thought, seemed rather jealous of each other. On the other

* *Life for Life's Sake: A Book of Reminiscences* (New York: Viking Press, 1941) pp. 324–5. Editor's title.

hand one must recognise their devotion in reading to or otherwise amusing their incapacitated hero.

I admired *Ulysses* as a work of originality and power, though I thought it over-laboured and prolix in parts, and more uniformly filled with pessimism and digust than is justified by the experience of life. If the last paragraph of the book may be interpreted as saying 'Yes' to life in spite of everything, it is too brief and belated after so many hundreds of pages of 'No'. And I lost interest in Joyce when he invented a complicated and polyglot language of his own, which concealed rather than expressed what he had to say. Just as *Ulysses* suffered from an excess of disgust typical of its epoch, so the fragments of this new book showed the other defect of a wilful darkness and difficulty, a veil not of profundity but of emptiness. It was a device for concealing the fact that the author had nothing more to say.[1]

NOTES

Richard Aldington (1892–1962), English poet and novelist.
    1. Aldington wrote about the 'deplorable' influence of *Ulysses* in his review, 'Mr James Joyce's *Ulysses*', *English Review* (London), 32 (April 1921) 333–41.

James Joyce*

GEORGE ANTHEIL

James Joyce loved music, and that is probably the only reason he and I became good friends. Certainly I was totally unprepared to understand his colossal stature as a writer.

My friendship with Joyce commenced shortly after the riotous concert at the Ballets Suédois.[1] During that concert Joyce had sat in a box near Erik Satie;[2] later he was to report everything that happened in Erik Satie's box up until the time they had turned the floodlights upon him and temporarily hurt his very sensitive eyes. Sylvia Beach introduced us one day in the bookshop, and he had come upstairs[3] to have some tea and look at my music manuscripts.

Around about my second or third year in Paris I very often journeyed over to the Right Bank, Montmartre, to spend the afternoon in the

---

* *Bad Boy of Music* (Garden City, N.Y.: Doubleday, Doran, 1945) pp. 150–5.

Moulin Rouge; it was for me a quite wonderful place whose atmosphere
had not changed an iota since the days of Toulouse-Lautrec or even
Offenbach. One day I took my courage in hand to invite Joyce to come
with me, and he did. He liked the place very much, and thereafter we
very often visited new places of interesting discovery together. One of
these was discovered by Joyce.

It so happened that both of us were very fond of Purcell, but hearing
Purcell in a Paris possessing its own Rameau was as difficult as getting
Gertrude Stein to say that *Ulysses* was a great work. Nevertheless there
was a French lady of great wealth and a centrally located mansion
whose particular Sunday delight was in giving performances of early
French, Italian and even English operas; she had these performed in
her own private theatre, and for her invited guests. Being extremely
French, and also of the old school, the new skyrocketing name of James
Joyce meant nothing whatsoever to her, and she could not be persuaded
to send him an invitation.

Whereupon Joyce immediately set his mental energies to work upon
means and methods of gate-crashing her house. I was usually his
companion on these expeditions. Her performances always took place
on Sunday morning, in a small churchlike structure which may have
been a private chapel before it became converted into a theatre; and a
good many various people came to them, so it was not too difficult to
crash the gate, particularly when the gate-crashing plans were conceived
by Joyce himself. He often wrote our 'scenario' out: what he was to
say, what I was to answer.

The French lady soon suspected us, however. At our third crash, a
performance of 'King Arthur', she cornered us, had us thrown out. I
have never been thrown out of a better place and in better company.

Joyce was good enough to take a deep interest in my own composition,
write several articles in French magazines upon my music (which
deeply impressed less prejudiced French persons than our lady of the
Purcell operas), and suggest writing an opera libretto[4] for me to set to
music.

We often used to discuss this libretto, in the course of which Boski
and I were often invited to his home.

Our first entry into the Joyce apartment was quite startling to us, if for
no other reason than that our own apartment was so unconventionally
decorated. The Joyce apartment, located near the Trianon Restaurant
where the Joyces habitually dined, was first of all a nightmare of
the conventional French wallpaper. French wallpaper is difficult to
describe, and I find myself at a loss except to say that, so far as I've
observed, it comes in two patterns, roseate syphilis and green gangrene.
When Boski and I first found ourselves projected into the Joyce
apartment we found it so utterly different from our own rather

ultramodern niche that we first had a mad impulse to giggle – an impulse which was immediately amplified by our discovery of a gas fireplace with two colour-retouched photographs above, one of Mrs James Joyce on the left, one of Mr James Joyce on the right.

The apartment was evidently a creation of Mrs Joyce's. Joyce, already blind enough not to be able to take great interest in visual detail, had let her have her way; and her way was a nice up-to-date Dublin bourgeois apartment. But for the wallpaper, it looked strangely out of place in Paris.

But Mrs Joyce was pure gold for all her lack of interior decoration. In her Irish way it was evident that she loved Joyce deeply without, however, quite understanding her genius husband. On many various evenings Boski and I heard her admonish him; once she asked him why in the world he didn't write 'sensible books that people can read and understand'; at another time she said, 'I just can't understand why you didn't become a banker instead' – and to us: 'You know James's father wanted him to become a banker'.

One evening Boski and I entered the apartment to hear her scolding him loudly for getting egg all over the bedspread and wondering audibly why in the world didn't he get up to work instead of sitting in bed all day writing (a thing I too like to do occasionally). She watched him like a hawk, administered to his every need, was undoubtedly the best wife a man like Joyce could ever have found.

She didn't understand him, but she did better, she loved him.

She was also a good mother to Joyce's two children, the daughter resembling her and the boy resembling Joyce. His daughter, then seventeen, was slender, willowly, beautiful only as Irish girls can sometimes be beautiful – in a sort of fey way; Andrea King, today, reminds me somewhat of her. The boy, Giorgio, was then being encouraged by Joyce to become an opera singer – Joyce's frustrated ambition. Giorgio, incidentally, had a fairly good voice; we often went through various opera scores together for Papa's benefit.

Which, in turn, reminds me that, excepting Mrs Joyce's, the household language was Italian. The children had been brought up in Italy (Trieste) and spoke the language like natives. It was curious to hear the lovely girl skip unconcernedly from a rich Irish-accented English to the beautiful round sentences of the Italian language.

Italian, apparently, was a sort of secret society between Joyce and his two children to which Mrs Joyce had not been admitted – and which she did not mind.

Joyce's madness was opera, preferably Purcell, but if no Purcell was available, just opera. On one occasion he even managed to drag me to the Paris Opéra to see *Siegfried*, on which occasion I became violently ill at my stomach – which is the way Wagner invariably affects me (particularly the way in which Wagner used to be done on the Paris Opéra stage). Another one of Joyce's madnesses was Irish singers; almost any Irish opera singer travelling through Paris could be assured of Joyce's support; he was always in the front row applauding loudly. On occasion, after a glass or two of white wine, he could be persuaded to sing himself; at such moments he displayed a really splendid if somewhat untrained tenor voice; he could have become a good singer had he chosen to do so.

Conversation with Joyce was always deeply interesting. He had an encyclopedic knowledge of music, this of all times and climes. Occasional conversations on music often extended far into the night and developed many new ideas. He would have special knowledge, for instance, about many a rare music manuscript secreted away in some almost unknown museum of Paris, and I often took advantage of his knowledge.

I also timidly approached him concerning a deplorable lack in my previous education; in my youthful high-school and Philadelphia days I had read plenty of American and Russian novelists, but hardly any French or English. What should I read? He advised me to start with two books of Stendhal's, *The Red and the Black* and *The Charterhouse of Parma*. He might just as well have stopped there, for these two novels have, since, become my favourite books, reread not once but perhaps ten or eleven times.

I did not understand Joyce's last *Work in Progress* very well, but was ashamed to admit it. Joyce, however, presumed that I understood everything, invariably gave me each new book as it was issued – with appropriate autograph. With *Ulysses* he even gave me a copy of his basic plan – which is today one of my most valued possessions.

When his works appeared in German, he autographed them for Boski. He spoke German flawlessy, as he spoke French, Italian, English and Spanish. He also spoke some Russian – how well, I would not know. (Boski is responsible for reports on his Italian and Spanish.)

One of the things which most deeply impressed me about Joyce was my old concierge's veneration for him. At one time or another she had seen at close range most of the greatest names in literature going in and out of Sylvia's bookshop, but she rated none of them so highly as Joyce. As I knew the old lady to be particularly astute about humanity in general, I felt sure that she had given him the closest study; later, however, I discovered that her admiration for him was based on the fact that he so exactly resembled the picture of William Shakespeare which had been painted on Sylvia's shop sign, 'The Shakespeare Bookshop' [*sic*].[5]

History will probably provide a hundred verbal portraits of Joyce. I will not bother to paint a further word picture except to note that when one first met Joyce one had rather the impression of meeting William Shakespeare just before he lost his hair. His features were delicate and finely drawn. He wore a fine Shakespearean goatee – as did Satie and Pound. (Elliot Paul and Ernest Hemingway were only occasional goateers at that period.)

On the surface he was respectable and old-fashioned, had immaculate manners – incidentally a most unusual characteristic in the Paris Latin Quarter of all periods.

Beneath he was typically Irish, full of sly fun, daring practical jokes and mad expeditions.

Once, for instance, he insisted upon our taking Sylvia's partner, Mlle Adrienne Monnier, all the way to the Right Bank and the Moulin Rouge because he wanted to shock the otherwise unshockable cocottes who inhabited the Moulin Rouge. Adrienne had long ago decided she looked best in a rather exact adaptation of nun's attire, so she always wore a grey full dress down to her ankles with white starched collar and cuffs. Adrienne was also a bit over on the stout side, so she really looked better in this costume – but extremely like a real nun.

After we'd gotten her into the Moulin Rouge we went around to all the cocottes, whispering that we had just managed to lure a genuine nun out of the nearby convent and moreover were about to transport her with us to America – for unspeakable high jinks, of course.

Adrienne's placid, spirituelle, unlipsticked and unrouged face, completely unaware of whatever we might be whispering, added credence to this otherwise unparalleled information – information well calculated to cause a sensation in the Moulin Rouge – because, no matter how unshockable a French 'fille de joie'[5] might be, there is just one matter completely sacred to her: a nun. No matter how low she ever sinks, the purity of her more spirituelle sisters is like a pure flame that must not be made fun of.

They were all really outraged, and Joyce and myself had quickly to spirit poor unsuspecting Adrienne out of the place before the girls become violent.

NOTES

George Antheil (1900–59), American concert pianist and composer. He became a friend of Joyce; played old English music at his birthday parties; and set his lyrics for *The Joyce Book*, published to celebrate his fiftieth birthday.

1. The concert took place on 4 October 1923.
2. Eric Satie (1866–1925), French composer.
3. Antheil lived in a small flat directly over Sylvia Beach's bookshop.

4. Based on Byron's *Cain*.
5. Sylvia Beach's bookshop was called 'Shakespeare and Co.'
6. Prostitute.

A Study of James Joyce*

ELLIOT PAUL

I first saw James Joyce in a small room of the old Pleyel establishment on the lower slope of Montmartre. A group, including Ezra Pound and Ernest Hemingway, had gathered there to hear George Antheil's arrangement of his *Ballet Mécanique* for the player piano. Nearly everyone was standing, for there were very few chairs, but Joyce, whom I recognised at once from the photographs which had appeared in various newspapers and magazines, had placed one of the small folding seats near the only window and was sitting with his face turned towards the light. His attitude showed that he was listening intently and was trying to isolate himself from the slight commotion of the crowd.

Joyce's face is as familiar to others as it was to me. His forehead is high and narrow, he wears a small pointed beard of the style known as a 'goatee', his air is detached and languid. A few artists, after a struggle with Sylvia Beach (who protects him from callers with a zeal which amounts at times to fury), have drawn him from life and two painters have painted portraits of him, but very badly. I think the reason that photographers succeed so well with Joyce while artists portray him so falsely lies in the fact that the latter depend too much upon eyes and Joyce's eyes, except when they are obscured by thick glasses, look unmistakably weak, as they are. This physical misfortune affords the key to much of his life and his work.

A Portrait of the Artist as a Young Man makes it clear, although it never states the fact directly, that its author had trouble with his eyesight even in his early years. Stephen Dedalus, as Joyce calls himself, did not care for athletic games, he was shy and supersensitive and had the keen ambitions which often go with a sense of physical inferiority. Joyce has never been blind, but for the last several years he has seen outlines dimly and for reading purposes has been obliged to use strong complicated lenses. Since the war he has had to submit to an almost

* Extracted from 'Farthest North: a Study of James Joyce', *Bookman* (New York) 75 (May 1932) 156–7, 159–60.

continual series of operations in order to retain what sight he has. The result is that his hearing and his memory have developed abnormally.

Mrs Joyce, a simple candid Irish woman, is very patient with her nervous husband, but she has little appreciation of his work. One of her sincere regrets is that he did not pursue a career on the concert stage.

'James Joyce, the *writer*,' she once said regretfully to a friend. 'And to think that once he sang on the same stage with John McCormack!'

In their living room not long ago, Mrs Joyce remarked without the slightest ironical intent that she had nothing to read and wished she could get the works of some of the 'good Irish humorists'. Joyce glanced at me slyly and smiled. It is no secret that his wife has not read the major part of his writings. After she had left the room he took up some proof sheets of *Work in Progress* and said, rather wistfully:

'I think this is funny, don't you? At least, I mean it to be.'

I replied that I found it very amusing, as I did, although nearly all the pages I remembered as being humorous he himself had explained to me, syllable for syllable. He knew this as well as I did, and yet he was almost childishly pleased by my complimentary remark. The abuse which has been heaped upon him from all quarters of the world has done its work, in making him over-susceptible to praise and to blame. Once, I know, he went to bed for two days because a man for whom he had not the slightest artistic regard wrote disparagingly of his recent efforts. When a mutual friend told him that James Stephens had found his *Anna Livia Plurabelle* musical, Joyce's face lighted with joy which diminished only slightly when the friend added that Stephens had also said that he was sure the general public would never understand it. The next time I called, I found Joyce peering through his spectacles into one of Stephens's books, I believe it was *The Crock of Gold*, and trying out of gratitude to like it. He shook his head doubtfully and put the volume away.

'It's all right, but it isn't *written*,' he said. 'I don't see why almost anybody couldn't do that.' . . .

The first time I called at his apartment after thorough preliminaries had been gone through by Miss Beach, our talk had not got fairly started when a clap of thunder sounded. Joyce's manner underwent an astonishing change. He tried unsuccessfully to remain seated and as he pulled down the window shades and turned on the lights he told me that Mrs Joyce had taken advantage of my presence in order to attend a movie and he expressed a nervous hope that I would not find it necessary to leave the place until she had returned. I was glad to be of service and as I saw him shudder and recoil I realised that hearing a thunder-clap was an experience which depended for its intensity upon the state of one's nerves and the sensitivity of one's eardrums. In considering Joyce's aural impressions, the normal man must raise his own to the uth degree.

When it became apparent that the shower was not going to pass quickly, Joyce asked me if I would mind sitting with him in an inside room, so we took two of the dining-room chairs into the narrow hallway, closed all the doors and sat there while the thunder rumbled outside and the lights blinked as the lightning clipped the current. All this time, Joyce said not a word, except to utter ejaculations of dismay from time to time.

In the midst of the storm, Mrs Joyce returned, wet and alarmed, and was much relieved to find me there. She told me that the year before, after consulting all their friends and the travel agencies to find a place in which their vacation be spent without fear of thunderstorms, she and Mr Joyce had selected Holland. The first evening at Amsterdam ushered in the worst electric storm the Low Countries had ever seen and a church steeple just across the street from the Joyces' hotel was struck by lightning and shattered. They took the first train back to Paris and it took Joyce several weeks to recover from the shock.

NOTE

Elliot Paul (1891–1958), American writer.

Visits from James Joyce*

NANCY CUNARD

Soon he came to the point: Sullivan, a very great Irish singer. Now, Sullivan was not getting the recognition he deserved and this must be set right at once. Well, Lady Cunard, my mother, was a very great friend of the orchestra leader, Sir Thomas Beecham, who should be made to realise that Sullivan must be engaged forthwith. Had Beecham ever heard of him? I could not say. Why was Beecham not interested? Well, what he, Joyce, wanted me to do was to use all my influence with Lady Cunard so that Beecham should hear, and engage Sullivan. I presume Joyce thought this quite simple. What he probably did not

* *Nancy Cunard: Brave Poet, Indomitable Rebel, 1896–1965*, ed. Hugh Ford (Philadelphia, Penn.: Chilton Book Co., 1968) pp. 81–2.

know was that my relations with her were not of the friendliest; at any rate, I had no 'influence' with her whatsoever – as I now tried to make clear. Joyce would have none of that and brushed it aside. I assured him that I would, of course, tell her that he had come to see me about the matter; more than that I could not possibly do. I thought he seemed annoyed and did not believe me. Sullivan *must* be engaged. And when I reminded him that he knew Lady Cunard himself and that she would be likely to listen to him, that too was brushed aside, and somehow, I did not feel like recalling to him that she had been very instrumental indeed, in 1917 or so, in obtaining public recognition for his great talent as a writer, recognition that could not have been more official, and on a financial plane, too. Joyce went on: Lady Cunard was in Paris now, Thomas Beecham as well, or soon coming, Sullivan was in Paris, and so they must be brought together. I must have said that this was more than I could do, but that he could accomplish it, if only he would get in touch with Lady Cunard; or why not directly with Sir Thomas? I fancy Joyce liked none of this. Obviously his mind had been made up: I, and I alone, must be the approach. 'How displeasing it is to be put in a false position – maybe he has taken offence,' I though, as I sprang off the bed to try and guide him discreetly to the door after the half-hour's conversation. It was horrifying to see him grope, miraculous to see his adroit descent of the stairs, the tall, cathedral-spire of a man. As for Lady Cunard, would she even listen? She did not listen much.

And then, two weeks later or so Joyce suddenly reappeared at 15 rue Guenegard, near the Seine, where I ran my Hours Press. It was towards evening and several of us were there, although I cannot remember just who. I know we ran forward to greet him: would he not take a drink with us in our local bistro, perhaps even have dinner? I had talked to my mother, I told him; she had seemed to understand and had said she would tell Beecham, but there was nothing definite to go on, and, really, he himself should get in touch with her. Meanwhile, would he not sit and have a little drink with us? No, he would not. The point was Sullivan, who *must* be engaged for grand opera. Could I not realise the urgency of this? If I had tried already, I should try now much harder. And then he dropped a hint that, if things went well on the score of Sullivan, a little piece of writing might perhaps come to me for publication at the Hours Press. (The honour was materially cancelled out by my knowledge that the Press would soon be closing down.) In the end, a few days later, Sullivan did sing and was heard by Beecham.[1] But what happened? I have a vague memory of some kind of complicated fiasco occurring that evening, and myself not even on the outer edge of it. How peculiar is this episode. I suppose it throws one of a million lights on Joyce, on the sincerity of his friendship for the singer, on his brooking no denial, while his tenacity was certainly revealed to me. That Joyce's manner with friends was very different to his formal way with me during these two unexpected apparitions, was easy to believe. How much I should have liked to observe the moment at which he became more human. At dinner, for instance, he 'mellowed' a great deal, it was said. Who used that word? Robert McAlmon, who would talk and talk about the 'Big Four'. Joyce, Pound, Eliot and Wyndham Lewis, in the early twenties – soon after the time I just knew Ezra and T. S. Eliot and Lewis rather well, all three. It is on record that Joyce 'mellowed' over good wine and conversation. I saw him icy. How unfortunate that what brought us together at all was that erroneously conceived 'use your influence with your mother'.

NOTE

1. The much importuned English conductor Sir Thomas Beecham (1879–1961) consented to attend *Guillaume Tell* with Lady Cunard at the end of September 1930.

James Joyce: a Sketch*

DESMOND HARMSWORTH

Joyce's blindness was at its worst in the early thirties when I undertook to make a drawing of him. He had undergone a dozen operations without anesthetic (for an hour or two after one of them he was practically insane, he told me). I did not know Joyce well at that time and was not very experienced with sitters.

I arrived at his apartment in the avenue Saint-Philibert, in Auteuil, laden with papers, pens, brushes, inks, charcoal and a field easel, and was ceremoniously received at the door by Joyce himself. It was a small flat conventionally furnished in Louis XVI style, and the dining room, which he decided was appropriate for the work, was filled by a table and an armchair in which he sat with his back to the window, explaining that the light was too much for his eyes. I laid out my equipment on the table and turned to the sitter, who immediately

* *Harper's Bazaar*, April 1949, 128–9, 198.

clapped his hand over his mouth. Waiting for the mouth to be uncovered, I directed my attention to the eyes. As with many people who have to use very thick lenses, the impression of Joyce's blindness was increased by the great enlargement of the iris: one could see that he could not see.

Joyce was a restless sitter. No sooner had I began to study the eyes and the forehead than these were covered by his hand and I examined the mouth, whereupon the hand (with its numerous, apparently symbolic rings) descended again to the lower half of the face. This ballet, or battle, continued for three hours and reduced me to that state of dithering ineptitude known to all portraitists who are not temperamentally related to the Rock of Gibraltar.

There were intermissions, of course. I was relieved when Joyce's son Giorgio burst in on us. They had some rapid conversation in Italian, the private language of the Joyce household. Giorgio anxiously scrutinised one of his father's eyes, delivered some remarks on the subject, and went. Then Joyce brought from a voluminous pocketbook a frayed newspaper photo. It reproduced a seventeenth-century portrait of a French seigneur, the Duc de Joyeux. 'As an artist, do you not see a resemblance to myself there?' Joyce asked. You can almost always discover some sort of likeness if you concentrate hard enough. I suppose, but beneath the curlicues of the duke's wig I saw little that suggested Stephen Dedalus. It was his belief, Joyce explained, that a branch of the house of Joyeux crossed to England with the Conqueror and thereafter settled the Joyce country in Ireland. And so it may have been. If it wasn't, Joyce's mythopoetic power was enough to make it so, and of that I shall have something to say.

We returned to the agonising business of drawing Joyce, and the more the session progressed, the more I realised I was getting nowhere. My paper bore blots and scratches which portrayed only my frustration. 'Let's see what you've done,' said Joyce. I was a good deal embarrassed to expose my paralysed scribble and relieved when he said he could not see it at even the closest range. 'I think that's the collar, isn't it?' he asked me. 'I like that; it looks like part of a monk's habit.'

Presently it was time for tea. Mrs Joyce brought it to us on a tray. Joyce asked her opinion of my work. 'Och. I know nothing of this modern art,' she said in her melodious low voice.

Further sweating on my part availed nothing: my nerve was gone. As if he knew I was wasting my time and his, Joyce now drew from his pocket a sheaf of galley proofs. He handed me a bunch of them and asked me to oblige him by reading to him, since he could not do so for himself. I struggled inharmoniously through a chapter of *Work in*

Progress (now *Finnegans Wake*), understanding nothing but its relevance to the Battle of Waterloo. 'Keep right on: don't stop!' Joyce commanded whenever I was at a loss to pronounce a word. At first he was attentive; then he began to grin; soon he was slapping his thigh and laughing aloud – not, as I at first thought, at my inadequacy, but at his own jokes.

I carried my miserable drawing home in defeat. After dinner and some unearned but needed drinks, I took a fresh paper and drew Joyce in a couple of dozen lines and fewer minutes. The inner eye works all the time, faithfully recording, while the conscious mind is helplessly floundering.

After that, we saw much of the Joyces: at the avenue Saint-Philibert and the Giorgios', at Moune and Stuart Gilbert's, at our own place on the Quai Bourbon in the Ile Saint-Louis, and in the restaurants Trianon and Fouquet's.

On such occasions Joyce was not unconscious of being a star, and he knew the dramatic value of a delayed appearance on the stage. Once arrived, he would sit with an air of resignation and world-weariness accented by raised eyebrows and creased forehead. But his melancholy reserve fell away when he warmed to one of the conversations in the room (he heard all of them at once).

He was not the Irishman of rounded periods and irrepressible epigrams, but, thanks to his vast store of knowledge and exact memory, could talk easily and to the point of every subject. He expressed himself succinctly with sometimes a note of the classroom. His face crinkled into a heralding smile when he came up with a joke, and he made sure that it was received in good condition. Once, when he made a pun on my name he was at pains to assure me that it was unpremeditated.

A frequent guest was the Franco-Irish opera singer Sullivan. Joyce was then devoting much time and persuasiveness to the advancement of the singer's fortunes. These efforts on Sullivan's behalf were perfectly unselfish but not disinterested. Sullivan, a big man with a big singing voice, was an ingredient of the composite Irish hero who haunted Joyce's creative and myth-weaving dream: success and minstrelsy were valuable components of the synthesis. Sullivan and Giorgio (another powerful voice) would be called upon, and Joyce would be perfectly happy.

My mother, a Dubliner, once cajoled Joyce till he went to the piano himself. He sang song after song – the ones, no doubt, that old Dedalus obliged with in the pubs. It is said that Joyce would have liked to be a professional singer if his voice had been of concert strength. It was a tenor whose beauty can be imagined, perhaps, by anyone familiar with the recording of *Anna Livia Plurabelle*. The voice was sweet, but the style of delivery was startling in its wildness and mockery. He seemed to tap a private source of Panic laughter. It was a separate art of Joyce's, and it did not deserve to perish.

The Trianon was in the place de Rennes, opposite the front of the Montparnasse railway station. 'Poor blind Jemmie', who liked jokes on himself and even on his blindness, told me how he once descended from a taxi, groped toward the lighted window of the restaurant and finally put his palms to the glass to get his bearings. A passing urchin, thinking him drunk, called out: *'C'est pas de la blague, vous savez!'* [1]

The atmosphere of this restaurant was sympathetic to Joyce at the time, and he dined there almost every night. We sometimes joined the party. He was generally known to the personnel as Monsieur James. It was one of those places that specialise in regional dishes (not, indeed, that Joyce sampled any of them: he could not be said to dine in any real sense), and its pride was *cassoulet*, a nourishing combination of duck, sausage and beans. Its other speciality was the only known Breton wine, Muscadet de Nantes. Joyce had a remarkable taste for far-fetched wines and he liked them light, white and flowery, all of which good Muscadet is. He needed its persuasion to help him, glass by glass, from the withdrawn and melancholy mood which he seemed mainly to inhabit. 'Ireland sober is Ireland stiff', says *Finnegans Wake*. It was true of Joyce, in a sense. Without wine or music or the spark of lively conversation, he was shrivelled; with one of these he entered a free world. I do not mean that he got drunk; certainly not; he got communicative and, eventually, gay.

At the start of dinner he wore a somewhat pained expression. He could eat nothing except perhaps some toast with a bit of caviar on it. The atmosphere was dominated by the precipitous, wrinkled brow which, like that of the American buffalo, seemed too heavy for the body supporting it. Conversation was tentative, intermittent and brief. There was a general air of constraint. The scene was not very happy.

But Muscadet was cooling in the pail. Presently it was pourable. We all came to, a bit, after the first glass. 'I'd like to have seven tongues, Mrs Harmsworth,' said Joyce, 'and put them all in my cheek at once.'

'Do you known why an Englishman always laughs three times at a joke?' from me. 'Once when he hears it, once again when it is explained to him and a third time when he sees the point.' Loud bang of laughter from Joyce.

When Dublin became obsessive, Joyce was inclined to draw all and sundry into the web his mind was ever weaving around that city.

'Do you not feel that Dublin is your town – your, shall I say, spiritual home?' 'Well no,' from me dully; 'I'm a Cockney, even if most of my antecedents were in Ireland.'

'Yes, but don't you think that you feel that Dublin . . . ?' 'Ah, let him alone. Jimmie,' said Mrs Joyce. 'Can't you see he doesn't think he's a Dubliner'. We had ordered champagne by now.

'Yes but . . . ?' 'Let him alone!'

'Your Uncle Northcliffe,[2] now, was he not born in Chapelizod? You know, by the way, that Chapelizod is the Chapel of Isolde?' Northcliffe was born in that town on the Liffey near Dublin, of an English father and an Irish mother; he was a poor boy who made good and got himself known in the world; and he was powerfully built and had some musical aptitude. He must therefore be incorporated in the mythopoetic giant who embodied so many other men, including William Martin Murphy, founder of the *Irish Independent*, and the Duke of Wellington and James Joyce himself.

'Didn't you tell me your father was at Trinity? Well now, haven't you a feeling that Dublin . . . ?' 'It's time to go home, Jimmie.' Nora Joyce was gentle but firm, and it was after midnight.

On the sidewalk, while they waited for their taxi, Joyce executed a few brisk ballet steps. He wore a broad smile.

NOTES

1. It's not a joke, you know!
2. Alfred Harmsworth, Viscount Northcliffe (1865–1922), journalist and newspaper proprietor.

James Joyce in Paris*

MARGARET ANDERSON

James Joyce was grown up before he left his twelfth year, I suppose. I don't mean grown up in the sense of living his life consciously. No one of my acquaintance has ever practised that unique activity. Joyce became a man early in the sense that very early he had defined what his personal situation was to be in respect to his fellow man. His focus

* *My Thirty Years' War: The Autobiography, Beginnings and Battles to 1930* (New York: Horizon Press, 1969) pp. 244–8.

on his own particular drama was clearly defined in his mind – the difference that becomes the tragedy.

James Joyce and his wife came to see us in Ezra's studio. Joyce was like a portrait of my father as a young man – the same gentle bearing, the same kindliness, the same deprecating humour in the smile, the same quality of personal aristocracy.

In one respect the meeting was a surprise to me. I had been prepared to see a sensitive man but I immediately felt Joyce's strata of sensitisation as beyond any possibility of immediate appraisal. He gave me the impression of having less escape from suffering about irremediable things than anyone I had ever known. It was an impression borne out by nothing that he said so much as by the turn of his head, the droop of his wrist, the quiet tension of his face, his quick half-smile. It is borne out by the irremediable facts he must accept. No writer has such need of his eyes as Joyce – the revision of five or six proofs of his vast books cannot be done by anyone else and would strain a perfect eyesight. And Joyce's eyesight is failing.

James Joyce talks little. He curtails his wit, his epithet, his observation by stopping short in the middle of a pungent phrase and saying: 'But I am being unkind'.

Sometimes he tells stories like this one:

Some friends were eager that he and Marcel Proust[1] should meet. They arranged a dinner, assured that the two men would have much to say to each other. The host tried to start them off.

'I regret that I don't know Mr Joyce's work,' said Proust.

'I have never read Mr Proust,' said Joyce.

And that was the extent of their communication.

I have seen no contemporary comment that does justice to Mrs Joyce. She is charming. She is good drama. Her Irish mockery and personal challenge furnish Joyce with a continual, necessary and delightful foil. She teases and tyrannises him. There is an undercurrent in her voice that makes her mockery at once exasperating, exciting and tender.

She must be at ease to show her quality. She has a feeling of inferiority before 'intellectuals', though she would not mince words in expressing her scorn of them. She was quickly at ease with Jane[2] and me, seeing our appreciation. Nora Joyce is one of those women a man loves forever and hopes one day to take effectively by the throat. She has spirit and independence which she has been willing (one feels not without rebellion) to subordinate to her devotion to a man she considers great in spite of 'his necessity to write those books no one can understand'.

The Joyce household also comprises a son and daughter whom their parents are enthusiastically manipulating into a singer and a dancer. But the interest of the family is clearly focused in the older generation.

Our talk that first evening at Ezra's was disappointing. It was one of those gatherings of people who have a great deal to say to each other, in which the very interest of the things to be said imposes a doubt in advance that they can or will be said. Fortunately there were other evenings in which we all achieved a measure of being ourselves, especially when the wine helped Joyce to tell of his curious telepathic experiences in putting real life into his stories so that people often wrote asking how he dared expose their personal tragedies; and Nora begged him to 'come home now or you'll be talking and feeling too much and who'll be taking care of you to-morrow?'

As we left Ezra's Joyce asked us to dine with them the next night. A look of distress crossed his face.

'I'm afraid it will have to be in a restaurant. We are leaving soon for the summer and the portraits of my family have been taken down from the dining room.'

He was deeply troubled by the lack of an ancestral background for dinner. We assured him that it would not derange us seriously.

We dined with the Joyces *en famille*. They were living in an apartment overlooking the Trocadero. It was not large enough to house Joyce's notebooks. He was working at a great disadvantage, having had to leave most of his library and trunks of notes in Italy. His weary way of referring to the notebooks made a tragedy.

The domesticity of the household was reduced to a minimum by the Joyces' custom of addressing the servant in Italian and using this language among themselves for all incidental conversation of the put-on-your-coat-if-you're-going-out-or-you'll-catch-cold type. This cleared away the underbrush and left space for continuity of talk.

'Though I rarely try to talk any more,' said Joyce, 'I have been too wearied by people asking me to have some more soup in the midst of conversation. I have come to feel that sustained conversation is impossible. In my books I have my revenge.'

Joyce doesn't consider it a valid excuse for people to say they can't read him because he is too hard to understand. When he was a young man he wanted to read Ibsen – wanted it so much that he learned Norwegian in order to read him in the original. He feels that people can make the same effort to read him. He sees no reason why he should make it easier for them.

Joyce was already working on a book which since 1927 has been running serially in *transition* under the title of *Work in Progress*. It is now (1930) half finished. In 1923 he could not yet talk of it – to talk put him off the writing. But later he read certain passages to me. One of the most beautiful was the episode of the Dublin women washing clothes in the river, a stone on one bank, a tree on the other, the names of six hundred rivers flowing through the text, the feeling of all life flowing through the women's hands with the water.

NOTES

Margaret Anderson, editor of the *Little Review*, an American avant-garde magazine which began to serialise *Ulysses* in March 1918, and which was later prosecuted as a result.

1. Marcel Proust (1871–1922), French novelist.
2. Jane Heap, co-editor of the *Little Review*.

I Saw Joyce Only Once*

KATHERINE ANNE PORTER

I saw him only once. When I first went to Paris, in February 1932, he was already world-famous, half-blind, surrounded by friends all faithful to him, apparently, but jealous of each other, watching him for signs of favour, each claiming to be first, trying to prevent any one new from coming near him: and on the outer rim of this group was a massed ring of eager followers trying to get into the sacred circle: it was pretty grim to witness even from a safe distance: but he had reached that point of near defencelessness against the peculiar race of people who live in reflected glory: I did not wish to see him, or to speak to him – what was there to say? And it was no doubt true that no new acquaintance could do more than disturb or bore him. But I never went near him, and this idea of him was presented to me as the true state of affairs by Sylvia Beach, Eugene and Maria Jolas, by Ford Madox Ford, by all of the many persons I knew there who had known Joyce, and befriended him for years. I think, too, that most of them had quarrelled more or less among themselves about Joyce, and in a way, with Joyce himself. Sylvia most certainly had good cause for her

* Extracted from 'From the Notebooks of Katherine Anne Porter', *The Southern Review*, 1 (July 1965) 571–2. Reprinted in her *Collected Essays and Occasional Writings* (New York: Delacorte Press, 1970) pp. 299–300. Editor's title.

belated resentment of his callous use of her life; but no one I knew was really easy in regard to him: he seems to have been a preposterously difficult man to get along with. His blindness was like the physical sign of his mind turning inward to its own darkness: after all, if the accounts now given are true, it seems not to have been the optic nerves but his teeth: and at last his intestines killed him.

One evening a crowd gathered in Sylvia's bookshop to hear T. S. Eliot read some of his own poems. Joyce sat near Eliot, his eyes concealed under his dark glasses, silent, motionless, head bowed a little, eyes closed most of the time, as I could see plainly from my chair a few feet away in the same row, as far removed from human reach as if he were already dead. Eliot, in a dry but strong voice, read some of his early poems, turning the pages now and again with a look very near to distaste, as if he did not like the sound of what he was reading. I had been misled by that too-often published photograph showing him as the young Harvard undergraduate, hair sleekly parted in the middle over a juvenile, harmless face. The poet before us had a face as severe as Dante's, the eyes fiercely defensive, the mouth bitter, the nose much grander and higher bridged than his photographs then showed; the whole profile looked like a bird of prey of some sort. He might have been alone, reading to himself aloud, not once did he glance at his listeners.

Joyce sat as still as if he were asleep, except for his attentive expression. His head was fine and handsome, the beard and hair very becoming to the bony thrust of his skull and face, the face of 'a too pained whitelwit', as he said it, in the bodily affliction and prolonged cureless suffering of the mind.

NOTE

Katherine Anne Porter (1890–1980), American novelist and short-story writer.

Homage to James Joyce*

EUGENE JOLAS

James Joyce reached the half-century mark in February of this year. It is a mile-stone in the literature of the world.

Joyce dominates his age as few writers have done. He has revolutionised literary expression. He has shaken the static world of phenomena to its foundation.

His work is not big in quantitative output. But *Dubliners*, written in his early twenties, followed by the *Portrait of the Artist as a Young Man* and *Ulysses*, created before he was forty years old, represent a gigantic architecture of a subjective–objective cosmos. Any one of these works would have sufficed to make the reputation of a great writer.

The as yet untitled *Work in Progress* is now being added by him to his life-work. A herculean task. A work without parallel in modern literary history. The English language here reaches heights not achieved since Shakespeare.

A life without sensational events is the background of this creative production. A life of exile for the most part. A life devoted exclusively to the flights of the spirit. A life of solitude, of pessimistic withdrawal.

From the moment he first tried to get a public hearing, there developed a sullen resistance against Joyce. He would never compromise. The publication of *Dubliners* was held up, when Dublin respectability seemed to be menaced. It was suppressed in Dublin after many delays in publication and it was not until several years later that it saw the light of day in London. The *Portrait of the Artist as a Young Man* aroused the fury of ecclesiastical cliques. *Ulysses* was considered to have inaugurated the 'sewage epoch', and was banned in America and England, to the everlasting disgrace of the intelligence of both countries. *Work in Progress*, during its publication in *transition*, was received for the most part, with catcalls and hisses.

Only a short time ago, both England and America once more played true to form. When Mr Harold Nicolson, who had been invited[1] by the British Broadcasting Company to speak before the microphone on the subject of current literature, suggested a discussion of the work of James Joyce, every attempt was made to prevent his carrying out his

---

* *transition* (Paris), no. 21 (March 1932) 250–3.

intention. After certain humiliating obstructions – which resulted in a sabotage of his first lecture – Mr Nicholson was finally allowed to give the talk, on condition that he make no mention of *Ulysses*. In America, Mr Joyce's predicament of not being able to copyright his book, has made it possible for a band of swindlers to imitate in every detail the only existing edition, published by Miss Sylvia Beach, and to distribute it as the original, all over the country, at book-leg prices.

While a small circle of well-wishers, including Miss Harriet Weaver, Miss Margaret Anderson, Miss Jane Heap, Messrs T. S. Eliot, Ezra Pound, Valéry Larbaud and John Quinn, were taking up the cudgels for his work, Mr Joyce was reviled, calumnied and misinterpreted by a herd of critics who would have done honour to the Spanish inquisition. The following letter by Sir Edmond Gosse which was shown at the *Exposition des Cent Ans de la Vie Française*, in celebration of the hundredth anniversary of the *Revue des Deux Mondes*, speaks volumes anent the revolting hypocrisy of the official critics:

Au catalogue,   Gosse (Edmond)
No. 416   Lettre autographe sur James Joyce

17 Hanover Terrace
Regent's Park
N.W.I.
7 June 1924

My dear Monsieur Gillet,
    I should very much regret your paying Mr J. Joyce the compliment of an article in the *Revue des Deux Mondes*. You could only expose the worthlessness and impudence of his writings, and surely it would be a mistake to give him the prominence. I have a difficulty in describing to you *in writing* the character of Mr Joyce's notoriety. It is partly political; it is partly a perfectly cynical appeal to sheer indecency. He is, of course, not entirely without talent, but he is a literary. . .
    (The rest of the letter is not visible)

I cannot forgo speaking here of my three years' association with James Joyce during the publication of *Work in Progress* in *transition*. Certainly no work was ever designed to create more misunderstandings between editor and author. There were none.

His meticulousness in the correction of proofs – not to mention the fact that correction, in his case, meant inevitably amplification and refinement of minutiae – made the editorial task an unusually hectic one. Particularly when one considers that we were printing four hours from Paris, and that nobody in the printing establishment spoke

English. There were always three, sometimes four and five sets of proofs. The fact, too, that at that moment Mr Joyce's sight was very bad occasionally necessitated the setting-up of proofs in an especially large type. (The condition of his eyes is now happily much improved, owing to the brilliant operation performed on them two years ago by Prof. Alfred Vogt of Zürich.)

I recall, among numerous similar happenings, one particular case, when a four-page addition had to be made after the first four hundred copies of the review had already been stitched. Everything was held up. The addition that had been announced by telephone came by the early mail and was rushed to the composing-room. During the day the completed copies were ripped apart, and by evening a sufficiently clean proof of the new text had been obtained for us to feel we could call it a day. For the second time the *bon à tiret*[2] was given. Just as we rolled slowly out of the printer's street, there arrived a telegraph messenger with a few more corrections. Despite the fact that the word 'Joyce' had become a verb of objurgation on the part of the 'typos', M Brulliard, the head of the establishment, showed an unusually intelligent suppleness, when called upon to accede to what many a printer might have dismissed as caprice. The telegraphic corrections were made, too. Possessors of *transition* no. 6 may have perhaps asked themselves why the page numbering of that volume should have started to stutter around page 106, which was followed by 106a, 106b, 106c, 106d, 106e, 106f. It was in order that the unforgettable 'Mookse and Gripes' might scuttle into their intended place.

Mr Joyce's reputation on the continent has grown by leaps and bounds during the last six years. The translation of his works into the principal European languages – particularly the French rendition of *Ulysses* by Auguste Morel, with the assistance of Valéry Larbaud and Stuart Gilbert, which was published by Mlle Adrienne Monnier – has started a plethora of critical estimates in almost every country. He is now profoundly influencing European writing.

About James Joyce, the artist, however, I should prefer not to go into details here. Many violent battles have already been fought around his name, and *transition's* attitude is sufficiently well-known for me to forgo any further commentary.

But on his fiftieth birthday, I should like to say how much *transition* sympathises with his titanic work and feels proud to have helped distribute his last creation. It seems appropriate, therefore, that *transition* make itself the mouthpiece of his friends in sending a message of greeting and admiration.

NOTES

Eugene Jolas (1894–1952), Franco-American publisher of the review *transition*, and a friend of Joyce.
1. In November 1931.
2. Ready for the press.

Homage to James Joyce*

PHILIPPE SOUPAULT

Neither time nor space can maintain an absolute value before a manifestation of the spirit. What can one say about a man's age? It is little more than the occasion for recollections, little more than a milestone.

It was therefore with surprise, with shock and admiration that I learned that James Joyce was only fifty years old. Already historians have seized upon this life for the purpose of disseminating their own viewpoints and suppositions. But Joyce's friends, more comprehending, are thinking of his health, of his sadness. And joining with them, I come to him strong in my friendship, and in the respectful and intimate affection which binds me to this unclassifiable man, to this man who is strong in his weakness, to this great writer who is, first of all, a man who suffers and smiles. Behind him move, as though against a stage curtain, the shadows of Dedalus, of Bloom, of Anna Livia.

Is it true? I no longer know if Joyce is fifty years old. On this day, like any other, I offer him my admiration, my faith and my friendship.

NOTE

Philippe Soupault (1897–   ), French writer who, with André Breton, founded the Surrealist movement in literature. He became a friend of Joyce and helped with the earliest French translations of *Ulysses*.

* *transition* (Paris), no. 21 (March 1932) 255.

Homage to James Joyce*

THOMAS McGREEVY

At first it seems odd that Mr Joyce should be only fifty years old. For already he is as much part of a slightly younger Irishman's background as O'Rahilly[1] and more so than Mangan or Synge or Mr Yeats. Mr Yeats has the nobility of passionate intellect and Olympian imagination and like Corneille and Goethe he has influenced his country, and goes on influencing it, from above. But Joyce! Joyce's nobility seems to me to be all heart, all loving interpretation. It is why he can afford to be so honest why he can say everything. He writes about human beings as the most enlightened and humane of father confessors might, if it were permitted, write about his penitents. For an Irish Catholic, his Dublin is the eternal Dublin, as Dante's Florence is the eternal Florence, Dublin meditated on, crooned over, laughed at, loved, warned, Dublin with its moments of hope and its almost perpetual despair, its boastfulness and its cravenness, its nationalism, its provincialism, its religion, its profanity, its Sunday mornings, its Saturday nights, its culture, its ignorance, its work, its play, its streets, its lanes, its port, its parks, its statues; its very cobbles, and the feet, shod and unshod, worthy and unworthy − if a charity like Joyce's permits the use of so final a word as 'unworthy' in relation to any human being − that walk them.

And if the Dublin of his earlier work is conscious Dublin with its memories, the Dublin of *Work in Progress* is subconscious Dublin with its half-memories, its legends, its fantasy. If *Ulysses* is Dublin moulded by the Church and all that the Church stands for, *Work in Progress* is the Dublin that immemorial nature created. It is because the author can identify himself with these two universal influences, even in relation to what, for anyone who cares about living, is a rather intolerable as it is a rather intolerant, strife-ridden, little town in the lesser of two unintellectually not very important islands off the coast of Europe and civilisation, that Joyce's work is of universal significance. Plutocratic provincialism and opinionated heresy may not grasp the fact − Joyce is still banned in England and America, and Ireland in so far as it is Anglicised, remains on the fence about him − but plutocratic provincialism and opinionated heresy do not stand quite as high as they did in

* *transition* (Paris), no. 21 (March 1932) 254–5.

the *stupide dix-neuvième*.[2] And so an Irishman of 1932 may feel that all of the world that signifies is with him in offering homage and affection to this young, still surprisingly young, compatriot who is not merely one of the greater glories of his own, but one of the most human writers of his time in any, country.

NOTES

Thomas McGreevy (1893–1967), critic and poet, graduate of Trinity College, Dublin, who was appointed English Reader at the University of Paris in 1926. He became a great friend of Joyce's and was the executor of his will. He returned to Ireland in 1941, and was Director of the National Gallery of Ireland from 1950 to 1964.

1. Presumably the Kerry poet Aogán Ó Rathaille (c. 1675–1729), one of the best-known Gaelic poets. See *An Duanaire 1600–1900: Poems of the Dispossessed*, ed. Seán Ó Tuama and trans. Thomas Kinsella (Mountrath: Dolmen Press, 1981) pp. 138–65.

2. Stupid nineteenth (century).

An Encounter with Joyce*

ARTHUR BLISS

I should like here to mention an encounter in Paris with James Joyce, arising out of the publication of *The Joyce Book*, a tribute to the author from a number of artists.[1] In his foreword Herbert Hughes jogs my memory.

This book, [he writes] has evolved out of conversations that took place in Paris in the autumn of 1929. The talkers were Arthur Bliss and myself. We were attending a festival of contemporary music arranged by Elizabeth Sprague Coolidge, and James Joyce had accompanied us to the Palais Royal where works of Bliss and Roussel and others were performed. The subjective association of chamber music – that is, of intimate music – with the poetry of Joyce was to us like the association of wind and wave, of light and heat; and the idea of this collaboration, urged maybe by the emotional incidence

* *As I Remember* (London: Faber & Faber, 1970) pp. 100–1. Editor's title.

of the festival, seemed to occur to us at the same moment. Let us, who are his friends, we said, make a volume of songs out of *Pomes Penyeach* and dedicate the volume to Joyce. We thought of selecting four or five. Our conversations were continued at Fouquet's and the idea expanded. It was decided that such a book of music would be incomplete, for *Pomes Penyeach* is a baker's dozen and the settings should be presented as such. There should, too, be a portrait, and poets, and writers of prose (also his friends) should join the musicians.

The handsome volume contained a pencil portrait by Augustus John, a poem by James Stephens, an essay by Padraic Colum, an appreciation by Arthur Symons, and settings of *Pomes Penyeach* by thirteen different composers. I chose the three-verse poem 'Simples' with the opening lines 'O bella bionda! sei come l'onda!' Joyce wanted a particular Italian refrain used for these words, and this probably accounts for the warm phrases in his letter to me:

> 42 rue Galilei,
> Paris VIII
> 3 March 1933

Dear Bliss,

I write to thank you for your contribution to the OUP. I like your song better than any other in the book. It's rich and ample and melodious, delightfully balanced in its movements. You have done my little song great honour. Please accept my warm thanks.

> Sincerely yours,
> James Joyce

I have a certain suspicion that with his Irish charm Joyce wrote a similar letter to each of the other contributors – perhaps he liked them all the best!

NOTES

Sir Arthur Bliss (1891–1975), English composer.

1. *The Joyce Book*, ed. Herbert Hughes (London: Sylvan Press) was published on 2 February 1933.

Joyce's Fiftieth Birthday*

ROLLO H. MYERS

It was, I think, through music that I made James Joyce's acquaintance. He was passionately interested in singing and especially in tenor voices. I had never met a case of this kind before: a highly cultured man of letters whose interest in music was almost exclusively confined to comparing the relative merits of operatic tenors and their ability to sustain (in the correct manner) 'high C's' and so forth in hackneyed operatic roles. Joyce knew a lot about voice production, and had a great fund of specialised knowledge concerning operatic tenors, past and present, and of every nationality. He would go to the Paris Opera to hear his favourite singer again and again; it was a matter of indifference to him what opera was being performed, and he would sit through many performances of the same work. *William Tell* was, I think, his favourite opera. In private Joyce would often sit down to the piano and sing, accompanying himself.

Joyce was something of a gourmet, and liked nothing better than to spend his evenings, nearly always with his wife or friends, in one or other of the numerous restaurants which flourished in those days in Paris where the food and cooking were really good. In the matter of wines his tastes were peculiar, but extremely definite. He had an antipathy to red wine, however noble the vintage, and would never in any circumstances, drink any. 'You might as well drink liquid meat', I remember him saying once. But for white wines he had what amounted to a passion. The finest types of white wine, he said, corresponded to the most ethereal and imaginative elements in man, releasing the mind from gross and mundane preoccupations. Not all white wines met with his approval – as I discovered one day to my cost. Being privileged to have him as my guest at a restaurant I had taken the precaution of ordering in advance some white Burgundy – Meursault or Montrachet – which I flattered myself was not half bad. But alas, no sooner had he taken the first sip – he was too blind to see the bottles on the table – than he exclaimed that this must be Burgundy, which he never drank.

In France Joyce had as many admirers as anywhere. Indeed, his position as a writer of European significance was emphasised in the

* Extracted from 'Memories of Le Boeuf sur le Toit', *The Listener* (London), 85 (25 February 1971) 243–4. Editor's title.

Twenties by Valéry Larbaud, one of the first French writers to appreciate his genius; and it was Larbaud who translated *Ulysses* into French – in itself a staggering feat. Philippe Soupault, who was then a young and ardent Dadaist, also translated Joyce, and I well remember one of those literary evenings in the Rue de l'Odéon, *chez* Adrienne Monnier (or it may have been at Sylvia Beach's Shakespeare & Co. across the road, where *Ulysses* first saw the light), when Joyce was the guest of honour and his French translators and admirers were present to hear him read passages from *Anna Livia Plurabelle* and other works. His soft musical voice, with its rich Irish burr, had a strange fascination, and his reading seemed to make what appeared obscure in print as clear as day, or rather to invest it with a meaning all its own, appealing to the ear as much as to the understanding.

Joyce was not a café man: when he left the privacy of his home, to which he was strongly attached, it was generally, as I said to dine in some carefully selected restaurant. But he also liked entertaining his friends at home, and I was invited on one or two occasions to his flat and met his wife, the delightful Nora, and his son Giorgio and daughter Lucia. On Joyce's fiftieth birthday, I went to a dinner party which Giorgio and his wife were giving in their flat. Joyce was in particularly good form, drank a great deal of wine and ended by sitting down at the piano and singing Irish songs to us in his high tenor voice. When it was time to go (it was now about 2 a.m.) the problem of transport arose. As it happened, there had been a taxi strike that day, but as I had come in my small car I naturally offered to drive Joyce and his wife home. The flat I remember well (I had cause to) was on the sixth floor, and the immediate problem was to conduct the great man safely down to street level. By this time he was not very steady on his legs, and I remember thinking, as I helped him down the long flight of stairs, what awful consequences a false step on my part might have. No sooner were we settled in the car than Joyce began to suggest that it would be a good idea if we went off to some café to finish off the evening. Nora, who was sitting behind us, did all she could to dissuade him, and begged me not to listen to him but to drive straight to their house – even if this meant pretending that we were in fact heading for the restaurant. When he finally found himself in front of his own doorstep and realised how we had deceived him, he submitted with good grace and was led away by Nora, who certainly knew how to handle him on these occasions – which I imagine were not infrequent.

Joyce*

VIRGIL THOMSON

Joyce and Stein,[1] I must explain, were rivals in the sense that, viewed near by, they appeared as planets of equal magnitude. Indeed the very presence of them both, orbiting and surrounded by satellites, gave to Paris in the 1920s and 1930s its positions of world-centre for the writing of English poetry and prose. Hemingway, Fitzgerald and Ford Madox Ford; Mary Butts,[2] Djuna Barnes and Kay Boyle;[3] Ezra Pound, e.e. cummings and Hart Crane worked out of Paris and depended on it for judgment, as often as not for publication too. And all were connected in some way to Stein or Joyce, sometimes to both.

The stars themselves came together just once – briefly and both consenting. That was at the house of the sculptor Jo Davidson. And since Joyce was by that time almost blind, Miss Stein went into another room to meet him, rather than that he should be led to her. But when they had approached, exchanged greetings and good-will phrases, they had nothing to say to each other, nothing at all.

It was through Sylvia Beach that I first met Joyce (at her flat, I think). But it was more in company with Antheil that I used to see him. When during the spring of 1926 Antheil's music and mine began to appear together on programs, Joyce always came to hear us and never failed to tell me that he liked my work. That the compliment was sincere I had no reason to doubt; that it was pleasing to me, coming from so grand a source, no one need doubt. Nevertheless when in the mid-1930s, after my opera *Four Saints in Three Acts*, for which Gertrude Stein had written the libretto, had received some recognition, Joyce offered me his own collaboration, I demurred, as Picasso had done, and for the same reasons. I did not feel like wounding Gertrude Stein, or choose to ride on both ends of a seesaw.

What Joyce proposed was a ballet, to be based on the children's games chapter of *Finnegans Wake*. He gave me a hand-printed edition of that chapter, with an initial designed by his daughter Lucia; and he offered me, for the final spectacle, production at the Paris Opéra with choreography by Leonide Massine. I did not doubt that a ballet could be derived from the subject. My reply, however, after reading the

* Extracted from 'Antheil, Joyce, and Pound', in *Virgil Thomson* (New York: Alfred A. Knopf, 1966) pp. 77–8.

chapter, was that though anyone could put children's games on a stage, only with his text would such a presentation have 'Joyce quality'. I did not add that in place of the pure dance-spectacle proposed, one could imagine a choreographed cantata using Joyce's words.

NOTES

Virgil Thomson (1896–   ), American composer, critic and organist, who studied in Paris in the 1920s. He returned to New York in 1940, where he was music critic for the *Herald Tribune*.

1. Gertrude Stein (1874–1946), American author.
2. Mary Butts (1892–1937), novelist.
3. Kay Boyle (1903–   ), American novelist and reporter; co-author with Robert McAlmon of *Being Geniuses Together, 1920–1930* (Garden City, N.Y.: Doubleday, 1968).

James Joyce in Paris*

HAROLD NICOLSON

I walked to James Joyce's flat in the rue Galilée. It is a little furnished flat as stuffy and prim as a hotel bedroom. The door was opened by the son. A strange accent he had, half-German, half-Italian – an accent of Trieste. We sat down on little hard chairs and I tried to make polite conversation to the son. Then Joyce glided in. It was evident that he had just been shaving. He was very spruce and nervous and chatty. Great rings upon little twitching fingers. Huge concave spectacles which flicked reflections of the lights as he moved his head like a bird, turning it with that definite insistence to the speaker as blind people do who turn to the sound of a voice. Joyce was wearing large bedroom slippers in check, but except for that, one had the strange impression that he had put on his best suit. He was very courteous, as shy people are. His beautiful voice trilled on slowly like Anna Livia Plurabelle. He has the most lovely voice I know – liquid and soft with undercurrents of gurgle.

He told me how the ban had been removed from *Ulysses* ('Oolissays',

* *Diaries and Letters, 1930–1939*, ed. Nigel Nicolson (London and New York: Atheneum, 1966) pp. 164–5.

as he calls it) in America. He had hopes of having it removed in London, and was in negotiation with John Lane. He seemed rather helpless and ignorant about it all, and anxious to talk to me. One has the feeling that he is surrounded by a group of worshippers and that he has little contact with reality. This impression of something unreal was increased by the atmosphere of the room, the mimosa with its ribbon, the birdlike twitching of Joyce, the glint of his glasses, and the feeling that they were both listening for something in the house.

He told me that a man had taken Oolissays to the Vatican and had hidden it in a prayer-book, and that it had been blessed by the Pope. He was half-amused by this and half-impressed. He saw that I would think it funny, and at the same time he did not think it wholly funny himself.

My impression of the rue Galilée was the impression of a very nervous and refined animal – a gazelle in a drawing-room. His blindness increases that impression. I suppose he is a real person somewhere, but I feel that I have never spent half-an-hour with anyone and been left with an impression of such brittle and vulnerable strangeness.

NOTE

Sir Harold Nicolson (1886–1968), English diplomat and author; husband of novelist Victoria Sackville-West.

James Joyce*

GERALD GRIFFIN

When, many years afterwards, I met him for the first time in Paris he was still the same slim Joyce of the Dublin days, his hair greying slightly and with just the *soupçon*[1] of an *imperiale*[2] on his chin.

He had considerably mellowed in many ways since I had last seen him in Dublin – he had mellowed environmentally, mentally and colloquially. He was now in quite comfortable circumstances – he was a ratepayer and a family man. He was too far away and too long away from Dublin to be interested in Free State economics, politics or culture.

* Extracted from *The Wild Geese: Pen Portraits of Famous Irish Exiles* (London: Jarrolds, 1938) pp. 27–8, 29–32, 44–5.

Green-garbed soldiers, the Gaelic League, the intensive insularity of the new Dublin, meant nothing to him. The Free State had not been in existence when he left Dublin – his was a Dublin that has passed away, the Dublin of Castle rule, vice-regal cavalcades, legions of lewd soldiers resplendent in red coats and clanking spurs, and cyclopean DMPs.[3]

His vocabulary too had mellowed – the old Anglo-Saxon monosyllables, and the mordant colloquialisms, had been eliminated. In fact, so mellowed had his conversation become, that when I returned to Paris again about a year late, I ventured to suggest that if he brought out an edition of his *Ulysses* with Private Carr's terse obscenities and Maria Tweedy Bloom's malodorous monologue expurgated, his book would become accessible to thousands of readers who were anxious to buy it. I had hardly come out with my ill-timed suggestion when I regretted it. Joyce looked at me with cold hauteur for fully a minute, and then replied: 'Griffin, I'm like Pilate. *Quod scripsi, scripsi.*'[4]

I panickily tried to divert the conversation into other grooves, but Joyce replied with such frigid and preoccupied terseness to my remarks that, to cover my embarrassment, I pretended that I had suddenly recollected an appointment elsewhere, and hastily fled back to my hotel. . . .

After he had given me the details of the result of the *Ulysses* lawsuit in the American Court at dinner at Les Deux Trianons one night, Joyce speedily changed the trend of the conversation. He is never very happy talking either about himself or his literary work. Furthermore, he is one of the most kind-hearted and loyal of friends, and during that dinner was very preoccupied about rumours of the declining health in New York of Tuohy, the Irish painter, who before going to America had done a magnificent life-size canvas of his father, the 'Simon Dedalus' of *Ulysses*. Incidentally that painting is the first object that greets the eye on entering Joyce's flat.

Later on during dinner he outlined for me a scheme which he was concocting to secure an audience for the famous Irish tenor, John Sullivan, who, he declared, was not receiving the recognition that was his due. 'Going through the score of *Guillaume Tell* with him,' Joyce said enthusiastically, 'I was astonished at the range of his voice. He sings 456 Gs, 93 A flats, 92 As, 54 B flats, 15 Bs, 19 Cs and 2 C sharps. In all Europe you will not find another singer to reach that record.'

From John Sullivan the conversation drifted to Édouard Dujardin, whose *Les Lauriers Sont Coupés* first inspired Joyce with the idea of that adaptation of the technique of the *monologue intérieur* which has had such far-reaching reactions on the style of latter-day novelists. Joyce had already on former occasions, generously acknowledged to many people, including myself, that he owed his inspiration to Dujardin, but it was at that dinner in Montparnasse that I heard for the first time all the details of what passed between the venerable pioneer of the 'silent monologue' and his disciple.

As a youth of twenty on his way to Paris, Joyce was reading an old copy of *Les Lauriers Sont Coupés* to while away the tedium of the train journey. He was so fascinated by the technique and the theme of the long-forgotten book that he made several unavailing attempts during the course of the years that followed to get in touch with the author. *Les Lauriers Sont Coupés* was originally published in 1887 when the symbolist movement was at its height, and both it and its author had lapsed into oblivion, when, as a result of Joyce's enthusiastic intervention, it was republished with a preface by Valéry Larbaud. In that preface the great French critic deals with the technique of the unspoken monologue as used by Dujardin and Joyce. At a dinner given to celebrate the re-publication, after thirty-seven years, of *Les Lauriers Sont Coupés*, Dujardin embraced Joyce with Gallic effusiveness, exclaiming with tears in his eyes: 'Vous m'avez rendu ma jeunesse'.[5]

And now as I am on the subject of Joyce's big-hearted generosity and loyalty to his friends, I shall touch on an incident of my own experience illustrating this splendid trait in his make-up. Having heard some six years ago, through some indirect channel, that I was having some trouble with my eyes, he wrote to me at once, expressing his sorrow, and he advised me as to the choice of a specialist. His solicitude was all the more touching, as he was at that time suffering himself from acute eye trouble, and was about to face one of a series of tedious operations.

Next to his literary work, music is Joyce's greatest interest in life. He has a fine tenor voice, and in his youth once thought seriously of taking up singing as a profession. Some Dublin friends of mine have told me that they cherish copies of an old programme of a concert, in which the singers' names are given as (1) Mr James A. Joyce, (2) Mr John McCormack.

On one occasion when Joyce and myself went to High Mass at Westminster Cathedral, I noticed that he listened with rapt attention to the music – it was Taverner's Plainsong. When the service was over he analysed both the chanting and also the organ performance of Sir Richard Terry meticulously, and commented on flaws which had eluded my crasser and less-sensitive ears. The *Ite, Missa Est* especially, he found too tenuous and spiritless. 'It should have rung out more like a triumphal chant,' he said, swinging his ash-plant with the same dramatic *élan* with which he had brandished its prototype many years previously when he was denouncing Yeats, Moore and Co. outside the National Library in Dublin.

I have heard Joyce singing old Irish 'Come-all-yes' and folk-songs, as well as comic songs of his own composition both in Paris and in London. In London I heard him singing both in my own flat in Bloomsbury and in the Euston Hotel where he was staying with Mrs Joyce and his daughter, Lucia. He sometimes played his own accompaniments. On other occasions he sang while our mutual friend, Herbert Hughes, the Irish composer, played for him.

Incidentally, Joyce's reason for always staying at the Euston Hotel when he comes to London is that it is the nearest point of contact that he can have with Ireland. 'I feel,' he said to me, 'that I am near Number Thirteen platform – the Irish Mail – (*absit omen!*).[6] I cannot return to Dublin. I would get an iron welcome there – to put it mildly – for my attitude towards the Catholic Church and especially towards the Jesuits!'

But despite his gibes at the Catholic Church and the Jesuits, Joyce is eternally obsessed by that faith from which he broke away many years ago. The 'agenbite of inwit' is eternally cropping up both in his works and in his conversation. 'Je crois, mais je crois en gémissant,'[7] said Pascal, and it is my definite impression that Joyce disbelieves *en gémissant* – that he out-Pascals Pascal and out-Calvins Calvin in the mental anguish he undergoes in brooding over religion.

That obsession about religion runs right through his autobiographical novel, *A Portrait of the Artist as a Young Man*. In the last chapters of the book we hear Cranly saying: 'It is a curious thing, do you know, how your mind is supersaturated with the religion in which you say you disbelieve.' And Stephen Dedalus (who is Joyce) did not succeed in shaking off the shackles of the Catholic Church and of Ireland when he exclaimed: 'I will not serve that in which I no longer believe, whether it call itself my home, my fatherland or my church, and I will try to express myself in some mode of life or art as freely as I can and as wholly as I can, using for my defence the only arms I allow myself to use, silence, exile and cunning.'. . .

Some seven years ago I witnessed a striking instance of Joyce's equanimity under a very unflattering criticism of the technique of *Work in Progress* in the late Harold Munro's Poetry Book Shop in Bloomsbury.

'To be perfectly frank with you, Mr Joyce,' said Munro with deprecatory embarrassment, 'I can't make head or tail of your *Anna Livia Plurabelle*. A friend of mine suggested that it was intended to be read backwards, starting from the end of the book, and that one day you would reveal this clue to the enigma for the benefit of your readers. And indeed it seemed to convey just as much sense – or rather as much nonsense when I tried this method as when I read it in the normal way.'

I glanced sharply at Munro at this point, and realised at once that he was not being cruelly jocose at Joyce's expense. There was a pathetically bewildered expression on his face.

'Munro is an honest critic,' said Joyce after we had left the shop. 'At least he has tried to understand my work, and regrets that he has been unable to do so. He has not suggested that I am indulging in a colossal hoax.'

That is Joyce as he is now – tolerant of all criticism, confident that he is right, yet sensitive to the last degree. The truculent, almost swashbuckling, hard-swearing, seedy-looking young Dubliner has merged into the mellow, genial, quiet, well-dressed man of poise and distinction. Aloof and frigid to gate-crashing journalists, he is the soul of hospitality and generosity to his personal friends.

NOTES

1. Dash, touch.
2. Small beard under the lip.
3. Members of the Dublin Metropolitan Police.
4. What I have written I have written.
5. You have restored my youth.
6. May the omen augur no evil.
7. I believe, but I believe with pain.

James Joyce: a First Impression*

JAMES STERN

At the fall of that grim year, 1934, Nora and James Joyce were living in a furnished apartment on the rue Galilée, a residential district a couple of blocks from the Etoile. The day was cold, sunless, the time the fearful hour of four. Hiler,[1] that huge man – painter, pianist, teacher, writer, clown, whom Bob McAlmon has described as 'rather like a handsome frog' – appeared distracted.

'*Quelle horreur! Quelle idée!*' he groaned. 'James Augustine Aloysius Joyce, he won't want to have us around!'

* *A James Joyce Miscellany, Second Series*, ed. Marvin Magalaner (Carbondale, Ill.: Southern Illinois University Press, 1959) pp. 93–102.

'Hell, man,' exclaimed Bob, 'come off it. You said you wanted to draw the old man's head. The idea's okay with him.'

'And what,' I asked, 'could Joyce have to say to me?'

'You'll make him think of Bloom,' replied Bob with a grin.

'Oh, he'll get something out of you, don't worry. He'll quiz you . . .'

The Joyces' apartment was on the fourth floor. At our ring a door opened slowly, and there he stood. At first glance he struck me as smaller, frailer, than I had imagined. Dressed in a peacock-blue velvet jacket and dark trousers, he held himself in the position of the blind – chin raised, head tilted slightly back.

Raised barely above a whisper, his voice – that tenor to which as a young man he considered devoting his life – sounded excessively tired, the voice of a sufferer in whose presence, as in hospitals, one feels instinctively all sounds should be muffled. His hand, too, suggested the hand of a recluse, an invalid – bony yet soft to the touch, conveying on the instant a marvellous gentleness.

In my mind's eye I can see but one book in that dim, depressing, impersonal sitting-room.

It was to the single book, which lay alone on a grand piano, that he – while Hiler and I seated ourselves on the sofa, and Bob on a chair – slowly, his hands out, fingering the furniture, soundlessly in slippers, made his way.

The volume was large, of many pages, and clearly new, possibly unopened. Joyce leaned over it, touched it with his long fingers, lifted it as though it were beyond price, then laid it down.

'Is that the American edition?' asked Bob, getting up.

Joyce said nothing, simply turned and handed the book to his friend with the faintest, barely perceptible, sign of a smile. He then sat down in a chair opposite the sofa, facing the light, so that Hiler, in his corner under the window, had a full view of his features.

Now that they were clearly visible, these features resembled so much those of the drawings and photographs I had seen that I had the sensation of having known him – and better than by sight – for years. Only the brow seemed even higher than I had thought, the grey-black hair thicker, the expression of the face in repose more sad.

'A dreadful thing has happened, McAlmon,' said Joyce, in that faraway, Anna Livia Plurabelle voice. 'I have to be fitted.'

'Fitted?'

'Nora insists that I have a new suit. Let us try not to think of it. But I warn you, it can happen – any minute.' He glanced towards the door, as though expecting to hear it burst open and the fitter spring into the room.

'McAlmon tells me, Stern,' he suddenly said, 'that you were born in Ireland.'

Because the eyes behind the round, heavy, loose-lensed spectacles seemed to be directed at a spot a little above my head, it struck me only then that he could not see me.

'Yes,' I answered, 'I spent my youth in southern Ireland.' And I told him where.

He raised his head, as though chasing a memory, then repeated the name of the place.

'There's an abbey, is there not,' he asked, 'a Cistercian monastery of that name?'

'There is,' I replied, surprised. 'It's a ruin, of course – a couple of miles from where we lived.'

I was about to ask if he knew its history when he continued his questions: 'That's famous hunting country round there. Were your people hunting people?'

'They were,' I told him.

'Did they go in for racing, too?'

'No,' I said. 'But my brother does. He's a great race rider. Lives in County Cork.'

'Is that a fact?' Joyce remarked with sudden interest. 'In what condition would the Irish people be, do you think, without racing?'

'I don't like to think of it,' I replied, and I began to feel at ease. 'In our part of the world they used to say that the British put an end to the Rebellion by threatening to ban racing throughout the country!'

'Ha!' exclaimed Joyce, almost loud, 'I never heard that one! Tell me, did y'ever know the Cremin family from round Fermoy way? Their son must be about your age.'

'I didn't,' I replied. 'My family left after the Troubles. It's the older people I know and remember best.'

'What about Sir Francis Becher now? He must have lived near your place?'

'Oh, he did,' I said. 'My people knew him well.'

'Tell me of him,' said Joyce eagerly, clasping his hands and smiling to himself. 'I never met him. Wasn't he a very gruff kind of a man?'

I glanced at Bob, who urged me on with a wink. 'Oh, he was,' I began. 'A regular tyrant at times. Big, six-foot three or four, he was bald and very fat. He ate enormously. Sometimes, after hunting, his wife used to ask us in to tea.

'Once, when there were some ten to fifteen guests at the table, an aunt of ours found herself sitting next to him. Being very hungry, she and most of the other guests readily accepted the suggestion of fried eggs. When the footman brought them in – six plates of them on a silver salver – Francis sniffed. "Whatcha got there?" he howled at the footman. "Eggs, Sir Francis," answered the man. "Bring 'em heeah!" bawled Francis. Whereupon he devoured the lot.'

Since I am not, by nature, a story-teller, the silence that greeted this little anecdote made me turn hot with embarrassment. Then I noticed that Joyce, sunk in his chair, his hands up to his mouth, was shaking – with silent laughter.

'And what did Francis do then?' he inquired, recovering.

'He called for jam,' I said. 'And when the footman brought two pots of jam, Francis howled that when he demanded jam he meant not two bloody pots but twelve bloody pots. So the footman brought twelve pots!'

'Ha!' laughed Joyce, 'a terror of a man! Didn't he write a book one time on how to shoot big game?'

'I didn't hear of him ever writing a book,' I replied. 'But on shooting he might have – for though he was cross-eyed or had a wall eye, I forget which, he was a great man with a gun. I remember watching him once when he didn't know it. It was one winter during the Troubles, when all firearms were strictly forbidden.

'I saw a kind of mound of rushes rising slowly from the ground. Just as I thought it would fall, from out of the middle of it sprang an object, black, long, thin, and – bang! – a shot, then another, shattered the silence. Before the echoes and reverberations had died away, I heard the splash of a bird hurtling into the water, a thud as another fell on land, then a howl of fury as I saw the cloak of rushes collapse – and there stood Francis, in shirt and breeches, his gun raised above his bald white head, bellowing a stream of curses at his dog.'

'That's grand!' explained Joyce, clasping his hands in a soundless clap. 'What were they – duck?' When I told him yes, 'Go on, man,' he urged, 'tell us more! Wasn't he very fond of cricket?'

'He was,' I confirmed, 'he even played it in the house.'

'Ha?'

'On the billiard table.'

Suddenly the door opened. A woman stood there – tall, grey-haired, dignified. She greeted Bob. Then: 'Come on, Jim,' she said 'He's here.'

Joyce let out a groan. Then he looked up in my direction. 'But what did they play with?' he asked.

'Matches,' I told him. 'Three Swan Vestas made a wicket, and the ball, I believe, was a piece of cork, cut round and very small.'

'Jim,' called Nora Joyce, 'did ye hear what I'm after sayin'? The tailor's here. Another week, an' ye'll not be fit for the street!'

Groaning, Joyce rose slowly from his chair. 'And what about the bat?' he asked.

'Oh, the bat . . .' I began.

But Nora had had enough. 'Ah, come on outa that!' she urged, and with his hand in hers she drew him, shuffling, from the room.

NOTES

James Stern (1904–   ), novelist.
   1. Hilaire Hiler.

The Joyces*

GIORGIO JOYCE

The Giorgio Joyces have been living quietly in and around town since they arrived with their small son on the Bremen last May. Giorgio is the son of the famous James Joyce, but he has no prose work in progress himself. He's a bass singer. He made his radio début in November as George Joyce, because he doesn't like the name Giorgio – it was given to him because Italian was the language spoken in Trieste, where he was born in 1905. He has sung twice on the radio so far – a Mozart aria, a Tschaikowsky song, two old Irish ballads. His father sent him radiograms wishing him luck. James, who started out to be a singer himself, is proud of Giorgio's voice and hopes he will be a great concert singer some day.

Giorgio won't talk about his father's work, but he told us some interesting things about the author's way of life, speaking with a slight accent. (He lived in Trieste till he was nine, in Switzerland during the war, and has been in Paris since 1919. He and his father always converse in Italian.) James Joyce's eyesight, his son says, is much better than it used to be, but he can see only with his left eye, the right being entirely blind. A few years ago he had to write with blue crayon on huge sheets of white paper, but now he uses pen or pencil on any paper that is handy. He can typewrite, using one finger on each hand, but uses a typewriter only for his infrequent correspondence, never for manuscripts. His friends drop in and type his manuscripts – he hates professional secretaries and has never hired one. His friends also read to him, out of dictionaries, encylopedias and other reference books. When he wants something read to him for relaxation, he usually asks for Ibsen. He has never had a line of Gertrude Stein read to him and seems to have no interest in her work. The two have met, but that's all. The only thing Joyce reads for himself is his *Work in Progress*. He reads parts of it aloud to his friends, chuckling now and then, going back and rereading sometimes passages he especially likes. He never reads from *Ulysses* or any other of his old works, being bored with them after they are written and published.

Joyce sees very few people. He never goes to literary teas or other parties, but gives three a year himself – at Christmas, New Year's, and on his birthday, 2 February. Only his small circle of intimates are invited to these parties. Joyce always sings Irish songs for them, playing his own accompaniment. His voice is tenor and his favourite song is 'Molly Brannigan'. (His son, incidentally, doesn't play the piano.) Joyce gets up around nine, writes a little, but spends most of the morning telephoning. He actually likes talking on the phone, and chins with his friends by the hour. Before lunch he plays and sings, and afterward works until five o'clock. He has been at his new book for years; nobody knows when it will be finished,[1] but Giorgio thinks it's about half done. After five, Joyce takes a walk, alone. He detests dogs and wouldn't walk with one. There are no pets at all in his household, which consists of himself, his wife (who was Nora Barnacle) and his other child, Lucia.

Joyce's favourite restaurant in Paris is Fouquet's. He likes the opera, the theatre (never misses a Thursday matinée), song recitals and even the movies. His favourite opera is *William Tell*, which he has heard dozens of times. The only thing he drinks is white wine. At present he is in Zürich. Giorgio had a letter from him recently. It began 'Dear Oigroig and Neleh'. That's backward for Giorgio and Helen, the latter being Mrs Oigroig. It ended 'With much love, Obbab'. Obbab is backward for Babbo which means Daddy in Italian. Babbo has been James Joyce's family nickname for thirty years.

NOTES

Giorgio (George) Joyce (1905–1976), Joyce's only son.
  1. *Finnegans Wake* was published in May 1939.

Worth Half-a-Dozen Legations*

KENNETH REDDIN

The first time I met Joyce he was living in the Rue de Grenelle. I went down armed with a box of Olhausen's black puddings. I did this on Paddy Tuohy's advice – I mean on the advice of my friend, the late Patrick Tuohy, RHA,[1] at that time living in Paris, having completed the now famous portrait of Joyce's father and one of Joyce himself. Tuohy wired me just in time. James's birthday was approaching. He loved Olhausen's black puddings. They recalled his student days in Dublin. So I came armed with them, and Tuohy and I enjoyed them, too, that night in the Rue de Grenelle.

The strongest man is he who stands most alone. Ibsen's dictum was especially true of Joyce in letters. He stood aloof from other writers, having set them a new fashion in prose. He remained completely islanded in his own consciousness, or rather in that of the Dublin of thirty years ago. In that consciousness he worked slowly, laboriously, with his failing sight, like a spider at the intricacies of his web. External contacts occurred, but unless they were relevant to the world of Dublin he had created he took no interest in them.

In his linen coat, his legs tucked under him on the divan, leaning back to ease the pain in his eyes, or listening to your news of the new Dublin, he looked a little bored and exotic. And the blond face, the neat moustache and the air of personal aloofness were a little chilling, conveying mostly that your news was no news at all to him. Which was probably true. His flat was full of Irish newspapers – even provincial ones – and I remember his quoting quips made by witnesses in my own court in Kilmainham.

One night, dining in a restaurant – I think it was the Trianon, opposite the Mont Parnasse Station – he took Tuohy and myself on (as the phrase is) in an effort of photographic memory. After twenty years' absence he challenged us, who had just left Dublin, to name the shops from Amiens Street Station to the Pillar. First one side, and then down the other. Mostly he was three or four shops in front of us. When Tuohy and I left a gap, he filled it. When we named a new proprietor,

* *Irish Times* (Dublin), 14 January 1941, p. 6

he named, and remembered the passing of, the old. I remember his flat in the Rue de Grenelle, and, later, the one up off the Etoile. I remember them for him, for Mrs Joyce's beautiful Galway voice, her hospitality and constant good humour; remembered them for the good Irish whiskey they provided, for the Dublin street ballads sung by the host himself, and for the ever-changing sense of a Dublin transported abroad.

I was the Irish delegate to the International Congress of PEN in Paris in 1937. Immediately I arrived Joyce rang me. He subsequently attended one of the meetings, receiving an ovation, and delivered a speech on the pirated editions of *Ulysses* in America. At the banquet held at the close of the Congress he personally organised an Irish table, presided at it and, again receiving an ovation from a very distinguished literary gathering, made a short speech in reply to the toast 'Ireland'. Afterwards in the foyer in the hotel a whole world of writers surrounded him.

Joyce was worth half a dozen Irish Legations in any country he had chosen to live in. All European writers knew of him, and he took care to let them know that he was Irish. In making Dublin famous he made Ireland famous in European letters.

NOTE

Kenneth Reddin (1895–1967), Irish novelist, playwright, and District Justice.

James Joyce in Paris*

MARY COLUM

Joyce loved restaurants, liked being among the crowd in them, and would go for long stretches to the same restaurant every evening for dinner, entertaining his friends lavishly. For years he frequented the Trianons, near the Montparnasse station, where he had a favourite table and a favourite waiter, Norbert, who frequently, when he was alone and drank too much, escorted him home. Once, in the absence of his wife on a vacation, he invited a number of friends to dinner,

* Extracted from *Life and the Dream* (Garden City, N.Y.: Doubleday, 1947) pp. 385–9. Editor's title.

where everybody drank a great deal of champagne, and Joyce, departing in an expansive mood, presented an array of bowing waiters, who had not been attached to his table, with a hundred francs each. I, backed by either the proprietor or the headwaiter, collected the hundred-franc bills from the waiters, giving them ten francs instead. As they had performed no service, even this might be called extravagant. We all escorted Joyce, whose continuous smile showed how happy he was over the whole proceedings, home in a couple of taxicabs. One of us put him to bed. I fished up an envelope, put in it the hundred-franc bills I had retrieved from the waiters, placing the whole under a clock on the mantelpiece for him to find in the morning.

The last time we were in Paris, in 1938, he had exchanged his old restaurant, Trianons, for Fouquet's in the Champs Elysées, which had the clientele of a New York night club and was filled by the world of fashion, of art, of the theatre and the cinema. When any visitors came over from Dublin he would invite them to dinner at a restaurant: he was so happy when any Dubliner understood his work and liked it, especially if he was a non-literary personage. Once when we were in a café in Montmartre, a Dubliner who recognised my husband came over and spoke to him. He was over in Paris to attend a football match between an Irish and a French team, one of those teams that our friend Abel Chevalley had fostered: like many simple Dubliners he was soaked in *Ulysses* though he made no pretence of literary sophistication. Immediately we knew he was the very type Joyce would like, and I telephoned to ask if we might bring him round. Joyce was alone in his apartment; it was Sunday, and the family had gone somewhere. He answered enthusiastically, 'Bring him right over'. The Dublin citizen was a little dazzled, but he was delighted to come. What particularly fascinated Joyce was that this guest belonged to a family of old Dublin glassmakers, the Pughs, and represented an item he wanted for *Finnegans Wake*; the careful reader can find it there. He handed a copy of *Ulysses* to the guest and asked him to read a chapter aloud in the accent of a lower quarter of the city, the Coombe. The visitor produced something that enchanted Joyce and showed that he must have read parts of *Ulysses* aloud many times and could reproduce the exact low-down Dublin accent necessary for this particular episode. Joyce, obviously delighted, felt that here was a simple citizen for whom *Ulysses* was a national masterpiece. Once, I remember, when asked where he would like best to live, he said slyly, 'In a city of about half a million population, an old city built on a river with a woman's name.' 'And with a castle inside a courtyard,' I suggested, 'a villainous castle with a villainous history.' He nodded.

But any hopes he had that Dublin would give him some official recognition were vain: no Irish writer except Bernard Shaw received official recognition in our time, and he only when a very old man, after he had written a letter flattering to the government. Yeats was made a senator, but that was because he had been associated with the Nationalist movement all his life.

Joyce was a very lonely man who paid dearly for his fame, though, maybe, if he had not had the fame, things might have been even more desolate for him: he did actually enjoy the attention that his fame brought him. Like all outstanding figures, he aroused jealously and malevolence, and a prying into his private affairs with a misinterpretation of them. One to whom he had been kind and hospitable wrote the most poisonous attack on him that I have ever read on anybody: it not only concerned itself with Joyce, but with his family and friends, his father and his wife. How it ever got published I cannot understand. We kept it out of his way for years, but, eventually hearing of it, he insisted on procuring it; he was deeply hurt because of its effect of humiliating his family. Then he would receive the most violently insulting letters in answer to a simple request. No doubt he had what might be called a persecution complex, but really this was not surprising, for he was actually persecuted. Against all this, he had the most attached friends, for he was a reliable friend himself and would help one with any old thing – to find an apartment or a maid or a doctor, how to plan a journey or pick out a hotel. He gave a great deal of consideration to such things, and if any of his friends were ill he would shower them with attentions and gifts of wine. When we lived in Paris he would telephone every day to find out how we were and how things were going with us. On his side he expected a lot of attention and help of all kinds from his friends: he really was not very far from blindness, and consequently he had to have a great deal of help for *Finnegans Wake*, not only help in putting it together, but for the reading of the necessary obscure references, books of every kind from the *Arabian Nights* to old-time Dublin directories, from the works of Vico to that of some romantic lady author like E. Barrington, who dealt with picturesque historical figures: one volume of hers which particularly interested him I remember because it was about some collateral connections of my own; he examined me minutely concerning what the family traditions about them were, for it was such items that he worked into his scheme of *Finnegans Wake*.

Finnegans Wake, as his friend Eugene Jolas has pointed out, seemed in the end to be almost a collective work, so many friends helped him with the minutiae of it, though of course, the moulding of the material, the whole creative energy in it, the pattern, was Joyce's own. Stuart Gilbert, who wrote so much on his work, helped him regularly and tirelessly; my husband helped him whenever he was in Paris,[1] and of his help he was very demanding because of the Dublin connection and because of a native knowledge of the history, the personages, the topography that Joyce was putting into the work. In Joyce's study in his apartment in Square Robiac, he would have a bottle of white chianti on the table, a medley of books and notebooks, a gramophone somewhere near: surrounded by such items, he and his helper set to work. The amount of reading done by his helpers was librarious, as he might have written himself, as were the notebooks filled with the results of their reading which generally boiled down to only a line or a paragraph. His great helper outside the literary people was Sylvia Beach, who, with her friend, Arienne Monnier, had been the original publisher of *Ulysses*, an undertaking of great financial risk. They were certainly sound critics, because they knew what the book was about, and in the end they had a share in the author's fame.

I think Joyce was very demanding on both of them, especially on his great friend, Miss Beach: he never knew when his demands were too onerous, and then there were always a few people who tried to make a breach between them. Joyce had undertaken in his family life more than other men, because he was not only a genius but the one member of his family who had much practical sense. It was he who arranged every family detail, wrote every letter, engaged apartments, arranged for vacations, treatment of illnesses, and everything else, for he had a particularly helpless family. I am not sure that any of them ever read a thing he wrote – he told me once with amusement that he asked them where one could find samples of Irish humour, expecting that they might have found some specimens in *Ulysses*, but he found them innocent of the whole work. For all that, he loved them devotedly and had a united family life until the late 1920s. His son had married a beautiful American girl,[2] who not only had an independent income, but produced what Joyce wanted, a grandson who was named after the hero of *Portrait of the Artist*, Stephen, with the addition of his own name, James. His son, Giorgio, had no religious affiliations, and neither had his daughter-in-law, an American of Jewish descent, yet when their son was born they fell into the pattern of the French life around them and had the child baptised in a Catholic church.

It was a curious ceremony, with neither the father nor the mother showing any familiarity with religious ritual; my husband and I had been picked as godparents, but the grandfather was to be kept in ignorance of the whole proceedings, as it was felt he might disapprove of this recognition of a sacrament of the Church. Though I carefully schooled my husband in the questions and answers of the ritual, his French like Yeats's, being somewhat hazy, yet he got so mixed up in the '*Je renonce*'s', the '*J'accepte*'s', the '*oui*'s' and the '*non*'s' that when the priest put the routine questions as to whether, on behalf of the child, he renounced the devil and all his works and pomps, he promptly answered 'Non', so that to this day I am not certain whether Stephen James is a Christian, a pagan or a Manichaean heretic. Also, at a strategic moment, my mind slipped on a sentence in the Apostles's Creed, and, to crown all, the officiating priest wound up by asking graciously, 'Est-ce que l'enfant est le petit fils de M James Joyce, le célèbre écrivain?'[3] We were all panic-striken for fear the news of the ceremony would get into the papers and we would all be put on the carpet by Joyce, for at this period he believed all religion to be a sort of elegant traditional symbolism or else a sort of black magic. However, he did not hear of it until some years later, when I accidentally revealed it to him, but then it made no difference one way or another, for his mind had marched in another direction.

NOTES

Mary Colum (1887–1957), Irish critic and autobiographer; wife of Padraic Colum (1881–1972), the poet. The Colums lived in Paris and Nice from 1930 to 1933.

1. See, for example, Padraic Colum, 'Working with Joyce', *Irish Times* (Dublin), 5 October 1956, p. 5; 6 October 1956, p. 7.
2. Giorgio Joyce married Helen Fleischman on 10 December 1930.
3. 'Is the child the grandson of Mr James Joyce, the famous writer?'

Some Recollections of James Joyce: in London*

SYLVIA LYND

When I met James Joyce, he was engaged on *Work in Progress* and had just completed *Anna Livia Plurabelle*. At that first meeting at Scott's one Sunday evening he set out to be as strange and difficult as possible, for on that particular occasion he would speak no language but Italian, which the rest of the party unfortunately could not speak, and would address no one except his daughter and very few words to her. Our hosts were the Herbert Hugheses. There must have been plenty of lively

* Extracted from *Time and Tide* (London), 22 (25 January 1941) 65–6.

chatter at the table; but I remember only Joyce's obdurate silence and Joyce himself, tall, slim, delicate, with a high, narrow head (a typical Leinster man); eyes blue and blind, it seemed, behind thick glasses; finely-made hands, a slender neck, a chin-tuft and a pale check tie fastened with a little brooch in the form of a bee. He drank only white wine, and this later proved to be one of his characteristics. He would not eat, and this was characteristic too. At the end of the meal, he called for a banana, and afterwards, for a fan, with which he fanned himself a little; and when we rose to go, he put on a straw boater and a second pair of pebble spectacles, and wearing the two pairs came slowly out into Piccadilly, leaning for guidance on Herbert Hughes' arm.

Later that same evening, however, he talked in English quite naturally, and sang songs at the piano. We saw him several times that summer, the Joyces dining with us, we with them. He was always a disconcerting companion, because one could not tell from his unchanging face whether he had heard anything that was said, whether he liked or disliked it, whether he was going to speak or to remain silent. Mrs Joyce, dark and handsome, presided over Jimmy with dignified patience and severity. He was friendly, however, and he noticed more than he seemed to notice. At some point in the acquaintance he must have overheard me say that the book of his that I liked was *Dubliners*, for when we dined with him at the Trocadero, where he could get his favourite wine, a Swiss wine (but a very good wine, improbable as it may sound) he said that I must have a particularly nice pudding because I 'liked *Dubliners*'. 'Would you like an *omelette en surprise*?' I said I didn't know what it was. 'Then you must certainly have *omelette en surprise*,' and he ordered it from the waiter. In case anyone is as ignorant as I was until that evening, let me say that *omelette en surprise* is an ice baked inside a meringue, that it takes a goodish time to make, three-quarters of an hour or so, and that when it appears it is about the size of turkey. As no one at the table except Mrs Joyce and myself would eat any pudding, she and I had to do our best with this gigantic delight and very good it was. (I wish, in spite of the cold weather, that I had some of it now.) We were warried on that occasion not to say in Joyce's presence the word Sullivan, for Sullivan was a tenor with a higher voice than any other tenor and, in Joyce's opinion, a singer of unrecognised talent. Sooner or later, however, some fatal reference was made and Joyce was away on his hobby horse. He had with him in his pocket a manuscript in praise of Sullivan which he wanted to publish anonymously, and we discussed the possibility of Herbert Hughes being able to get it into the *Daily Telegraph*. John Dulanty, the other guest that night, showed me the manuscript under cover of the table: it said something about Sullivan's being a Kerry man, if I remember aright and that his lack of recognition was a matter of considerable keriosity. . . .

Joyce liked a large white plate for an ashtray, so that he could make sure of seeing it and not making a mess with his cigarette ash. He smoked innumerable cigarettes. His songs were old Irish and French airs, sad rather than merry. He had a pretty tenor voice, and a pretty speaking voice, too, but we did not really hear it till he had gone away and sent us his gramophone record of *Anna Livia Plurabelle*. What a fantastic martyr, but what a courageous man.

NOTE

Sylvia Lynd (1888–1952), poet and novelist; wife of Irish essayist and journalist Robert Lynd (1879–1949).

The Living Joyce*

LOUIS GILLET

Last Christmas I was supposed to visit the Red Cross in Geneva, and I wrote to him: 'See you again soon'. The trip, however, was made without me; I could leave only a month later; Joyce had died on the 13th of January.[1]

The following Sunday I arrived in Zürich. It was evening, a dismal evening of thaw, rain and glazed frost. On the wooded hill in back of the city, I had no trouble in finding the villa of Doctor Giedion.[2] I was received as a friend and the writer's son Giorgio gave me an account of his father's last moments. Friday night Joyce was awakened by a fierce pain. He was taken to a clinic. The X-ray revealed a stomach ulcer. Curiously enough, no one had ever suspected this. It was not the first time that such an attack had assailed Joyce, but it had been believed that the gnawing pains were of nervous origin and seemed to present no danger. Joyce ate obviously without appetite, he always toyed with his food as if searching for something, and would then push back his plate with a disgusted look: he could put up with almost no food. We knew him to be frail; nobody was alarmed. He enjoyed entertaining his friends at the restaurants, finding nothing too expensive and too refined for them; he was a regular customer of the Trianon

* *Claybook for James Joyce* (London and New York: Abelard-Schuman, 1958) pp. 80–1.

and Fouquet's where the luxury pleased him as a relaxation after his daily work, but at all these places he barely picked at his food, merely nibbling from his plate some leaves of salad or a piece of cake. He seemed to live on air. His overly delicate system could not endure our food, a most select meal was still too coarse for him. After the first mouthful he would light a cigarette, he had finished his dinner. We did not suspect him to be sick.

On Saturday morning Joyce underwent an emergency operation. He could not meet the challenge and died during the night, at 2 a.m. He was fifty-nine years old.

Giorgio opened a door. On a cushion in the parlour, pale against the black velvet, lay the head of his father. I had a shock: I had not believed I would see him again. A sculptor, M Paul Speck, had taken a casting. The imprint of the left ear lobe had blurred in the plaster. The face lived. His eyelids were closed, but this was not the pose of sleep. Under the short moustache which gave him a pout of disdain, a strange smile played on the edge of his lips. I have never seen him without his sombre myopic lenses which seemed to be part of his person. Now the mask appeared bare, abruptly confessing its truth. At the moment of death, a relaxation takes place, the face seems washed as if a hand had wiped the wrinkles of life from it. This occasionally imparts a spark of youth to the dead, whence the medieval belief that they all have in heaven the common and perfect age of thirty-three.

NOTES

Louis Gillet (1876–1943), French art historian. His relationship with Joyce is described in George Markow-Totévy, 'James Joyce and Louis Gillet', in *A James Joyce Miscellany*, ed. Marvin Magalaner (New York: James Joyce Society, 1957) pp. 49–61.

1. 1941.
2. Carola Giedion-Welcker.

James Joyce as Man and Artist*

C. P. CURRAN

With Joyce dead in Zürich, and an end made to a forty years' friendship, one's thoughts inevitably revert to the first meeting. It was at my first lecture at University College. The class was in English literature, and the lecturer began with Aristotle's Poetics, as seemed to me very right in the circumstances. Towards the end of the lecture the professor put in some remark about Stephen Phillips, who had just written *Paolo and Francesca*. He asked had anyone read it, and then immediately: 'Have you read it, Mr Joyce?' A voice behind me said 'Yes'; I looked around, and saw my first poet.

I grew very familiar with that figure in the next three years, and in my eyes it did not change much in the next forty. Tall, slim and elegant; an erect and loose carriage, an up-tilted, long, narrow head, with a chin that jutted out arrogantly; firm, tight shut mouth, blue eyes that for all their myopic look could glare suddenly or stare with indignant wonder; a high forehead that bulged under stiff-standing hair. Some of these items changed later. The elegant adumbration of a beard tentatively came and went, and the eyes that since then saw and suffered so much were obscured by powerful lenses; but the graceful figure and carriage remained the same, and the cane that replaced the famous ash-plant of his later Dublin days still swung casually, disguising but aiding the dimmed vision.

That is how he looked in Paris, where he lived in the years between the two wars, in different apartments from the Faubourg to the Invalides. The talk within might be as much in Italian as in French, but there were pictures by Jack Yeats looking down from the walls – pictures, I need hardly say, of Anna Liffey – and above them a great woodcarving of the Arms of Dublin, that once looked out on the Liffey herself. And gradually the spirit of Dublin would prevail. He would sing old Tudor songs and Dublin street ballads in an admirable tenor voice, trained years before in Dublin by Signor Palmieri when he won distinction at the Feis Ceoil in 1904. I once asked Joyce when was he coming back to Dublin. 'Why should I?' he said. 'Have I ever left it?'

* *Irish Times* (Dublin), 14 January 1941, p. 6.

And, of course, he never really had. He contained Dublin. His knowledge of the town by inheritance, by observation, by memory was prodigious, and he was at pains to keep his picture of it up to date. When he challenged me to mention some new feature of Dublin to justify his return I could only instance the new smell of petrol. If Dublin were destroyed, his words could rebuild the houses; if its population were wiped out, his books could repeople it. Joyce was many things, but he was certainly the last forty volumes of *Thom's Directory* thinking aloud.

In those eary days, as since, Joyce was a figure apart. It would be easy to exaggerate his apparent arrogance and reserve. If he seemed arrogant and aloof it was a defence. Silently or with some abrupt, devastating phrase he stood in fierce defence of his own integrity – his liberty to think differently. He was far and away the most mature of our student group. We were all conscious of it; cheerfully and disrespectfully aware that he was in correspondence with Ibsen, Arthur Symons and William Archer, and that his verse was beginning to appear in the *Saturday Review*, and his prose in the *Fortnightly*. He was just past eighteen then, reading Danish as well as French and Italian, and his early papers in University College were curiously highly wrought and recondite performances. The casual allusion to the Nolan in the first sentence of the 'Day of the Rabblement' is an instance of the out-of-the-way reading that kept us all guessing.[1] His literary idols of that time – never, I think, to be overthrown – were Dante and Ibsen, and I cannot help thinking that he saw himself in relation to the Ireland of his day as the disdainful Florentine or as Ibsen among the Norse Nationalists.

His later life belongs to world literature, where his influence has been as widespread, as profound and as disruptive as Picasso in painting. He was as great a master of English prose as Yeats was of English verse – that is to say, he was one of the two greatest figures in contemporary English literature. In his last work he chose to abandon the writing of English and to formulate his own idiom. He shattered the categories of time and space, and sought, by the incantation of sound and otherwise, enormously to extend the sensitiveness of our apprehension. The success or failure of this experiment may not be considered here, but it is relevant to the two points which I am content to isolate. The first is the constant preoccupation with Dublin to which I have sufficiently referred, the other is more significant. Joyce lived much of his life in desperate and tragic suffering. We have had in Ireland many generous artists who have not hesitated to mix in public affairs. Joyce was not one of them. To preserve his independence for the sake of his art was with him a passion. It led him to more than one painful parting and through much suffering. The fierce intensity of his will made his life a struggle against circumstance. He followed his inflexible purpose in poverty, in exile, in physical suffering, in good and ill, and even in the manner of his literary expression, with a sort of heroism not easy to understand and certainly not common. The integrity and independence of the artist may be vilified by a catchword. It was the essence of Joyce. One might like at this moment to dwell on his loyalty, his courtesy, his gaiety amongst friends, the galant companionship of his wife. In the end one comes back to this indomitable integrity of his, 'holding to ancient nobleness that high unconsortable one'.

NOTES

Constantine P. Curran (1883–   ) and James Joyce met as fellow students at University College and remained friends throughout Joyce's life.

1. The first sentence of Joyce's essay, 'The Day of the Rabblement', reads:

No man, said the Nolan, can be a lover of the true or the good unless he abhors the multitude; and the artist, though he may employ the crowd, is very careful to isolate himself.

The Nolan is Giordano Bruno of Nola (1548?–1600), a favourite philosopher of Joyce. His name is mentioned constantly in *Finnegans Wake*.

Sisters of James Joyce Mourn for Two Brothers*

Three sisters of James Joyce, the distinguished Irish writer, who died yesterday, talked of a double sorrow as they sat together last night in a top flat in Mountjoy Square, Dublin.

They had heard not only of the death of their brother, James, but also of another brother, Charles, who died at Hastings, Sussex, on Saturday.

One sister was Mrs Eileen Schaurek,[1] with whom James Joyce had

* *Irish Press* (Dublin), 14 January 1941, p. 6.

lived almost continuously in Trieste from 1910 to 1928.

The other sisters were the Misses Florence and Eva Joyce. Another sister, Mrs May Monaghan,[2] lives in Galway, and yet another is a nun in the Mercy Order, Sister Mary Gertrude, in New Zealand.

To their burden of sorrow is added their uncertainty about the fate of a third brother, Stanislaus, who was living in Trieste until the outbreak of war and of whom they have heard no news since.

James Joyce used to write regularly to his sisters in Dublin. 'He always expressed his love of Dublin and of the Dublin people, and often said that he would love to live here again,' said Miss Eva Joyce.

'Was Our Idol'

'He suffered much from rheumatic fever though, and the climate would not suit him.

'However some people may criticise what he wrote, he was our eldest brother and our idol, and to us, at least, his writings had the stamp of genius.

'He had the kindest disposition, hated show and publicity, and spent all his spare time with his family, enjoying trips with them in the French countryside.'

Mrs Schaurek, with whom James Joyce lived while he was working on *Ulysses* and later while he was engaged on his unfinished *Work in Progress*, told me:

'He seemed tireless; wrote everything in his distinctive, though spidery, hand. For leisure, would turn to the piano and sing in a clear tenor voice Irish melodies of the sentimental kind.

'They say he was anti-Catholic, but he never missed a service during all the Holy Weeks he spent with me in Trieste.'

NOTES

1. See Eileen Schaurek's earlier recollections of Joyce, p. 60.
2. See May Monaghan's later recollections of Joyce, p. 182.

Memoir of the Man*

ARTHUR POWER

It was with a shock that I read of the death of James Joyce in the *Irish Times* this morning. Bad news travels quickly even in war-time, and, in spite of the numerous difficulties, people have been asking since the surrender of Paris what had happened to James Joyce and where he was. Now we hear from Zürich that he is dead.

It is hard to write of a man whom one knew well, and who was a true and great friend, while still under the blow of his loss. For Joyce was a gentle and affectionate man who loved his friends, and, in turn, was loved by them. A stray and unknown Irish man in Paris, I experienced, for no other reason but affection, a constant kindness from him, while living very much alone there, for a number of years – years during which he was at the peak of his international fame: a fame which, though he appreciated it, never swerved him to forget the simple and real things of life – his family and his personal friends. His natural nobility was too great to have his balance of life upset by his rise to fame, though a fame as remarkable and widespread as any Irishman has experienced abroad.

A Simple Man

For though in intellect he was complicated by nature, he was a simple man: and a man of fine and delicate sensibility, as an artist must be. Indeed, his genius consisted of two main characteristics – great originality and great sensibility, which amounted to almost super-sensitiveness in his case. As a result, he avoided all excess and lived a very simple life. The programme of his day, when I knew him twenty and fifteen years ago, was generally as follows: He rose fairly late, unless there was purpose otherwise, and generally he went out to lunch in a neighbouring restaurant. After lunch he would return to his flat, somewhere about three, and work until six or seven in the evening; then he used to collect his family and go to dine at the restaurant of a Monsieur Casabelle, close the Gare Montparnasse. There he would dine sparingly: the chief interest of the dinner being in the wine, of

---

* *Irish Times* (Dublin), 14 January 1941, p. 6.

which he was a connoisseur. He would remain there until about nine-thirty, when he would return to his flat, near the Champs de Mars, where he used to remain until twelve or one in the morning discussing literature and various artistic personalities we knew. That was his day's programme, day after day, month after month, during that phase of his life.

As his sight was very bad, I used sometimes to read to him the press cuttings, criticisms of his work, which poured in from different agencies from all parts of the world. When I had read an article, to which he listened very intently, he would make no remark, just a non-committal exclamation. After reading about five or six of these he would stop me, realising, perhaps, that I found it irksome to constantly read praise of another man's work. Then we would broach a bottle of Clos de Saint Patrice, a wine he had discovered while on holiday in the Midi, and we would discuss current artistic events and personalities.

Dublin always formed the chief topic of the conversation. Mostly silent himself, an observant onlooker, he appreciated in these conversations all manner of wit and *feu d'ésprit*,[1] but he could not bear anything in the nature of loose or bawdy talk, and he never discussed women.

His Outlook

In general his outlook might be described as cynical – cynical in the sense that he did not think very much of his life. Indeed, I remember once on my way to dine with him at a restaurant near the Théâtre Odéon during a discussion turning in the street and asking him what his opinion was in regard to a future life. He just replied: 'I don't think much of this'.

And this melancholy was always with him – the melancholy of an idealist. You see it in *The [sic] Portrait of the Artist as a Young Man*, this poetic idealism always struggling against the darker forces of realism – an idealism which in the end is almost overcome in *Ulysses*. And that was the man, a sensitive and poetic idealist, at war – a tentative, but never a conclusive, war – against the dark forces of primitive nature. And as life went on he became more and more interested intellectually in the workings of these forces. But it was his intellect which took him on, not his nature; for the man himself remained detached from life. Indeed, I think he was the most detached man I ever knew – detached in his work and detached in his pleasure.

I often tried to push him into an avowal of faith, or of disbelief, on such vital issues as right and wrong, immortality or extinction; but I could never succeed. There was a common friend of ours, a French woman, an intellectual, who paraded herself very obviously as a

Communist, but she was often to be met dining at expensive restaurants. I asked him how she reconciled it; he shrugged his shoulders at my earnestness and said: 'People can reconcile anything.' That answer was typical of him. Over everything he maintained, by an effort of will often, a neutral opinion; the intellect in him appeared paramount. But underneath this exterior he lived a life of strong emotions, strong likes and strong dislikes. I remember once at a party in his flat, probably in yet another effort to draw him, saying to him: 'You are a man without feelings!' But I will never forget his looking up at me – his blue eyes greatly magnified by his strong glasses – with pained surprise, and saying: 'My God – I a man without feelings!'

But what always worried me was how a man of his refined and delicate sensibility could have written the things he did write in *Ulysses*. But I never got an answer from him. In one of my worst moods I hinted to him that he had done it to gain notoriety; but I had barely uttered it when I withdrew it all, convinced, as I was, from a thousand observations of his absolute integrity. He wrote what he did because he believed it should be written. And he spent years in obscurity and poverty because he would not change so much as a line of it.

The End

Now he is dead, at the age of 58. Death lately has been having rich harvestings among our poets, writers and artists – F. R. Higgins,[2] James Joyce, Sir John Lavery[3] – all within a week.

And no more shall I see him, or spend the Sundays with him as I used to spend them in the artificial grottos under the Palais Blue at St Cloud, drinking *café-au-lait* in the sunshine, looking out over the glass-like Seine, talking of the Dublin he and I knew, and arguing good naturedly over our differences, or spend the evenings in his flat – the room dominated by a big portrait of his father by Patrick Tuohy – near the Champs de Mars, when he would break off his conversation with me to speak to his son about some family business in Italian – for the Joyces, curiously enough, always spoke Italian to one another – the result of their long sojourn in Trieste. Nor will I accept again his kind and constant invitations to dinner at Casabelles; or hear, as when I was lying ill, alone in my studio, the sound of his light footsteps coming up the steep and narrow stairs to inquire after me.

A man's kindness is even more important than his greatness; and in my loneliness in Paris he was my constant friend – the man whom all the world was anxious to meet. And not only was he kind, but all his family as well; his wife, and his children; a charming and human family. Everywhere he went he carried Ireland and Dublin with him, in his mind and heart. He is gone, and Dublin remains, will remain; and yet the majority of the world only knows Dublin through the medium of his personality, the personality of James Joyce. Such is the function of the artist.[4]

NOTES

1. Probably a mistake for *jeu d'esprit*, 'witty or humorous trifle'.
2. Frederick Robert Higgins (1896–1941), Irish poet.
3. Sir John Lavery (1856–1941), Irish painter.
4. See Arthur Power's earlier recollections of Joyce, p. 81.

Joyce's Burial*

HANS GASSER

It was a ghastly winter day with lots of slush coming down from the sky, and there were no taxis any more, as the petrol rationing was very strict. Therefore I took a tram, and in this tram, going up the hill very slowly, there was assembled almost the whole funeral party. I did not know many people, but they were all talking about James Joyce. There was Lord and Lady Derwent; he was cultural attaché at the British Legation in Berne during the war, and there was his eye-doctor, and the secretary of Paul Klee, the painter.

We arrived at the cemetery[1] and were directed into the chapel. But, as James Joyce did not want to have a priest at his funeral, there was nobody there, and the attendants of the mortician did not know what to do, as usually in Switzerland one has a priest, either Catholic or Protestant. The main speech was given by Lord Derwent, who was usually very brisk but, I think, as he had to perform an official duty, he made a rather formal speech.[2] After this we went into the snow again, and the coffin was carried in front of us, and we walked right to the end of the wall, where the hole for the grave was dug.

Meanwhile in the distance there was the faint roar of the wild animals in the zoo, and we stood round the grave, and again didn't quite know what to do, because again there was no priest, and this

---

* Extracted from *Irish Literary Portraits*, ed. W. R. Rodgers (London: British Broadcasting Corporation, 1972) pp. 72–3. Editor's title.

time not even an official funeral speech. So we looked at each other in a very embarrassed way until a very, very old man turned up – obviously a man who hovers over the grave, as one sees in almost every churchyard, men who seem to just wait till they are buried themselves. A tiny man who obviously was deaf, because he went to one of those attendants of the mortician, who was holding the rope which went underneath the coffin, as the coffin was not yet sunk into the grave, and he asked, 'Who is buried here?' And the mortician said, 'Mr Joyce'. And again in front of the whole assemblance of mourners he seemed not to have understood it. He again asked, 'Who is it?' 'Mr Joyce,' the mortician shouted, and at that moment the coffin was lowered into the grave.

NOTES

1. Fluntern Cemetery, Zürich.
2. See Lord Derwent, 'James Joyce: "Hail and Farewell"', in *In Memoriam James Joyce*, ed. C[arola] Giedion-Welcker (Zürich: Fretz & Wasmuth, 1941) pp. 13–15.

I Met James Joyce's Wife*

KEES VAN HOEK

James Joyce died in Zurich in 1941; his widow still lives there.[1] Forty-five years ago, Joyce met the good-looking, auburn-haired girl who had come from Galway to earn her living in Dublin. The natural freshness, good humour and transparent honesty of Nora Barnacle captivated the budding genius, and within four months of their first meeting they set out together from the North Wall on that fabulous voyage through life, which has since become part of the history of literature.

As long as the fame of James Joyce will live, so long will Nora Joyce have her share in it. No other author – living or dead – is being written about so extensively, and that in many lands, as the great Dubliner.

* 'Vignette: Mrs James Joyce', *Irish Times* (Dublin), 12 November 1949, p. 5. Condensed as 'I Met James Joyce's Wife', *Irish Digest* (Dublin), 35 (February 1950) 23–5.

No biography fails to pay affectionate tribute to her all-important share in the ultimate success of that life.

She is in her sixties now, medium of height, somewhat plumpish. The auburn tresses have long since turned to carefully coiffed grey curls. Her face is still as soft of cheek and as fresh of complexion as a colleen's; her eyes, under the long, silken lashes, are the blue of a Connemara lake. Most Irish in her is the longish upper lip and the soft, warm voice; well-nigh half a century of Continental wanderings (she speaks French, German and Italian fluently) has not blurred her endearing brogue.

Of late, arthritis is crippling her. She goes about slowly, at times painfully, with the help of a stick. Even that has not affected her serenity, her impeccable poise, her almost regal appearance, which strikes one most on meeting her. Not that there is anything stuck-up about it. She herself has dismissed her origin as humble, and her roguish humour never had time or temper for artificiality. She is what she has always been – her natural self.

Her brow is not noticeably high, yet it makes a very intelligent forehead, the mirror of a mind, the greatest asset of which is its sure instinctive wisdom and unobtrusive skill. Not an intellectual, she is one of the most intelligent women that one could meet, a shrewd, sound judge.

Her attitude towards life has been always essentially realistic, and thus she provided an ideal counterweight to her husband. Of her skill, not to say courage, the very life story of James Joyce bears eloquent testimony.

When they set out from Dublin on his hegira, years of poverty or penury lay in store for them before the world accepted him. It was all the harder, living in a far foreign land; the more so as the battle for their daily bread was ever overshadowed by an even harder battle that she had to help him to fight, for what can be more terrifying to a writer than a constant affection of his eyes?

Forty-one years they lived together. Every nook and cranny of Joyce's life has been illuminated by modern biographers. The one picture that emerges is one of ideal domestic happiness, an enjoyment of each other's company that never waned. Ever devoted to and considerate of each other, she made his home, kept his body and soul together. She had mastered the art of listening with a receptiveness which quickened his mind.

Later, when success came in torrential abundance, she guarded him against hangers-on and victimisers of genius, the 'head hunters', as she called them. But to those whose company stimulated her husband she was by unanimous testimony, an ideal hostess, her conversational *raillerie* as spirited as her cooking was excellent.

In his dedication to her of his first published work, *Chamber Music*, Joyce testified that 'his love is his companion'. The remembrance of that love is what she lives with, and the world's recognition of his genius. I spent a month last year in the same Zürich *pension* where she lives.

Thus I know that not a day went by without a letter or a cutting or a visit of someone wanting her to autograph one of his books. Thus I learned to know her generous, warm-hearted, humorous, lovable Irishness – so very Irish still, that she would good-naturedly upbraid me if I left the house too late on a Sunday morning to be in time for the beginning of Mass, for she herself is a practising Catholic.

Her son, Giorgio, visits her daily and frequently startles her anew by his striking similarity – in build, face and mannerisms – to his father. Her only daughter is in a sanatorium in France; her only grandson, Stephen Joyce, now a strapping boy of seventeen, is at College in the United States.

Hers is a lonely life, and once a week she goes up to the Fluntern Cemetery. One morning I met her there by chance, sitting on a bench underneath the barren silver birches, gazing out on the city spread below along the lake against a backcloth of snow-covered Alpine peaks, and she remarked that the loveliest word in the German language is that for cemetery, *Friedhof*, 'homestead of peace'.

Last October she journeyed to Paris to stay with Mrs Eugene Jolas, who organised the Joyce Exhibition, which was so much the rage of Paris that it was even televised. Harriet Weaver, the English Mæcenas who enabled Joyce to work without financial worries in the later years of his life, came over for it and stayed with Sylvia Beach, who, as 'Shakespeare & Co.', was the original publisher of *Ulysses*.

The wealth of its exhibits showed how Dublin, eternally metamorphic and beautiful, was ever in Joyce's mind. All its exiled son's work is an invocation of Dublin and its people. It is as symbolic as a liturgy, as telling as the ring which was James Joyce's most precious present to his wife, and which Nora Joyce always wears: a big, magnificently set aquamarine – the stone symbolic of the River Liffey – the present commemorating the day he wrote *finis* to *Finnegans Wake*.

NOTE

1. Nora Joyce died on 10 April 1951.

James Joyce's 'Nurse' Remembers*

PETER LENNON

'I won't get out. I will not!' Sylvia Beach sat up in her highbacked chair and thumped the armrests vigorously with her fists; her eyes, alert and quick as a teenager's, darted around the cluttered room looking for someone to glare at. 'What does a man want with 500 houses?'

'What does he want with them?'

'Speculation! It's happening all over Paris now. They buy up all these old houses where the rents of the apartments are still very low because you are not allowed to increase them, and then they give the tenant a chance to buy his apartment. But at a huge sum! If you haven't the money, you get out. So it looks as if he will get me out.

'I have been here since the First World War. When they interned me during the Second World War I closed Shakespeare and Company down below and later moved up here. I have lived now for forty-two years in the old book shop or up here.'

The chilly old apartment was swamped with books. Everywhere you turned there were books; on shelves, under your feet, scattered across the tables, strewn on the floor. And clutters of pictures everywhere. Joyce with his eye-patch; a handsome young Hemingway; Eliot frowning, thin lipped; Ezra Pound reclining languidly in a chair; Scott Fitzgerald sitting on the doorstep of the bookshop smirking at a stout, stolid Adrienne Monnier.

'Is there nothing you can do?'

'What can I do? I never had any money. You don't make money off books – unless you write a best-seller and they are rare. And how can I make money at my age?'

'How old. . . ?'

'Oh, you needn't be cautious asking me my age,' she cut in. 'I'm seventy-four. I think when you have managed to last that long you should be proud of it. I am. There is nothing wrong with me either . . . Except that I am a bit deaf.'

You had the feeling that if you asked her to do a jig, she'd be up

* *Irish Digest* (Dublin), 74 (June 1962) 61–4. Condensed from the *Guardian* (London).

like a shot. A friend told me that quite recently he had seen her
swinging away at a pile of wood with an axe nearly as big as herself.
She was watching me closely and came out with a direct answer to my
thoughts: 'Joyce always said that I had great energy. Let's hope, he
would say, Sylvia's energy will never diminish. And it hasn't!

'Do you know, he was nearly going to take this place one time. When
I was living downstairs in the bookshop he sent his son to have a look
at it. But it wasn't modern enough for him. There is no bathroom, you
know. He had very high-falutin' ideas.'

'I thought he never had much money?'

'He hadn't – not until towards the end when Miss Weaver took care
of him. She never wanted it to be known how much she gave him but
I can tell you it was a perfect fortune. But when he came here from
Trieste he had nothing.

'I helped him a lot. But he was very demanding and spent money
like water if he had it. Every time he travelled with his wife and family,
he always put up at palaces. He liked the grand style.'

'He was supposed to have had a beautiful singing voice?'

'He thought so, anyway. He thought that he and John McCormack
should have had twin careers.

'You know anyone who took up with Joyce had to take care of all
his problems. He was very demanding. He thought that people had
nothing else to do but read his books. If you did anything for him you
did everything. Just like a nurse with a child.' She laughed.

'Sometimes I would want to get away for a few days to a little cottage
I had in the country but Joyce would want me to stay and take care of
his business. When I would go he would pursue me. He would bombard
me with letters and telegrams. I never saw such a man! He was a
perfect octopus!'

'Didn't people get tired of his demands?'

'Ah no! We liked him too much. And he was perfectly charming.
Mind you, he was not liked at dinners and things like that because he
had no small talk, but with people he knew, he was a delightful man.
And then he was a great worker.

'In Trieste he worked for hours in the Berlitz to support his family
and then wrote his books at night. Nothing could put him off – even
failing eyesight. He still worked on when he was practically blind. I
helped him because he helped himself. He was never a slacker. If he
was,' she said with the air of a severe schoolmistress, 'I would never
have helped him. He did great work . . . *Finnegans Wake* – you could
swim around in that! I thought Yeats was pale beside him.'

'Did you not publish anyone else?'

'How could I? I was too busy with Joyce. D. H. Lawrence wanted
me to publish *Lady Chatterley's Lover*, but I didn't want to. He had his

publisher and people to take care of him: Joyce had no one. . . . In any case I did not like his work. It was all preaching, preaching. . . . It's nobody's duty to go in for sex if he doesn't want to, is it?

'They always said that Joyce was very nice the way he would never say a bad word about anyone else's writing, but the truth is they never existed for him. He only read his own work. Of course, he had reading he loved, and when, for example, his daughter was illustrating Chaucer,[1] he would read Chaucer, but he never read the new stuff . . .

'But towards the 'thirties I did get a bit tired. He was having all this trouble with pirated editions of *Ulysses* in America, and he wanted me to go over and take care of his affairs. He did not like it when I would not go, but how could I?'

'Did he not get any help from Ireland?'

'Not at all. People don't realise that for those years between the wars he was entirely out of touch with Ireland. He would write to a friend to check a name of a street or a public-house, but that's about all.'

'And you never went to Ireland?'

'I never had time while Joyce was alive. But when I had an exhibition of the 'twenties in London a couple of years ago, I rushed over to have a look at Ireland. For me Ireland was so much Joyce and Joyce so much Ireland.'

'They are turning the Martello Tower into a Joyce Museum and opening it on 16 June. Are you going over?'

'Yes, I know. Bloomsday. I was the one who called it Bloomsday. I didn't invent much but I did invent that. . . . I would like to go over. I think we all should go over, Samuel Beckett, Stuart Gilbert. . . . But how can I with this trouble with the apartment?'[2]

She led me out into the stone-flagged hallway. An oil stove took the chill out of the great cluttered room inside but the heat did not come out this far. 'Be sure now,' she said, 'not to make out that I said Joyce was full of faults. He had faults like anyone else, but he was a delightful man – and then, not everyone has genius.'

NOTES

1. Lucia Joyce's decorative alphabet was used in *A Chaucer ABC*, which was published privately in July 1936.

2. Although Sylvia Beach said she would not be going to Dublin for the opening of the James Joyce Museum, she was there according to the *Irish Times* (Dublin), 16 June 1962, p. 10 ('An Irishman's Diary'). Incidentally, Sylvia Beach herself has a short piece on that same page, entitled 'Portrait of the Artist'.

Sister*

MAY JOYCE MONAGHAN

Miss Steloff introduced us, and Mrs Monaghan, sitting down on a blue-painted bentwood chair that stood amid a great clutter of books, said politely, 'Oh, I've had a wonderful time over here, and met so many interesting people. Mme Steloff has been very good. The big event, of course, was the meeting of the Joyce Society. Maria Jolas was there, and Padraic Colum interviewed me with a tape recorder, asking me for my recollections of my brother.'

We inquired of Mrs Monaghan whether she was often interviewed in Dublin on the subject of her brother.

'No, not really,' she said. 'I think people over here are much more interested in my brother than the people of Ireland are. In Dublin, people don't talk so much about him. The literary section there, they're not so interested in him. It takes the Americans, with their enthusiasm. Quite a few American people have come to see me from time to time to ask me questions about my brother. Of course, they want to know what I remember about him, and what he was like at home; they want to know whether the family recognised when he was young that he showed signs of becoming famous in the literary field. Being interviewed about my brother is not easy for me. The main reason is that I was so much younger than Jim – eight years younger – and I was just a child when he was a grown student. When you're growing up in a family, you're not looking for this, that, and the other thing that in future you're going to tell about. There were ten of us at home, and because I was so far down in the family, I suppose, Jim and I weren't really intimate. But he was very gentle with me. He was a warm man. He wasn't cold, as some people have implied. Like shy people, he would build up a wall. But he had great warmth. Jim had a very good voice. He was a tenor. He liked to sing Moore's melodies, and he would often sing things from *Aïda* and *Tosca*. My father sang well, too. Jim was very proud of Father; he was amused by his wit. In *A Portrait of the Artist as a Young Man*, he portrayed my father as a character and a wit but a man who squandered money. Father was a man-about-town, and, like a lot of such men at that period, he drank a good deal and would spend a lot of time at the Ormond Hotel or at the old Brazen

* Extracted from the *New Yorker*, 40 (14 March 1964) 35–6.

Head,[1] which is still there, I think. About my mother I think Jim had remorse. He hurt her badly by his way of life. She always was ambitious for him. She knew that he was very clever and probably would make a name in writing, but she was saddened by his falling away from the Church. I think my father would have preferred it if Jim had taken a more ordinary way of life. I was only fourteen when my brother left Dublin. He was very much in the public eye by then. When the *Portrait* was published, it really embarrassed us a lot to see the family details given to the public. Later, when *Ulysses* came out, the rest of the family were shocked quite a bit, too. But we were always proud of Jim, even if we were embarrassed by what he produced. I've read through his books, except for *Finnegans Wake*. I can't read *Finnegans Wake*. I've heard portions read and I could make sense of those parts, but I can't read it myself. The books I understood best were *Dubliners* and the *Portrait*.

'The last time I saw Jim was in 1909 or 1910,[2] when he came back to Dublin from Trieste for a brief stay. In later years, I didn't have much contact with him, even through the post. He sent cards, mostly, and unfortunately we didn't keep any. He didn't write much to anyone in Dublin, you know. What he generally wrote was greetings from himself and his family at birthdays and at Easter, and they'd all sign their names. His son, Giorgio, lives in Munich now – he works for a bank, I think – and his daughter, Lucia, is still in a hospital in England, where she has been for years. Of our family, there are just myself and my two sisters now – Florence, who lives in Dublin, and Margaret (we always called her Poppy), who is a nun in New Zealand. In Dublin, I live with my son, who works in a bank, and my four grandchildren, and they do keep me on the go.'

NOTES

At the behest of the James Joyce Society, one of Joyce's sisters, Mrs May Monaghan, paid a visit to New York from her home in Dublin. Her principal hostess was Mrs Frances Steloff, the founder of the Society and the proprietor of the Gotham Book Mart, where this interview with Mrs Monaghan took place. Mrs Monaghan died in 1966.

1. The Brazen Head continued until 1985.
2. In 1909.

Ecce Puer*

STEPHEN JOYCE

We met up with James Joyce's grandson, a blue-eyed, redcheeked fifteen-year-old, in an apartment on Central Park West the other afternoon. He bears the name Stephen, as did a famous character of his grandfather's before him. Young Stephen was spending his Easter holidays from Andover with his uncle, Robert N. Kastor,[1] treasurer of the Camillus Cutlery Company, who has been supervising his career since he arrived here from Zürich in December. With a lilt that almost hid the merest hint of a Teutonic accent, Stephen told us right off that he hadn't read any of his grandfather's works except a handful of poems, among them 'Ecce Puer', in which Joyce sang of the death of his father and the birth of Stephen. 'I don't think I'm old enough to read James Joyce,' Stephen told us, 'and anyhow English is my worst subject. I think mostly in German now, because I've been studying that language in Switzerland. In English, I like Wild West stories by Zane Grey. My favourite poem is 'Sohrab and Rustum'. When we were in St Gérand-le-Puy, near Vichy, before the Germans came in 1940, Grandfather lived quite near, and he used to drop in before breakfast to talk to me about Greek mythology. I'm afraid I've forgotten most of it now.' 'Do you remember who Dedaius was?' we inquired. 'Wasn't he a Greek in a big battle with somebody?' said Stephen. 'More or less,' we said tactfully. 'Grandfather told me a lot of old Irish stories, too,' young Stephen continued. 'There was one about two giants – an Irish giant named Finnegan and an English giant – and they got into a fight and one pulled up a piece of Ireland and the other pulled up a piece of England and then they threw the pieces at each other, and the pieces made the Isle of Man. Grandfather was always buying me candy, which made my father scold, but Grandfather went on giving it to me anyhow. Grandfather had a hard time living in France before the Germans took all of the country, and it was only the money he got through the American Embassy that made it possible for us to get to Zürich. My father, you know, is Giorgio Joyce, who has a good bass but isn't known to the world, so I guess we all depended on Grandfather. He had a fine tenor himself – he didn't know whether he wanted to be a writer or a singer when he was young – and you

* *New Yorker*, 23 (5 April 1947) 26–7.

can find out what I say is true if you listen to his records of *Finnegans Wake*.' Stephen's father who was given an Italian name because he was born in Trieste, is a professional concert singer.

Stephen, we discovered as we went along, could, from a hereditary standpoint, stroll right into *Ulysses* without feeling very much out of things. He's Irish on his father's side, Jewish on his mother's,[2] and a Catholic, although his father isn't a churchgoing man; neither was his grandfather, for that matter. In Zürich, to which the Joyces repaired just before the Nazis moved into unoccupied France, and where James Joyce died when Stephen was going on nine, Stephen attended a Catholic school – apparently a more attractive one than the Jesuit establishment described by Joyce in *A Portrait of the Artist as a Young Man*. 'I must say,' said Stephen, 'I liked Zürich better than I like America, but perhaps that's because I've only been here a short while. I was on the soccer team of my school there,' he added with a note of satisfaction. 'I've learned it's soccer, not football, since I came here.'

Mr Kastor arrived at the apartment at this point and reached full oral spate on the subject of James Joyce almost before he had removed his coat. 'He was a simple man,' said Mr Kastor, 'never excited, and I still like to think of the times at my sister's house when he would sit there with a glass of white wine in his hand and a smile on his face listening to Maria Jolas play the piano. His diction was as easy as yours or mine, but he had six or seven languages at his beck and call. He always wrote with a shelfful of dictionaries, putting everything down in longhand, and often splattering his pages with ink because of his poor eyesight. His eyes, though, weren't nearly as bad near the end of his life as they were in his middle years, and when Stevie used to take walks with him, he didn't even wear the patch over the left one, as he did when I first met him. He was bitter only about the reception of *Finnegans Wake*, which he expected to cause a lot more excitement than it did. He was sure both *Finnegans* and *Ulysses* were fine material for Hollywood movies, and he even made an outline for a movie of *Finnegans Wake*. His royalties, I suppose you know, were tied up in England and the United States by the war, and even now his widow is trying to get funds released from England to support herself in Zürich. All Joyce's American royalties go to his executors in London, and they are promptly frozen on arrival there.' 'All Grandfather's actual writings seem to have gone,' Stephen interrupted. 'Daddy possibly still has a copy of *Finnegans Wake* in Grandfather's own script – good handwriting, too – but all the others, except a poem to my grandmother, on parchment, were probably taken by the Germans.' 'Would you like to hear a recording Joyce made of *Finnegans Wake*?' Mr Kastor asked. We said we would, and the Irish tenor on the phonograph sounded sweet indeed as it told of Anna Livia Plurabelle.

NOTES

1. Helen Joyce's brother.
2. Stephen's mother was Helen Fleischman.

Additional Bibliography

The references in this list – arranged alphabetically – comprise secondary material, which may be of use in additional fields of biographical inquiry.

Antoni, Claudio, 'A Note on Trieste in Joyce's Time', *James Joyce Quarterly*, 9 (Spring 1972) 318–9 (the main historical and cultural aspects when Joyce lived there).

Barnes, Djuna, 'James Joyce', *Vanity Fair*, 18 (April 1922) 65, 104 (interview discussion of Joyce in Paris, by a fellow novelist).

Beach, Sylvia, 'Portrait of the Artist', *Irish Times* (Dublin), 16 June 1962, p. 10 (Joyce in Paris in the 1920s).

Benco, Aurelia Gruber, 'Between Joyce and Benco', *James Joyce Quarterly*, 9 (Spring 1972) 328–33 (the relationship between Joyce and his friend the Italian critic and publisher Silvio Benco, by Benco's daughter).

Benco, Silvio, 'James Joyce in Trieste', *Pergaso*, 2 (8 August 1930) 150–65. Reprinted as 'Ricordi di Joyce', *Umana*, 20 (May–September 1971) 6–12; in English translation as 'James Joyce in Trieste', *Bookman* (New York), 72 (December 1930) 375–80; and in *Portraits of the Artist in Exile* ed. Willard Potts (Seattle and London: University of Washington Press, 1979) pp. 49–58 (memoir by Joyce's close friend the critic and publisher).

Borach, Georges, 'Gespräche mit James Joyce', *Neue Zürcher Zeitung*, no. 827 (3 May 1931) 3. Reprinted in English translation as 'Conversations with James Joyce', *College English*, 15 (March 1954) 325–7; in *Meanjin*, 13 (Spring 1954) 393–6; in *London Magazine*, 1 (November 1954) 75–8; and in *Portraits of the Artist in Exile*, ed. Potts, pp. 69–72.

Bradley, Bruse, SJ, *James Joyce's Schooldays* (Dublin: Gill & Macmillan, 1982) (Joyce at Clongowes Wood College, 1888–91; and at Belvedere College, 1893–8).

Budgen, Frank, 'Further Recollections of James Joyce', *Partisan Review*, 23 (1956) 530–44. Reprinted in *James Joyce and the Making of 'Ulysses'* (Bloomington, Ind.: Indiana University Press, 1960) pp. 314–28.

——, 'James Joyce', *Horizon*, 4 (1941), 104–8 (obituary memoir and tribute).

——, 'Joyce and Martha Fleischmann: a Witness's Recollection', *Tri-Quarterly*, 8 (Winter 1967) 189–94 (Budgen was called on to play a part as figurant in the Martha Fleischmann episode in Joyce's life).

——, 'Mr Joyce', in *Myselves When Young* (London and New York: Oxford University Press, 1970) pp. 181–204 (recollections).

Carens, James F., 'Joyce and Gogarty', in *New Light on Joyce from the Dublin Symposium*, ed. Fritz Senn (Bloomington, Ind.: Indiana University Press, 1972) pp. 28–45 (Gogarty's relationship with Joyce, and his role as Buck Mulligan in *Ulysses*.

Churchill, Thomas, 'An Interview with Anthony Burgess', *Malahat Review*, 17 (January 1971) 103–27 (brief comments on Joyce's life).

Colum, Mary, 'A Little Knowledge of Joyce', *Saturday Review of Literature* (New York), 33 (29 April 1950) 10–12. Condensed as 'He Thought He Knew Joyce', *Irish Digest* (Dublin), 37 (September 1950) 39–41 (replies to Oliver St John Gogarty's attack on the 'Joyce legend' in his *Irish Digest* article, 'They Think They Know Joyce').

——, and Padraic Colum, *Our Friend James Joyce* (Garden City, N.Y.: Doubleday, 1958) (recollections by a couple who knew Joyce during all of his creative life).

Colum, Padraic, '[Homage to Joyce]', *transition* (Paris), no. 21 (March 1932) 244 (poem).

——, 'In Memory of James Joyce', in *Twelve and a Tilly: Essays on the Occasion of the 25th Anniversary of Finnegans Wake*, ed. Jack P. Dalton and Clive Hart (Evanston, Ill.: Northwestern University Press, 1965) pp. 9–10 (poem).

——, 'The Joyce I Knew', *Saturday Review of Literature* (New York), 23 (22 February 1941) 11 (Letter to the Editor in reply to Gogarty's portrait of Joyce).

——, 'The Joyce I Knew', in *The Joyce We Knew*, ed. Ulick O'Connor (Cork: Mercier Press, 1967) pp. 63–91.

——, 'A Portrait of James Joyce', *New Republic*, 66 (13 May 1931), 346–8. Reprinted in *The Faces of Five Decades*, ed. Robert B. Luce (New York: Simon and Schuster, 1964) pp. 187–92. Expanded as 'Portrait of James Joyce', *Dublin Magazine*, 7 (April–June 1932) 40–8 (recollections of Joyce in Paris in 1929).

——, 'Working with Joyce', *Irish Times* (Dublin), 5 October 1956, p. 5; 6 October 1956, p. 7. Reprinted as 'I Worked with James Joyce', *Irish Digest* (Dublin), 58 (December 1956) 53–6 (recollections of Colum's help to Joyce).

Cowley, Malcolm, *Think Back on Us*, ed. Henry Dan Piper (Carbondale, Ill.: Southern Illinois University Press; London and Amsterdam: Feffer & Simons, 1967), *passim*.

——, 'When a Young American . . .', *Mercure de France*, 347 (August–September 1963) 57–9 (Sylvia Beach).

Crise, Stelio, *Epiphanies & Phadographs: Joyce E Trieste* (Milan: All'insegna del pesce d'oro, 1967) (an account of Joyce's sojourn and relationships in Trieste).

Cunard, Nancy, *These Were the Hours: Memories of My Hours Press, Réanville and Paris, 1928–1931*, ed. Hugh Ford (Carbondale and Edwardsville, Ill.: Southern Illinois University Press; London and Amsterdam: Feffer & Simons, 1969) pp. 115–17 (Joyce's promotion of the Irish tenor John Sullivan).

Curran, Constantine P., *James Joyce Remembered* (London and New York: Oxford University Press, 1968) (recollections by a close friend).

Dahlberg, Edward, *The Confessions* (New York: George Braziller, 1971), *passim* (recollections of Joyce in Paris).

Daly, Leo, 'James Joyce Interviewed by Leo Daly', *Hibernia* (Dublin), 36 (3 November 1972) 17 (imaginary).

Delimata, Bozena Berta [Schaurek], 'Reminiscences of a Joyce Niece', ed. Virginia Moseley, *James Joyce Quarterly*, 19 (Fall 1981) 45–62 (memories of Joyce, Nora, Stanislaus and family in Trieste in the late teens, by the daughter of Joyce's sister Eileen Joyce Schaurek).

——, 'Uncle Jimmy Remembered', *Irish Times* (Dublin), 2 September 1971, p. 10 (the daughter of Eileen Joyce Schaurek interviewed by Maeve Binchy).

Edel, Leon, 'The Genius and the Injustice Collector: a Memoir of James Joyce', *American Scholar*, 49 (1980) 467–87 (memories of brief contacts with Joyce in Paris, 1929–31; and of a visit to Nora in Zürich, in 1946).

——, *James Joyce: The Last Journey* (New York: Gotham Book Mart, 1947). The last chapter is reprinted as 'James Joyce: The Last Journey', *Story*, 32 (Summer 1948) 139–47 (provides a sketch of Joyce's last days in Zürich and of his funeral).

'Eine Erinnerung an James Joyce', *Weltwoche* (Zürich), 17 January 1941, p. 5 (a recollection of Joyce).

Ellmann, Richard, 'The Hawklike Man', in *Eminent Domain: Yeats Among Wilde, Joyce, Pound, Eliot and Auden* (New York: Oxford University Press, 1967) pp. 29–56 (surveys Yeats's and Joyce's few meetings, reactions to each other's work, mutual respect and occasional cross-influences).

——, *James Joyce*, 2nd edn (London and New York: Oxford University Press, 1982) (the standard biography of Joyce).

——, 'James Joyce's Addresses', *American Book Collector*, 15, no. 10 (1965) 25–9 (Joyce's addresses throughout his life).

——, *James Joyce's Tower* (Dun Laoghaire: Eastern Regional Tourism Organisation, 1969) (Joyce's residence in the Sandycove Martello Tower and his use of the tower in *Ulysses*).

Fabricant, Noah D., 'The Ocular History of James Joyce', in *Thirteen Famous Patients* (Philadelphia: Chilton, 1960) pp. 128–38 (physician's account of Joyce's eye problems).

Finneran, Richard J., 'James Joyce and James Stephens: the Record of a Friendship with Unpublished Letters from Joyce to Stephens', *James Joyce Quarterly*, 11 (1974) 279–92 (an account of the relationship which began in 1909).

Fitch, Noel Riley, *Sylvia Beach and the Lost Generation* (New York: Norton, 1985).

Flanner, Janet, 'The Great Amateur Publisher', *Mercure de France*, 347 (August–September 1963) 46–51 (Sylvia Beach).

——, *Paris Was Yesterday, 1925–1939*, ed. Irving Drutman (New York: Viking Press, 1972) *passim* (recollections by a writer, with some references to Joyce).

——, 'That Was Paris', *New Yorker*, 11 March 1972, pp. 32–6 (recollections of Joyce and others in Paris).

Ford, Ford Madox, *It Was the Nightingale* (Philadelphia and London: J. B. Lippincott, 1933) pp. 290–4 and *passim* (Joyce, among his adulators, in Paris).

Francini Bruni, Alessandro, *Joyce intimo spogliato in piazza* (Trieste: La Editoriale Libraria, 1922). Reprinted in English translation in *James Joyce Quarterly*, 14 (Winter 1977) 127–59; and in Willard Potts (ed.), *Portraits of the Artist in Exile*, pp. 7–39 (a fellow Berlitz teacher with Joyce records his memories of their association).

Frank, Nino, 'L'ombre qui avait perdue son homme', in *Mémoire brisée*, vol. I (Paris: Clamann-Lévy, 1967) pp. 27–64. It is an expanded version of 'Souvenirs sur James Joyce', *Table ronde* (Paris), 23 (November 1949) 1671–93, part of which was published in Italian translation as 'L'ombre che aveva perduto il suo Uomo', *Il Mondo*, 2 (3 June 1950) 11–12; (10 June 1950) 11–

12. A selection appeared as 'La joyeuse partie de campagne de James Joyce', *Figaro littéraire*, 8 May 1967, p. 27. Reprinted in English translation in Willard Potts (ed.), *Portraits of the Artist in Exile* pp. 74–105.

Freund, Gisèle, 'En rouge et en noir', *Figaro littéraire*, 20 January 1966, p. 8 (recollections by a French photographer).

——, and V. B. Carleton, *James Joyce in Paris: His Final Years* (New York: Harcourt, 1965) (numerous photographs of Joyce and his contemporaries, with a brief summary of his last years, 1938–41).

Fulford, Robert, 'The Rising Cult of James Joyce', *Toronto Daily Star*, 21 August 1965, p.22 (interview with Harry Pollock).

Furbank, P. N., 'Svevo and James Joyce', in *Italo Svevo: The Man and the Writer* (Berkeley and Los Angeles: University of California Press, 1966) pp. 78–91 (discusses the relationship between the two writers in Trieste).

Galli, Lina, 'Livia Veneziani Svevo and James Joyce', *James Joyce Quarterly*, 9 (Spring 1972) 334–8 (the relationship between Joyce and the wife of Italo Svevo, the Triestine novelist and Joyce's friend).

Giedion-Welcker, Carola, 'Begegnungen mit James Joyce', in *Schriften 1926–1971: Stationen zu einem Zeitbild*, ed. Reinhold Hohl (Cologne: M. du Mont Schauberg, 1973) pp. 53–74. A shortened version of the recollection in *Weltwoche* (Zürich), no. 388 (18 April 1941) 5. Appeared in English translation as 'James Joyce in Zurich', *Horizon* (London), 18 (September 1948) 207–12. Reprinted in *The Golden Horizon*, ed. Cyril Connolly (London: Weidenfeld & Nicolson, 1953); in *Irish Digest* (Dublin), 32 (January 1949) 47–8; and in Willard Potts (ed.) *Portraits of the Artist in Exile*, pp. 256–80 (provides a general account of Joyce's years in Zurich).

——, 'Eine Ausstellung zum Gedächtnis von James Joyce', *Basler Nachrichten* (Basel), no. 494 (18 November 1949) 1 (an exhibition in memory of Joyce).

—— (ed.), *In Memoriam James Joyce* (Zürich: Fretz & Wasmuth, 1941) (includes memoirs and tributes by Heinrich Straumann, Lord Derwent, Carola Giedion-Welcker and Armin Kesser).

Gillet, Guillaume, 'Un diner en ville', *Figaro littéraire*, 20 January 1966, p. 9 (an account of a dinner with Joyce in Paris, by the daughter of the critic Louis Gillet).

Gillet, Louis, 'Adieux à Joyce', *Paris-Soir*, 15 January 1941. The following recollection by Gillet, 'Joyce vivant', with some additional material, appeared as 'Recuerdos de James Joyce', *Sur*, December 1941, pp. 28–42; January 1942, pp. 53–65. Both recollections were included in *Stele pour Joyce* (1941; rpt. Paris: Editions du Sagittaire, 1946). Reprinted in the English translation of that volume, *Claybook for James Joyce* (London and New York: Abelard-Schuman, 1958) pp. 75–9, 80–119 (recollections by the conservative critic).

Glassco, John, *Memoirs of Montparnasse* (New York: Oxford University Press, 1970) (recollections of a visit to Joyce in Paris).

Gluck, Barbara R., *Beckett and Joyce: Friendship and Fiction* (Lewisburg, Penn.: Bucknell University Press, 1979) pp. 19–40 and *passim* (discusses Joyce's relationship with Samuel Beckett).

Gogarty, Oliver St John, *As I Was Walking Down Sackville Street* (London: Cowan; New York: Reynal & Hitchcock, 1937) pp. 293–9 and *passim* (amusing anecdotes concerning Joyce by the original of Buck Mulligan in *Ulysses*).

——, 'James Augustine Joyce', *Dallas Times Herald*, 3 April 1949, section 4, pp. 8, 10 (an unfavourable portrait of Joyce as a writer).

——, 'James Joyce as a Tenor', in *Intimations* (New York: Abelard, 1950) pp. 58–69 (Joyce as singer and patron of singers).

——, 'Joyce as a Joker', in *Start from Somewhere Else* (New York: Doubleday, 1955) pp. 82–5 (Joyce's ability to compose limericks).

——, *Rolling Down the Lea* (London: Constable, 1950) pp. 116–19 (anecdotes concerning Joyce).

——, 'They Think They Know Joyce', *Saturday Review of Literature* (New York), 33 (18 March 1950) 8–9, 36–7. Condensed in *Irish Digest* (Dublin), 37 (July 1950) 19–23 (intemperate attack on Joyce).

Gogarty, Oliver, Jr, 'The Tower: Fact and Fiction', *Irish Times* (Dublin), 16 June 1962, p. 11 (Martello Tower at Sandycove).

Goldman, Arnold, 'Stanislaus, James and the Politics of Family', in *Atti Del Third International James Joyce Symposium* (Trieste: Universita Degli Studi, 1974) pp. 60–75 (comparisons between James Joyce and his brother).

Graham, Rigby, *'James Joyce's Tower', Sandycove* (Wymondham, England: Brewhouse Press, 1975) (includes brief comment on the Martello Tower Joyce rented and later used as the opening setting for *Ulysses*).

Gregory, Horace, 'A Portrait of the Irish as James Joyce', in *Spirit of Time and Place: Collected Essays* (New York: Norton, 1973) pp. 250–5 (surveys the contradictory elements of the Irish character as combined within Joyce).

Guggenheim, Peggy, *Out of This Century* (New York: Dial Press, 1946) *passim*.

Halper, Nathan, 'How Simple: a Tale of Joyce and Pound', *Partisan Review*, 44, no. 3 (1977) 438–46 (discusses Joyce's relationship with Ezra Pound).

Helwig, Werner, 'Erinnerung an James Joyce', *Merkur* (Stuttgart), 24 (July 1970) 693–5 (recollections of Joyce).

Hemingway, Ernest, *Selected Letters of Ernest Hemingway*, ed. Carlos Baker (New York: Charles Scribner's, 1981) *passim* (includes several references to Joyce).

Hoffmeister, Adolf, 'James Joyce' and 'Osobnost James Joyce', in *Podoby: Napsal a Nakreslil* (Prague: Československý Spisovatel, 1961) pp. 71–8 and 118–26. An Italian translation of 'Osobnost James Joyce' was published as 'Un incontra con James Joyce', *Europa letteraria*, 2 (February–April 1962) 55–63. Both recollections appear in the French translation in Hoffmeister's *Visages écrits et dessinés* (Paris: Editeurs Français Réunis, 1963) pp. 39–47 and 48–60; and in English translation in Willard Potts (ed.), *Portraits of the Artist in Exile*, pp. 121–7 and 127–36.

——, *Păriz & Okoli* (Prague: Československý Spisovatel, 1967) *passim*.

Holloway, Joseph, 'An Account of Joyce's Interview with AE', in *A James Joyce Miscellany, Second Series*, ed. Marvin Magalaner (Carbondale: Southern Illinois University Press, 1959) (Joyce and George Russell).

Huddleston, Sisley, 'Shakespeare and Company', in *Paris Salons, Cafés, Studios* (Philadelphia: Lippincott, 1928) pp. 208–20 (recollections of Joyce in Paris in the 1920s).

Imbs, Bravig, *Confessions of Another Young Man* (New York: Henkle-Yewdale, 1936) *passim* (recollections of literary life in Paris, with references to Joyce).

James Joyce Quarterly, 9 (Spring 1972) 307–49: 'Joyce and Trieste Issue' (includes memoirs and essays by Claudio Antoni, Aurelia Gruber Benco, Lina Galli, Stelio Mattioni, Mario Nordio, Nora Franca Poliaghi, Niny Rocco-Bergera, Antonio Fonda Savio and Letizia Fonda Savio).

Jolas, Eugene, 'My Friend James Joyce', *Partisan Review*, 8 (March–April 1941) 82–93. Reprinted in *James Joyce: Two Decades of Criticism*, ed. Seon Givens (New York: Vanguard Press, 1948) pp. 3–18.

Jolas, Maria, 'Joyce en 1939–1940', *Mercure de France*, 109 (May–August 1950) 45–58 (an account of Joyce at Saint-Gérand-le-Puy).

——, 'Joyce's Friend Jolas', in *A James Joyce Miscellany*, ed. Marvin Magalaner (New York: James Joyce Society, 1957) pp. 62–74 (memoir and account of Joyce's friendship with Eugene Jolas).

—— (ed.), *A James Joyce Yearbook* (Paris: Transition Press, 1949) (includes memoirs by Heinrich Straumann, Paul Léon and Philippe Soupault).

Joyce, Giorgio, 'My Father', *Sunday Press* (Dublin), 18 June 1967, p. 17 (interview in Dublin by Maud Lennox).

[Joyce, John Stanislaus], 'Interview with Mr John Stanislaus Joyce [Joyce's father]', in *A James Joyce Yearbook*, ed. Jolas, pp. 159–69 (possibly by Flann O'Brien, doubtless spurious).

Joyce, Stanislaus, *The Meeting of Svevo and Joyce* (Udine, Italy: Del Bianco Editore, 1965) (lecture given in May 1955 in Trieste on the relationship between the Italian writer Italo Svevo and Joyce).

——, *My Brother's Keeper: James Joyce's Early Years*, ed. Richard Ellmann (New York: Viking; London: Faber & Faber, 1958) (unfinished autobiography of Joyce's younger brother).

——, 'Open Letter to Dr Oliver Gogarty', *Interim*, 4 (1954) 49–56. Also as an 8-page pamphlet, *An Open Letter to Dr Oliver Gogarty* (Seattle: University of Washington Press, 1954) (responds to inaccuracies in Gogarty's 'They Think They Know Joyce').

——, *Recollections of James Joyce, by His Brother, 1941*, trans. Ellsworth Mason (New York: Gotham Book Mart, 1950) (brief biographical summary, with personal asides).

Kahane, Jack, *Memoirs of a Booklegger* (London: Michael Joseph, 1939), *passim* (recollections by the publisher who published *Haveth Childers Everywhere*, a fragment of *Finnegans Wake*).

Kain, Richard M., ed., 'An Interview with Carola Giedion-Welcker and Maria Jolas', *James Joyce Quarterly*, 11 (1974), 94–122 (from the Fourth International James Joyce Symposium, Dublin, 1973).

Kempf, Roger, 'Ma première impression de vous', *L'Arc*, no. 36 (1968) 63–66 (Martha Fleischmann).

Kerr, Alfred, 'Joyce in England', trans. Joseph Prescott, in *A James Joyce Miscellany*, ed. Magalaner, pp. 37–43 (conversation with Joyce in 1936, principally concerning the censoring of *Ulysses*).

Kettle, Thomas M., 'Review [of *Chamber Music*]', *Freeman's Journal* (Dublin), 1 June 1907, p. 5 (includes a brief recollection of Joyce at University College).

Kuehl, John, 'A la Joyce: The Sisters Fitzgerald's Absolution', *James Joyce Quarterly*, 2 (Fall 1964) 2–6 (the extent to which Scott Fitzgerald read and used the words of his idol, James Joyce).

Lansdell, Sarah, 'An Adventure in Color', *Louisville Courier-Journal Magazine*,

29 August 1965, pp. 33–9 (the artist Henry Strater, with some of his recollections of Joyce).

Le Fèvre, Frédéric, 'Une heure avec M Valery Larbaud', *Les nouvelles littéraires*, 2 (6 October 1923), 1–2 (Larbaud's views on Joyce).

Lennon, Michael J., 'James Joyce and the Tenor Sullivan', *Hibernia* (Dublin), 16 October 1959, p. 11; (23 October 1959) p. 11 (Joyce's promotion of John Sullivan).

Léon, Lucie [Lucie Noel], *James Joyce and Paul L. Léon: the Story of a Friendship* (New York: Gotham Book Mart, 1950) (Account of Joyce's relationship with his friend, 1928–1940, by Léon's wife).

——, 'Seed Cake for Tea', *Irish Independent* (Dublin), 12 February 1965, p. 13 (interview with Paul Léon's wife).

Léon, Paul, 'In Memory of Joyce', Poésie (Paris), no. 5 (1942) 35–40. Appeared in English translation in *A James Joyce Yearbook*, ed. Jolas, pp. 116–25; and in *Portraits of the Artist in Exile*, ed. Potts, pp. 286–91.

'Les Treize', 'Les Lettres', *Intransigeant* (Paris), 23 February 1933, p. 2 (hypothetic conversation between Joyce and Cesar Abin).

Lidderdale, Jane, and Mary Nicholson, *Dear Miss Weaver: Harriet Shaw Weaver, 1876–1961* (New York: Viking, 1970) (a biography of Joyce's patroness, publisher and friend).

Lyons, John B., *James Joyce and Medicine* (Dublin: Dolmen Press, 1973) (physician's clinical examination of Joyce's physical ill health and emotional disorders).

McCarthy, Mary, 'Exiles, Expatriates and Internal Emigres', *Listener* (London), 86 (25 November 1971) 705–8 (describes Joyce's characteristics as a exile).

MacDiarmid, Hugh, *The Company I've Kept* (London: Hutchinson, 1966; Berkeley: University of California Press, 1967) *passim*.

——, *In Memoriam James Joyce, from A Vision of World Language* (Glasgow: MacLellan, 1956) (poetic tribute to Joyce).

Maddox, Brenda, *Nora: The Real Life of Molly Bloom* (Boston: Houghton Mifflin, 1987).

Magee, William K. [John Eglinton], 'A Glimpse of the Later Joyce', in *Irish Literary Portraits* (London: Macmillan, 1935) pp. 153–8 (recollections of a visit in Paris).

Markow-Totevy, Georges, 'James Joyce and Louis Gillet', in Marvin Magalaner (ed.), *A James Joyce Miscellany*, pp. 49–61 (Joyce's friendship with the critic Gillet, who championed Joyce's work).

Materer, Timothy, 'James Joyce and the Vortex of History', in *Vortex: Pound, Eliot and Lewis* (Ithaca, N.Y. and London: Cornell University Press, 1979) pp. 163–97 (Joyce's relationships with the Vortex group).

Mattioni, Stelio, 'My Friend, James Joyce', *James Joyce Quarterly*, 9 (Spring 1972) 339–41 (an Italian writer becomes a 'friend' of Joyce only through his admiration of Joyce's works).

Mayoux, Jean-Jacques, *Vivants, piliers* (Paris: Julliard, 1960) *passim*.

Meagher, James Anthony, 'Stories of Joyce and Myself', *Hibernia* (Dublin), 6–26 June 1969, p. 19 (anecdote about Joyce in Paris in 1925).

Mercanton, Jacques, 'Les heures de James Joyce', *Mercure de France*, 348 (1963) 89–117, 284–315. Reprinted, with slight changes, in book form, *Les heures de James Joyce* (Lausanne: Editions l'Age d'Homme, 1967). Appeared in English translation in *Kenyon Review*, 24 (Autumn 1962) 700–30; 25 (Winter 1963) 93–118; and in Willard Potts (ed.) *Portraits of the Artist in Exile*, pp. 206–52 (memoir of Joyce in Paris in the late 1930s, by a French journalist and friend).

Meyers, Jeffrey, 'James and Nora Joyce', in *Married to Genius* (New York: Barnes and Noble, 1977) pp. 74–91 (the course of the Joyces' marriage).

Modern Fiction Studies, 18 (1972) 3–129: 'Italo Svevo' (special issues on Joyce's Triestine associate Svevo).

Moseley, Virginia, 'Joyce and the Bible: the External Evidence', in *Ulysses: Cinquante ans après*, ed. Louis Bonnerot (Paris: M. Didiet, 1974) pp. 99–110 (Joyce's familiarity with the Bible is proved by the official curricula for Irish education and by recollections of Joyce's classmates).

Myers, Rollo H., 'Some Recollections of James Joyce', *Time and Tide* (London), 22 (25 January 1941) 66.

Nichols, Lewis, 'Joyce', *New York Times Book Review*, 7 February 1960, p. 8 (recollection of a New Year's Eve party in Paris).

Nicolson, Harold, *The Desire to Please* (London: Constable, 1943) pp. 136–9 (recollection of a 1934 visit with Joyce in Paris).

O'Brien, Conor Cruise, 'Joyce's Ireland', *Saturday Review* (New York), 50 (11 March 1967) 56–7, 88 (describes the houses in which Joyce lived and the buildings which figure in his writings).

O'Brien, Edna, 'Joyce and Nora: a Portrait of Joyce's Marriage', *Harper's*, 261 (September 1980), 60–4, 66, 68–73 (Joyce's relations with Nora).

O'Connor, Ulick, 'Beneath the Mask of James Joyce', *Irish Digest* (Dublin), 56 (April 1956) 51–3. Condensed from *Time and Tide* (London) (as a student, Joyce seems to have had two personalities: one which he created for the public, and the other his real one, which he concealed beneath the mask).

——, *The Times I've Seen: Oliver St John Gogarty – A Biography* (New York: Obolensky, 1963) pp. 59–93 (Joyce's relationship with Cogarty).

—— (ed.), *The Joyce We Knew* (Cork: Mercier Press, 1967) (memoirs by Joyce's contemporaries Eugene Sheehy, William G. Fallon, Padraic Colum and Arthur Power).

O Laoi, Pádraic, *Nora Barnacle Joyce: A Portrait* (Galway: Kennys Bookshops, 1982).

O'Mahony, Eoin, 'Father Conmee and His Associates', *James Joyce Quarterly*, 4 (1967) 263–70 (history of the schools Joyce attended).

O'Neill, Michael J., 'The Joyces in the Holloway Diaries', in *A James Joyce Miscellany, Second Series*, ed. Marvin Magalaner (Carbondale: Southern Illinois University Press, 1959) pp. 103–10 (comments on Joyce and his father, in the diary of the Dubliner Joseph Holloway).

'Onlooker', 'The Man Who Thinks There Is Too Much Literary Talent in Ireland', *Irish Press* (Dublin), 29 July 1966, p. 10 (Fritz Senn).

O'Sullivan, Seumas, 'The "Forty-Foot" Forty Years Ago', in *Essays and Recollections* (Dublin: Talbot Press, 1944) pp. 112–17 (an account of life in the Martello Tower at Sandycove).

Parandowski, Jan, 'Spotkanie z Joycem', in *Dziela wybrane*, vol. III (Warsaw: Czytelnik, 1959) pp. 468–77. A German translation, minus the first paragraph, was published as 'Begegnung mit Joyce', *Deutsche Rundschau*, 83 (1957)

279–84. A portion of the recollection appeared in *Umana*, 20 (May–September 1971) 46–8. Reprinted in English translation as 'Meeting with Joyce', in Willard Potts (ed.), *Portraits of the Artist in Exile*, pp. 154–62.

Pearl, Cyril, *Dublin in Bloomtime: The City James Joyce Knew* (New York: Viking, 1969 (biographical backgrounds).

Phillips, Nancy, 'Jim Joyce – a Beautiful Voice', *Telegram* (Toronto), 11 February 1964 (interview with Mrs May Joyce Monaghan, Joyce's sister).

Pinker, James, 'James Pinker to James Joyce, 1915–1920', in John Firth (ed.), *Studies in Bibliography*, 21 (1968) 205–24 (letters from Joyce's literary agent, with prefatory comments and annotations by Firth).

Potts, Willard (ed.), *Portraits of the Artist in Exile: Recollections of James Joyce by Europeans* (Seattle and London: University of Washington Press, 1979) (contributions by Alessandro Francini Bruni, Silvio Benco, August Suter, Georges Borach, Nino Frank, Philippe Soupault, Adolf Hoffmeister, Ole Vinding, Jan Paradowski, Louis Gillet, Jacques Mercanton, Carola Giedion-Welcker, Paul Ruggiero and Paul Léon).

Pound, Ezra, *Pound/Joyce: The Letters of Ezra Pound to James Joyce*, ed. Forrest Read (New York: New Directions, 1967) (also includes running commentary by Read and his 'Introduction' on Joyce's relationship with Pound).

Power, Arthur, 'At a Party with James Joyce', *Irish Digest*, 51 (September 1954) 27–9. Condensed from the *Irish Tatler and Sketch*.

——, *Conversations with Joyce*, ed. Clive Hart (New York: Barnes & Noble; London: Millington, 1974) (reconstructions of the art critic's conversations with Joyce, chiefly on literary topics, from contemporary notes).

——, 'Conversations with Joyce', *James Joyce Quarterly*, 3 (Fall 1965) 41–9 (encounters in Paris in 1921).

——, 'James Joyce – the Man', *Irish Times* (Dublin), 30 December 1944, p. 2.

——, 'The Joyce I Knew', in O'Connor (ed.), *The Joyce We Knew*, pp. 95–123 (tribute).

Queneau, Raymond, 'Une traduction en joycien', in *Bâtons, chiffres et lettres* (Paris: Gallimard, 1950) pp. 171–3.

Quinn, Edward, *James Joyce's Dublin, with Selected Writings from Joyce's Works* (London: Secker & Warburg, 1975) (collection of photographs of Dublin locales, captioned with extracts from Joyce's writings).

Quinn, John, '"Quinnigan's Quake!" John Quinn's Letters to James Joyce, 1916–1920; 1921–1924', ed. Myron Schwartzman, *Bulletin of Research in the Humanities*, 81 (1978) 216–60; 83 (1980), 27–66 (description of, and quotations from, the correspondence between Joyce and his New York legal and literary defender, concerning *Ulysses*).

Raimondi, Giuseppe, 'Qualcosa su James Joyce', in *Lo scrittoio* (Milan: Edizioni 'Il saggiatore', 1960) pp. 129–33.

'Recollections of the Man', *Envoy* (Dublin), 5 (May 1951) 73–8 (four extracts from Joyce's obituaries in the Irish papers).

Rees, Leslie, 'Clongowes, The Tower and a Meeting with James Joyce', *Meanjin Quarterly*, 27 (September 1968) 328–35 (recollections of a meeting in 1936, by an Australian writer).

Reid, Benjamin L., *The Man from New York: John Quinn and His Friends* (New York: Oxford University Press, 1968) *passim* (Joyce's relationship with the New York lawyer and literary patron).

Richards, Grant, 'Grant Richards to James Joyce', Robert Scholes (ed.), *Studies in Bibliography*, 16 (1963) 139–60 (letters from Joyce's publisher, with prefatory and interspersed commentaries.

Rocco-Bergera, Niny, 'A Contribution on the Study of Jealousy in Italo Svevo and James Joyce', in *Atti Del Third International James Joyce Symposium* (Trieste: Universita Degli Studi, 1974) pp. 25–30 (comparison between the personalities of the two writers).

——, *Itinerary of Joyce and Svevo Through Artistic Trieste* (Trieste: Aziendo Autonoma Soggiorno e Turismo, 1971) (tourist guide to Joycean landmarks, prepared for the Third International James Joyce Symposium).

——, 'James Joyce and Trieste', *James Joyce Quarterly*, 9 (Spring 1972) 342–9 (an account of Joyce's Triestine sojourn).

Rodgers, W. R., ed., 'A Portrait of Joyce as a Young Man' and 'A Portrait of the Artist in Maturity', in *Irish Literary Portraits* (London: British Broadcasting Corporation, 1972) pp. 22–47 and pp. 48–74 (edited transcriptions of BBC interviews with several of Joyce's contemporaries, recorded in 1950).

Russell, George [AE], 'Joyce an "Arrogant Youth"', *New York Times*, 7 February 1928, p. 12 (Russell's views on Joyce and others in a lecture at Town Hall in New York on 'Some Personalities in the Irish Literary Movement').

Ryan, John (ed.), *A Bash in the Tunnel: James Joyce by the Irish* (Brighton, England: Clifton Books, 1970) (memoirs, biographical commentaries, and critical essays).

Scholes, Robert, and Richard M. Kain (eds), 'The Artist as a Young Man', in *The Workshop of Daedalus* (Evanston, Ill.: Northwestern University Press, 1965) pp. 111–237 (accounts of Joyce's family and education, and reprinted sketches of the young Joyce by ten memoirists).

Slocombe, George, *The Tumult and the Shouting* (London: Heinemann; New York: Macmillan, 1936) pp. 220–1 (recollections of Joyce in Paris in the 1920s).

Soupault, Philippe, *Profils perdus* (Paris: Mercure de France, 1963) pp. 49–70. A portion of the recollection was published as 'Portrait de l'artiste à Paris', *Lettres françaises*, 16–22 February 1961, pp. 1, 3. An earlier version, with some additional matter, is contained in *Souvenirs de James Joyce* (Paris: Charlot, 1945). A brief excerpt from the latter volume was translated in *A James Joyce Yearbook*, ed. Jolas, pp. 126–9. Reprinted in Willard Potts (ed.), *Portraits of the Artist in Exile*, pp. 106–18 (recollections by the French surrealist poet and novelist).

Staley, Thomas F., 'Composition of Place: Joyce and Trieste', *Modern British Literature*, 5 (1980) 3–9 (Joyce's life in Trieste).

——, 'James Joyce in Trieste', *Georgia Review*, 16 (Winter 1962) 446–9 (interview with a woman who had been a maid for Joyce during part of his stay in Trieste).

Stark, Helmuth, 'Eine Begegnung aus dem Jahr 1915', *Akzente*, 8 (April 1961) 155–7 (recollections of Joyce in Trieste in 1915).

Steloff, Frances, 'In Touch with Genius', *Journal of Modern Literature*, 4 (1975) 803–4 (the founder of Gotham Book Mart and a champion of Joyce's work recalls a party she gave at her bookshop to celebrate the publication of

Finnegans Wake); 848–56 (recollections of the foundation and activities of the James Joyce Society).

Straumann, Heinrich, 'Last Meeting with Joyce', trans. Eugene Jolas and Maria Jolas, in *A James Joyce Yearbook*, ed. Jolas, pp. 109–15. Originally appeared in *Du* (Zürich), (December 1948) (visit and conversation with Joyce in Zürich in late 1940).

Sullivan, Kevin, *Joyce among the Jesuits* (New York: Columbia University Press, 1958) (Joyce's relationship with the Jesuits, through the years of his education at Clongowes Wood, Belvedere College, and University College).

Suter, August, 'Some Reminiscences of James Joyce', *James Joyce Quarterly*, 7 (Summer 1970) 191–8. Reprinted in Willard Potts (ed.), *Portraits of the Artist in Exile*, pp. 61–6 (recollections of Joyce in Zürich and Paris, by a Swiss sculptor).

Svevo, Italo, 'Ricordi zu James Joyce', *Fiera letteraria* (Milan), 27 March 1927, p. 8 (recollection of Joyce in Trieste).

Svevo, Livia, *Vita di mio marito* (Trieste: Zibaldone, 1950) (the relationship between her husband, the Italian writer Italo Svevo, and Joyce).

Tegenbosch, Lambert, 'Ontdekking von Eindhovense Huisvrouw,' *De Volkskrant* (Amsterdam), 22 November 1969, p. 27 (interview with Bernardine Wijffels-Smulders).

Téry, Simone, *L'Ile des bardes* (Paris: Ernest Flammarion, 1925) pp. 213–17 (recollections of Joyce in Paris).

———, 'Rencontre avec James Joyce, Irlandis', *Les nouvelles littéraires*, 4 (14 March 1925) 6 (a meeting with Joyce in a restaurant in Paris).

Tindall, William York, *The Joyce Country*, rev. edn (New York: Schocken, 1972) (photographs of Dublin and environs, with quotations from Joyce's work).

Trilling, Lionel, 'James Joyce in His Letters', *Commentary*, 45 (February 1968), 53–64 (Joyce's obscene letters).

Tuoni, Dario de, *Ricordo di Joyce a Trieste* (Milan: All'Insegna del Pesce d'Oro, 1966) (recollections by Trieste painter and writer and friend of Joyce).

Vinding, Ole, 'Et interview med Joyce', *Forum: Tidsskrift for Teater, Musik, Literatur, Film*, no. 1 (February 1941) 21–2. Shortened version in *Perspektiv*, 6 (Summer 1959) 14–16; reprinted as 'James Joyce i København', in *Vejen til den halve verden* (Copenhagen: Gyldendalske Forlag, 1963) pp. 198–209. Appeared in English translation as 'James Joyce in Copenhagen', *James Joyce Quarterly* 14 (Winter 1977) 173–84; and in Willard Potts (ed.), *Portraits of the Artist in Exile*, pp. 139–52.

Wagner, Geoffrey, 'Master Joys and Windy Nous', in *Wyndham Lewis: A Portrait of the Artist as the Enemy* (New Haven, Conn.: Yale University Press, 1957) pp. 168–88 (Joyce's relationship with Lewis).

Walsh, Louis J., 'With Joyce and Kettle at U.C.D.', *Irish Digest* (Dublin), 12 (June 1942) 27–9 (Thomas M. Kettle).

Weaver, Harriet, 'Harriet Weaver's Letters to James Joyce, 1915–1920', John Firth (ed.), *Studies in Bibliography*, 20 (1967) 151–88 (includes introductory note and annotations by Firth).

W[ekker], H[erman], 'Cultus Wordt een Industrie', *De Tijd* (Amsterdam), 13 December 1969, p. 3 (interview with Fritz Senn).

Weygandt, Cornelius, *Irish Plays and Playwrights* (Boston: Houghton-Mifflin, 1913) pp. 121–2 (an account of Joyce's meeting with George Russell).

Index

(The figures in parentheses after entry numbers indicate the number of references. Mc is treated as if spelt Mac. Works by Joyce are listed under Joyce, James.)

John, Augustus, 104, 116, 144

Jolas, Eugene, xv, xvii(n), 95, 114(2), 136, 138–41, 162

Jolas, Maria, 95(3), 115, 136, 178, 182, 185

Joyce, Charles (brother), xxvii, 93, 170

Joyce, Eileen (sister). *See* Schaurek, Eileen Joyce

Joyce, Eva (sister), 63, 64, 171(2)

Joyce, Florence (sister), 171, 183

Joyce, George (brother), xxi

Joyce, Giorgio (son), xxii, xxiv, xxvi(2), xxvii, 39, 49, 50, 55(2), 62, 63, 66, 84, 87, 88, 95(2), 99, 100, 107, 115(2), 122, 130(2), 131(2), 134, 146(2), 148, 157–8, 163(2), 166, 167, 178, 180, 183, 184

Joyce, Helen (daughter-in-law), xiv, xxiv, 164, 186(n)

Joyce, James:

born, xviii; baptised, xx; frequent moves by family, xx; at Clongowes Wood College, xx(2), 9; at Belvedere College, xx, 2, 3(2), 4, 5(2), 9(2), 61; at University College Dublin, xviii(n), xx, xxi(5), 6, 10(2), 17, 20(n), 33, 53, 168, 169; projects a newspaper called 'The Goblin', 39; writes articles and reviews, xxi, xxii, xxiii(2), 46, 53, 121; opens Volta Cinema, xxiii(2), 14, 15, 36, 39, 46, 58; as a businessman, xxiii(4), 36, 39, 58, 59; as a journalist, 39, 41; as a banker, xxii(3), xxiii; as a clerk, xxiv; as a reader, 3; as a lecturer, xx(2), xxi, xxiii, xxiv(2), 10; as an actor, 9, 12, 38; as a teacher of English, xxii, xxiii(3), xxiv(3), xxv, 36, 39, 46, 47(n), 49, 50, 53, 57, 58, 59, 65, 91; at Berlitz School, xxii, 36, 39, 50, 51, 53, 91, 180; in Martello Tower, xxii, 23, 34, 43(n); in Dublin, xxi(5), xxii(3), xxiii(5), xxiv(2), 1–45; in Mullinger, xxi; in Galway,

xxiii; in London, xxi, xxiv, xxvi(2), 45, 152, 164–6; in Glasgow, xx; in Bognor (Sussex), xxvi; in Pola, xxii(2), 50; in Trieste, xxii(3), xxiii(2), xxiv(2), xxv, 21, 34, 36, 39, 41, 42, 44, 45–60, 91, 92, 103, 171; in Rome, xxii, 53(2); in Florence, xxiii; in Locarno, xxv(2); in Padua, 53(2); in Zürich, xxii, xxiv(2), xxvii(2), 26, 49, 53, 54, 55, 59, 66(2), 67, 69–78, 84, 93, 97, 103, 158, 166, 168, 172, 175–6, 178, 185; in Paris, xxi, xxii(2), xxv, xxvi(2), xxvii, 14, 19, 39(2), 54, 55, 61, 67(3), 68, 79–164; in Flushing, 26, 27, 31; in Holland, 127; in Belgium, 93; his apartments, 121, 122, 135, 148, 150, 154, 163; his appearance, 2, 12, 22, 32, 36, 37, 45, 48, 55, 57, 59, 71, 82, 108, 149, 153, 154, 168; his figure, 22, 32, 37, 71, 96, 165, 168; his neck, 32, 165; his head, 71, 82, 96, 98, 168; his hair, 71, 137, 154, 168; his face, 22, 32, 37, 71, 82, 96, 101, 119, 124, 125, 131, 134, 137, 154, 159, 165; his beard, 22, 32, 36, 71, 82, 86, 124, 125, 137, 149, 168; his nose, 46, 101; his chin, 32, 168; his mouth, 82, 168; his eyes, 12, 22, 32, 37, 45, 48, 51, 57, 71, 82, 83, 101, 125, 155, 165, 168; his looks, 35, 174; his hands, 82, 96, 101, 130, 154; his handshake, 112; his handwriting, 92; his clothes, 32, 37, 55, 71, 76, 86, 112, 148, 154, 165; his ash-plant and cane, 151, 168; his fine voice, 1, 12, 26, 35, 36, 46, 49, 52, 58, 84, 95, 98, 111, 115, 123, 131, 146(2), 148, 151, 154, 158, 166, 168, 171, 180, 182; his conversations, xv(5), 32, 37, 42, 55, 57, 58, 109, 123, 129, 131, 132, 134, 135, 148, 150, 152, 173, 174; his laughter, 73; his smiles, 97, 133, 134(2), 141, 185; his